I0438766

MR. PRESIDENT

*Internet Columns Addressed Directly
To President Barack H. Obama*

By Hermie Rotea
Author of Marcos' Lovey Dovie

* No-Holds-Barred
* Frank • Factual • Fearless

*As Published in Philpress
*And Huffington Post

Foreword

EDITORIAL POLICY
The Power of Truth

The state of journalism has drastically changed with the advent of computer and the Internet. Where before print and broadcast media dominated the industry, now online news providers have raised the bar. With few clicks of the keyboard, news and views are instantly read or publicized throughout the world. Millions of viewers around the globe have access to information basically at no cost. All one needs is a computer connected to the Internet.

But while the medium of transmission and communication has considerably changed and improved, the practice of journalism should remain the same. Journalists regardless of their systems of publication – newspaper, broadcast or Internet – have a duty to report facts and the truth. This may be easier said than done because of conflicting interests of corporate media owners, but at least that is the goal.

Traditionally known as the Fourth Estate, the journalistic profession ideally is expected to serve as a public watchdog not different from the time of Joseph Pulitzer, the acknowledged titan of American journalism in whose name and honor the most prestigious Pulitzer Awards for outstanding journalists are given yearly by Columbia University. Although he belonged to a different era, yet today's practitioners strive to emulate him. And rightly so.

For indeed Pulitzer was the epitome of what a journalist should be. He always crusaded for truth and exposed abuses in and out of government. A no-nonsense editor and publisher of the New York World and the St. Louis Post-Dispatch, he pioneered in investigative journalism and championed the cause of the common man. He tangled with presidents and spared no wrongdoer.

Now it may well be asked, what is the state of American journalism today? Are the principles of a free press and free speech being followed, or are they being compromised? There is no question that because of the current economic crisis and competition from the Internet, newspapers are hurting. Not a few have already folded up and those trying to survive have laid off not a few employees.

To survive, some prestigious daily newspapers have even published advertisements on their front pages, which was unheard of before. They have also cut pages, increased the price of a copy, and refocused their attention to community events to attract local following. But what is alarming is a proposal for the government to bail them out from their financial predicament by awarding them tax-exempt or nonprofit status.

That is anathema to the cause of journalism because it will kill media freedom and independence. Newspapers or journalists cannot and must not be beholden to the government or to political or business interests. If newspapers became captive of government bailout aid or corporate ownership, they would lose their reason for being. Truth would become a casualty.

Truth must not be abandoned or compromised. It has the power to change things for the better. Without journalists – be they print, broadcast, cable or Internet – serving as public watchdog, the government would turn more corrupt and abusive. The traditional adversarial relation between the media and the powers that be goes with the territory and cannot be taken for granted.

The power of truth must be preserved for the public's and the nation's good.

This is our editorial policy: To be factual, frank, and fearless. We don't belong to any political party, civic, legal, business or social organization. We consider journalism a labor of love. We believe that truth and independence are the key to freedom.

Finally, we subscribe to what Thomas Jefferson said, that when the people fear the government, that is tyranny. When the government fears the people, that is liberty.

About the Author

Author **Hermie Rotea** is the editor and publisher of **Philpress**, an Internet news and views agency based in Los Angeles County, California, United States of America, that features his online column, **"Mr. President"**, addressed directly to President Barack Obama, in his websites www.hermierotea.com and www.philpress.net.

Rotea studied journalism at the Far Eastern University in Manila and at the Newspaper Institute of America in New York City. He is author of two new books, **"Egypt & U.S. Cuddling of Dictators, Revolution Behind The Barricades"** which was released on February 15, 2011; and **"To UN: Indict Bush & Cheney for War Crimes"**, which was released in January 2011.

His two other previous books are: **"Marcos' Lovey Dovie" (1983, Los Angeles), and "I Saw Them Aim and Fire!" (1970, Manila)**, that landed him in the enemy blacklist of Philippine Dictator Ferdinand Marcos, which he considered like an Olympic gold medal.

The government subjected him to legal prosecution and political persecution. He escaped to the United States just before Marcos declared martial law in 1972. But fleeing to America was like jumping from the frying pan to the fire.

His request for political asylum was buried in the dead file without action and put him in legal limbo as a man without a country for 16 long years. He challenged the INS authorities to deport him, but they demurred.

So despite his undocumented status, the author published Philippine Press in Los Angeles and continued the crusade against Dictator Marcos in his community newspaper. He became a regular member of the Greater Los Angeles Press Club.

The author continued what he did in Manila, which included writing for the Manila Times, Philippines Free Press, Chronicle Broadcasting Network, Daily Record, and published the Daily News. He was elected a director of the National Press Club that book-launched his first book.

In the U.S., he had articles published in the Ed-Op pages of the Los Angeles Times and the Los Angeles Herald-Examiner and other news publications in the country. He wrote his second book, "Marcos' Lovey Dovie" on Catalina Island.

To settle his immigration status once and for all, the author later dragged the INS to court. The judge ruled in his favor and granted him political asylum the hard way. He belatedly became a naturalized U.S. citizen in 1994.

It turned out that America merely sheds crocodile tears for victims of pro-U.S. foreign dictators and makes a big joke out of the Statue of Liberty in New York harbor, at least in the author's case at the time.

But Dictator Marcos was also a shrewd politician. He contributed $10 million to President Reagan's reelection campaign. Emboldened, he ordered the arrest of US-exiled opposition leaders led by Senators Benigno Aquino Jr. and Raul Manglapus.

Then the tyrant lobbied with the White House for an extradition treaty between the United States and the Philippines so that they could be extradited to Manila and fed to Dictator Marcos' lion's den. Ironically, President Reagan approved the proposed extradition treaty, but the U.S. Congress led by Senator Edward Kennedy blocked it.

Suffice it to say, Martial Law followed the author to America. In 1983, he was indicted and tried in absentia before a military kangaroo court in Greater Manila on a trumped-up charge of rebellion to overthrow the government along with top exiled opposition leaders.

That same year Senator Aquino returned to Manila from U.S. exile for a dialogue with Marcos. But the dictator's soldiers assassinated him right at the Manila International Airport tarmac upon his arrival, which foreign reporters accompanying him witnessed live.

The event triggered the Philippine Revolution of 1986 that overthrew Marcos and catapulted Aquino's widow, Corazon Aquino, to the presidency in a snap election. U.S. observers caught Marcos cheating in the counting of votes. President Reagan facilitated his escape to Hawaii.

In the author's case, the Philippine Consulate in Los Angeles also instigated the filing of extortion case against him on a trumped charge, but a Superior Court dismissed the lawsuit as without merit.

Finally, the author was bombed out of his Beverly Blvd. office in Los Angeles when a bomb was mistakenly planted in his former annex office across the hall that he had just vacated to save on rent. At first the police ironically even suspected him of planting the bomb himself and subjected him to a lie-detector test. Although cleared, he felt burnt out and took a leave of absence from newspaper work after the Philippine revolution of 1986.

In his self-imposed exile from journalism the author disappeared from public sight. That prompted some sectors of the local community and Manila press to report that he had finally been killed by Marcos Gestapo agents in the United States, after eluding them for years, as they did to his fellow journalist, author and defector Primitivo Mijares.

In the author's book in progress, **"Martial Law Followed Us to America"**, along with a documentary**, "Exile: Ninoy Aquino's Journey to Martyrdom",** he spotlights the exiled Philippine Liberation Movement in the United States and U.S. bad foreign policy of cuddling foreign dictators, particularly White House's support of Marcos from President Nixon to Presidents Ford, Carter, Reagan and H.W. Bush.

Literary & Film Works of the Author

RPictures
www.rpictures.net • www.hermierotea.com
The World Is Our Stage
WELCOME LITERARY AGENCIES AND PRODUCERS!
Screenplays • Documentary • Books

RIZAL
GENRE – Historical action/drama similar to and better than GANDHI in story line.
LOGLINE – His pen is mightier than the sword. He gives his people hope, braves a firing squad, and leads his country to freedom. In his wake, an empire crumbles and changes world history forever! 119 pages. Read synopsis. Screenplay available.

DOVIE
GENRE – Action/Drama
LOGLINE – A Hollywood actress Dovie Beams is involved in a love triangle with Philippine President Ferdinand Marcos and First Lady Imelda Marcos. The government's worst sex scandal in history is caught on tape in the presidential bedroom and drags the United States into a diplomatic crisis

with earthshaking repercussion. Based on the book Marcos' Lovey Dovie. 112 pages. Read synopsis. Screenplay available.

GLORY
GENRE – Romantic Drama/Mystery
LOGLINE – A restaurant maitre d' encounters a boy she feels was her lover in a previous life. Since then she is caught in the vortex of a power struggle between religion and medical science, and between God and the devil as she pursues the mystery of reincarnation. Based on a true story. 90 pages. Read synopsis. Screenplay available.

NINOY
GENRE – Action/Drama
LOGLINE – A feature documentary of a political clash between pro-U.S. Philippine Dictator Ferdinand Marcos and opposiion leader Senator Benigno Aquino Jr. that explodes into assassination and revolution. The event catches the United States in a diplomatic dilemma and puts its foreign policy to a test. Read synopsis. 150-minute DVD video.

BUSH & CHENEY: THE UNINDICTED WAR CRIMINALS
BOOK – Former President George W. Bush and former Vice President Dick Cheney are the worst war criminals in modern history. They violated the U.S. Constitution and international laws relating to crimes against humanity by invading Iraq and Afghanistan without legal justification and on great deception. They are found "guilty" of genocide at public tribunals held in Tokyo, Brussels and Tacoma, Washington. Yet these fugitives from justice remain unindicted. Why? Read preview. Manuscript available.

MR. PRESIDENT
BOOK – A compilation of online regular columns addressed directly to Barack H. Obama and published on the Internet in a no-holds-barred style without fear or favor. It fills a gap left by mainstream media that abdicate their crusading role as public watchdog. Read preview.

MARCOS' LOVEY DOVIE
BOOK – Vanity Fair newsmagazine of New York in its book review by Tristan Vox writes: "More than once in history have people concluded that a ruler who cannot be reached by shame must be reached by bullet. This grim thought is occasioned by a slim volume, Marcos' Lovey Dovie by Hermie Rotea, that has, at long last, come into my hands. For years friends in the Philippines have praised it as required reading about Ferdinand and Imelda Marcos, and as the world's tackiest and tawdriest account of a tyrant. They were right on both counts." Available in brand new hardcover edition. Read review.

MARTIAL LAW FOLLOWED US TO AMERICA
BOOK – The United States merely sheds crocodile tears in treating exiled opposition leaders and press critics of Philippine Dictator Ferdinand Marcos

by cuddling him and making the Statue of Liberty in New York harbor a big joke. Behind their back the White House signs an Extradition Treaty with the tyrant to feed them to his lion's den in Manila. Read preview.

HERMIE ROTEA
Author & Screenwriter
P.O. Box 547, Harbor City, California, United States 90710
Email: hrotea@netzero.com
www.rpictures.net • www.hermierotea.com • www.philpress.net

Counterpoint -
The Interview to End All Interviews
With Hermie Rotea

Q: Well, look who's back! Where have you been all this time? Did you just return from planet Mars?

HR: Yeah. How did you know, smart aleck? Actually I just took a well-deserved vacation after there are no more Dictator Marcos in Manila and gestapo Consul Fernandez in Los Angeles to kick around.

Q: We missed your "bombs" or big headlines when you were gone. Now that you are back in action, does that mean happy days are here again?

HR: Not really. Just the same old thing. As they say, never a dull moment. This time though we cover the world. Through the Internet.

Q: What did you do while you were away?

HR: Actually like Evita Peron of Argentina, I never left. Just wrote another kiss-and-tell book.

Q: Another sexplosive book of the Marcos-Dovie kind?

HR: It's about George W. Bush and Dick Cheney, the unindicted worst war criminals in modern history.

Q: You always pick on the big guys. Why not pick on your own size?

HR: Because the bigger they are the more fun or challenge. That's my specialty.

Q: Yeah, but why them? They are no longer president and vice president. They are out of office already.

HR: Because they committed genocide in Iraq and Afghanistan. They violated the U.S. Constitution and international laws. They waged illegal, immoral, phony and reckless wars on terror that killed thousands of innocent victims and destroyed the two nations.

Q: Why don't you leave Bush and Cheney alone? Even President Obama don't seem to care what they did.

HR: Not only that. He is even following in their footsteps. Candidate Obama called Iraq a "stupid" war. President Obama now continues it. The same thing with Afghanistan.

Q: But he prefers to move forward, not backward. He doesn't want any distraction that may jeopardize his Universal Healthcare Reform. So what's wrong with that?

HR: As veteran White House journalist Helen Thomas has observed, Obama is very smooth and sleek. He has perfected the art of political double-talk.

Q: How is that?

HR: Under the U.S. Constitution, he is actually the top law enforcer of the United States. He is supposed to go after law violators, especially Bush and Cheney. So he goes around the problem by saying as you said that he prefers to move forward, not backward. At the same time he also says that nobody is above the law.

Q: So?

HR: Behind his political double-talk is his failure to perform his constitutional duty. He doesn't have to do it himself. He has U.S. Attorney General Eric Holder and his Justice Department to do the leg work.

Q: They are actually investigating CIA interrogators for water boarding torture of detainees at Abu Ghraib and Guantanamo Bay. So they are doing their job already.

HR: But they are just small fishes who merely followed orders from Bush and Cheney. They are the big fishes that Obama should go after, not the CIA agents.

Q: Do you think that will happen?

HR: Of course not. Not with Obama who dances around the problem and passes the buck to famed California prosecutor Vincent Bugliosi, author of the best-selling book *The Prosecution of George W. Bush for Murder*.

Q: What about that book?

HR: Bugliosi argues that Bush can be prosecuted in the United States for the murder of over 4,000 American soldiers who died in Iraq after he invaded and occupied that country "under false pretenses."

Q: But is not the United Nations the proper venue for war crimes?

HR: Normally, yes. But the UN is also politics-ridden and is afraid to rock its own boat, so to speak. Besides, the UN Security Council has jurisdiction over war crimes. And the United States is one of five permanent-member states that have veto powers. So that is out of the question.

Q: So how can Bugliosi prosecute Bush for murder?

HR: Although it is the duty of the president's U.S. attorney general and his justice department to perform that task, Bugliosi has laid out the legal framework and incontrovertible evidence for any state or county prosecutor to use to indict Bush for murder and conspiracy to commit murder.

Q: But has not the passage of time rendered the issue moot?

HR: With murder, there is no statute of limitation. In fact, Bugliosi has already announced in a recent radio interview that Bush will be indicted in California.

Q: How come I did not know about that book?

HR: Because the American mainstream media censored it. They blocked reviews and news about his book. They even refused to accept paid advertisements promoting the book. Only the foreign press picked it up.

Q: But why?

HR: Because the mainstream media adore President Obama like a rock star and want to stay cozy with him. American journalism is dying or is already dead. Joseph Pulitzer must now be squirming in his grave.

Q: What can be done to resurrect it?

HR: That is why there is now the Internet as a grass-roots alternative which has virtually made the mainstream media obsolete in terms of independence and immediacy. Their elitist monopoly and supremacy of news and views are over.

Q: How so?

HR: Internet journalists in the Blogosphere have become news and opinion leaders by default or failure of mainstream media to perform their duty as public watchdog. They have reneged from their journalistic duty to probe for facts and truth. That is how presidents and governments get away with murder. That is how the people suffer from abuses by corrupt elective and appointive officials. With a dead or dying free press, journalism and democracy have become a farce.

Q: What about your own book? What is the title and what is it about?

HR: The title is self-explanatory: *Bush-Cheney War Crimes*. As I said in the preview. the enormity and gravity of their war crimes are staggering. What they committed during their eight years in power may be compared to what Dictator Adolf Hitler of Germany and Admiral Hideki Tojo of Japan committed during World War Two. Hitler exterminated the Jews and overrun Europe, while Tojo's imperial military bombed Pearl Harbor and butchered conquered nations of Southeast Asia. My book is considered too hot to handle.

Q: Final question.

HR: Shoot.

Q: Why are the contents of your websites hermierotea.com and philpress.net the same?

HR: Good query. It is because Hermie Rotea and Philpress are alter egos of each other. They are inseparably linked or are one and the same. Philpress is the abbreviation of Philippine Press I used to publish as a print newspaper based in Los Angeles, California. Now Philpress is an Internet news and views service that covers the world with unlimited viewers or readership, thanks to electronics science and the Blogosphere.

© September 21, 2009

Public Feedback
In the Spirit of Free Press and Free Speech

Dear Hermie:

Glad to know you are back in action. We have not heard from you in a long time. Where have you been? Long time no hear.

We missed your crusading newspaper in Los Angeles, California. You left a void in the arena of public opinion.

Welcome back!

Wow, you mean the world is your stage now? Your foray into Internet journalism must be more exciting. More power to you!

Your "Mr. President" regular online column bristles with the same punch and no-holds-barred action that had been your trademark.

Since you have no more Dictator Marcos to kick around, now you are taking on, gosh, no less than President Barack Obama!

I was pleasantly surprised to chance upon your website while surfing Google and, lo and behold, there you are!

I used to read your column and newspaper in which you ceaselessly attacked Dictator Marcos like a punching bag.

Take it easy on Obama. You must admire the guy for making history as the first black president of the United States. Only in America!

Can you imagine a black or Muslim being elected president or prime minister in England, France, Germany, or Israel? No way! Only in America!

Anyway, welcome back to the battlefield! But take it easy, guy!

Marc
Honolulu, Hawaii

Table of Contents

1

Sarah Palin Book *Going Rogue* is a Declaration of War Against Her Critics and Serves Notice of Her Presidential Run

MR. PRESIDENT:

After reading the 413-page bestselling book *Going Rogue* by former Alaska Gov. Sarah Palin with an open mind and without preconceived notion, one can safely conclude the following:

1. Palin may run for president in 2016.
2. Palin will run as a Republican, but if need be, as a third-party independent or Tea Party candidate, possibly against Democratic Hillary Clinton.
3. Palin's supporters believe she is destined to be the first woman president of the United States.
4. The millions of readers who read her book in addition to her conservative Republican base are her formidable voters base.

4a. *Going Rogue* (meaning playfully mischievous) intentionally annoys, if not dares, her critics to do their worst and then have the last laugh.

5. Based on public record, Palin has more executive and legislative experience than Obama and Biden combined. She ran the nation's biggest state and managed a $14 billion budget. Before that she served as a city mayor and two-term council member.

6. Therefore, contrary to what prejudiced critics say, Palin is qualified to be U.S. president.

That, in a nutshell, is the inevitable observation one gets from reading *Going Rogue*. Her record of public service could pass a fact-check.

Mr. President, you made history in 2008 by your election as the first black president of the United States.

Next time around, the American electorate may welcome the idea or inevitability of the first woman to be elected president of the United States following in your footsteps.

In the case of Sarah Palin, what she claims may seem self-serving although her government accomplishment is a matter of public record.

So Mr. President, "A View from Alaska" by Dewey Whetsell, author of *Fire and Ice* and *Lazarus on a Spur Line*, is reprinted here to help set the Sarah Palin record straight, as follows:

The last forty-five of my sixty-six years I've spent in a commercial fishing town in Alaska. I understand Alaska politics but never understood national politics well until this last year. Here's the breaking point. Neither side of the Palin controversy gets it. It's not about persona, style, rhetoric, it's about doing things. Even Palin supporters never mention the things I'm about to mention here.

1. Democrats forget when Palin was the Darling of the Democrats, because as soon as Palin took the governor's office away from a fellow Republican and tough SOB, Frank Murkowski, she tore into the Republicans' "Corrupt Bastards Club (CBC)" and sent it packing. Many of its members are now residing in state housing and wearing orange jumpsuits. The Democrats reacted by skipping around the yard, throwing confetti, and singing "La la la la" (well, you know how they are). Name another governor in this country who has ever done anything similar. But while you're thinking, I'll continue.

2. Now, with the CBC gone, there were fewer Alaska politicians to protect the giant oil companies here. So Palin constructed and enacted a new system of splitting the oil profits called "ACES." ExxonMobil (the biggest corporation in the world) protested, and Sarah told it, "Don't let the door hit you in the stern on your way out." It stayed, and Alaska residents went from being merely wealthy to being filthy rich. Of course, the other huge international oil companies fell meekly into line. Again, give me the name of other governor in the country who has done anything similar.

3. The other thing she did when she walked into the governor's office is that she got the list of state requests for federal funding for projects known as "pork." She went through the list, took 83 percent of them out, and placed them in the "when-hell-freezes-over" stack. She let locals know that if we need something built, we'll pay for it ourselves. Maybe she figured she could

use the money she got from selling the previous governor's jet because she saved by dismissing the governor's cook (remarking that she could cook for her own family), giving back the state vehicle issued to her (maintaining that she already had a car, and dismissing her state-provided security force (never mentioning -- I imagine -- that she was packing heat herself). I'm still waiting to hear the name of those other governors.

4. Even with her much-ridiculed "gosh and golly" mannerisms, she managed to put together a totally new approach to getting a natural gas pipeline built that will be the biggest private construction project in the history of North America. No one else could do it even if they tried. If that doesn't impress you, you're trying too hard to be unimpressed while watching her do things like this baking up a batch of brownies with her other hand.

5. For thirty years, Exxon held a lease to do exploratory drilling at a place called Point Thomson. It made excuses the entire time for why it couldn't start drilling. In truth it was holding it as an investment. No governor for thirty years could make it get started. This summer, she told Exxon she was revoking its lease and kicking it out. It protested and threatened court action. She shrugged and reminded them that she knew the way to the courthouse. Alaska won again.

6. President Obama wants the nation to be on 25 percent renewable resources for electricity by 2025. Sarah went to the legislature and submitted her plan for Alaska to be at 50 percent renewable by 2025. We are already at 25 percent. I can give you more specifics about things done, as opposed to style and persona. Everybody wants to be cool, sound cool, look cool. But that's just a cover-up. I'm still waiting to hear from liberals the names of other governors who can match what mine has done in two and a half years. I won't be holding my breath.

By the way, she was content to return to Alaska after the national election and go to work, but the haters wouldn't let her. Now, these adolescent screechers are obviously not scuba divers. And no one ever told them what happens when you continually jab and pester a barracuda. Without warning, it will spin around and tear your face off. Shoulda known better.

Author Dewey Whetsell, whose tribute to Palin above is incorporated in her book, served 24 years as chief of Fire/Rescue in Cordova, Alaska. He moved to Eagle River where he remains involved in disaster management. His website is www.deweywhetsell.com.

Sarah Palin, in her Epilogue and Acknowledgment, thanks all his supporters, campaign workers, well-wishers, including the 2012 Draft Sarah Committee, with an ominous statement, "I can't wait 'til we assemble again!"

A Ronald Reagan conservative disciple, Palin is succinctly described by her father Chuck Heath Sr.: "Sarah's not retreating; she's reloading!"

Mr. President, got that? Goodnight.

© Hermie Rotea/Philpress, November 24, 2009

2

Obama Must Stop U.S. Imperialistic Wars and Occupations of Foreign Nations and Neglecting the Needs of the American People

MR. PRESIDENT:

A U.S. State Department official, Matthew Hoh, has resigned in protest against the United States war in and occupation of Afghanistan, the first foreign service official to publicly quit over the issue.

The department's Senior Civilian Representative in Zabul Province in Afghanistan wrote a four-page resignation letter to Ambassador Nancy J. Powell, director general of the Foreign Service and director of Human Resources, stating his reasons.

"I have lost understanding of and confidence in the strategic purposes of the United States' presence in Afghanistan. I have doubts and reservations about our current strategy and planned future strategy, but my resignation is based not upon how we are pursuing this war, but why and to what end.

"To put [it] simply: I fail to see the value or the worth in continued US casualties or expenditures of resources in support of the Afghan government in what is, truly, a 35-year old civil war."

Mr. President, that speaks volume. Let him continue:

"This fall will mark the eighth year of US combat, governance and development operations within Afghanistan. Next fall, the United States' occupation will equal in length the Soviet Union's own physical involvement in Afghanistan. Like the Soviets, we continue to secure and bolster a failing state, while encouraging an ideology and system of government unknown and unwanted by its people.

"If the history of Afghanistan is one great stage play, the United States is no more than a supporting actor, among several previously, in a tragedy that not only pits tribes, valleys, clans, villages and families against one another, but, from at least the end of King Zahir Shah's reign, has violently and savagely pitted the urban, secular, educated and modern of Afghanistan against the rural, religious, illiterate and traditional.

"It is this latter group that composes and supports the Pashtun insurgency. The Pashtun insurgency, which is composed of multiple, seemingly infinite, local groups, is fed by what is perceived by the Pashtun people as a continued and sustained assault, going back centuries, on Pashtun land, culture, traditions and religion by internal and external enemies.

"The US and NATO presence and operations in Pashtun valleys and villages, as well as Afghan army and police units that are led and composed of non- Pashtun soldiers and police, provide an occupation force against which the insurgency is justified.

"In both RC East and South, I have observed that the bulk of the insurgency fights not for the white banner of the Taliban, but rather against the presence of foreign soldiers and taxes imposed by an unrepresentative government in Kabul.

"The United States military presence in Afghanistan greatly contributes to the legitimacy and strategic message of the Pashtun insurgency. In a like manner our backing of the Afghan government in its current form continues to distance the government from the people.

"The Afghan government's failings, particularly when weighed against the sacrifice of American lives and dollars, appear legion and metastatic:

Mr. President, Mr. Hoh's position against United States war and occupation of Afghanistan jibes exactly with what we have been saying all along against continued American imperialistic presence in foreign countries that do not want to be occupied by outsiders, particularly by U.S. troops.

Why, for heaven's sake, does the United States have to have 700 military bases in 130 countries? That is insane! The Military-Industrial Complex in America that produce weapons of mass destruction, along with the Corporate Oil Cartel, are the only ones that profit from wars in Iraq and Afghanistan, not the American people.

Not mentioned and censored by the American mainstream media that are complicit with the powers that be in Washington, is the U.S. oil interests in Afghanistan. It is a long and complicated plot, but the bottom line is that the United States is in Afghanistan for oil.

Yes, it is all about oil.

The oil company, Unocal of California, has built or is building an oil pipeline north of Afghanistan, Turkmenistan, Uzbekistan, Kazakhstan and Russia. Routes for such pipeline transport oil on a 42-inch pipe southward through Afghanistan for 1040 miles in the Pakistan coast. Such a pipeline cost about $2.5 billion and carries about one million barrels of oil per day.

This was not possible when the Taliban was in power in Kabul in 2001 amid different factions in Afghanistan. As the ruling faction, it pursued a nationalistic policy against foreign encroachment of the country's sovereignty.

With the Taliban running the government at the time, the United States could not implement the Unocal oil pipeline project. So then President George W. Bush and Vice President Dick Cheney plotted a regime change in Afghanistan and used 9/11 as a great deception to invade the country and overthrew the Taliban from power.

Bush and Cheney then handpicked Hamid Karzai, a Unocal representative and a 5-year Green Card immigrant in the United States, to be the U.S. puppet president of Afghanistan, who later was dubbed as a godfather of the opium trade there whose brother was also in CIA payroll.

Now Mr. President, you appear to have also embrace Karzai as U.S. puppet president of Afghanistan whose reelection is assured with the withdrawal of former Afghan Foreign Minister Abdullah Abdullah from the November runoff presidential election in protest against a farcical runoff election, just like the first one that the United Nations overturned.

Well, Mr. President, Hamid Karzai may be a son of a bitch, but at least he is now your son of a bitch. So what else is new from Bush's time? History repeats itself.

If as you said in your Cairo speech that Afghanistan is a war of necessity, Mr. President, you are making a terrible mistake. Heed the lesson of history.

Vietnam in its determination and struggle for independence successfully defended its sovereignty. The small country defeated the big powers -- China, France, and the United States -- in a succession of wars. After 100 years, Vietnam finally achieved independence.

U.S. President Harry Truman's pursuit of the Korean War cost him his reelection. So did President Lyndon Johnson who expanded the Vietnam War and lost his bid to be reelected.

In your case, Mr. President, if you escalate the Afghanistan war and occupation, you would suffer same fate of Truman and Johnson as a one-term president. Making the Bush War the Obama War, is your political Waterloo or road to hell.

Mr. President, be forewarned that Afghanistan is the graveyard of imperialism. Even the Soviet Union with 150,000 occupying Russian troops failed to conquer Afghanistan.

Even adding 40,000 American soldiers to the 68,000 already there as part of the U.S. military surge as General Stanley McChrystal has proposed, would not defeat the Taliban.

That is wishful thinking. For like Korea and Vietnam, Afghanistan and even Iraq are unwinnable wars. Wake up, Mr. President!

© Hermie Rotea/Philpress, November 1, 2009

Full Text of Matthew Hoh's Resignation Letter in Protest Against U.S. Afghanistan War is Reprinted in Full Here Due to Its Significance US Foreign Service Officer Matthew P. Hoh Senior Civilian Representative, Afghanistan

September 10, 2009

Ambassador Nancy J. Powell
Director General of the Foreign Service and Director of Human Resources
U.S. Department of State
2201 C Street NW
Washington, D.C. 20520
Dear Ambassador Powell,

It is with great regret and disappointment I submit my resignation from my appointment as a Political Officer in the Foreign Service and my post as the Senior Civilian Representative for the US Government in Zabul Province. I have served six of the previous ten years in service to our country overseas, to include deployment as a US Marine office and Department of

Defense civilian in the Euphrates and Tigris River Valleys of Iraq in 2004-2005 and 2006-2007. I did not enter into this position lightly or with any undue expectations nor did I believe my assignment would be without sacrifice, hardship or difficulty. However, in the course of my five months of service in Afghanistan, in both Regional Commands East and South, I have lost understanding of and confidence in the strategic purposes of the United States' presence in Afghanistan. I have doubts and reservations about our current strategy and planned future strategy, but my resignation is based not upon how we are pursuing this war, but why and to what end. To put simply: I fail to see the value or the worth in continued US casualties or expenditures of resources in support of the Afghan government in what is, truly, a 35-year old civil war.

This fall will mark the eighth year of US combat, governance and development operations within Afghanistan. Next fall, the United States' occupation will equal in length the Soviet Union's own physical involvement in Afghanistan. Like the Soviets, we continue to secure and bolster a failing state, while encouraging an ideology and system of government unknown and unwanted by its people.

If the history of Afghanistan is one great stage play, the United States is no more than a supporting actor, among several previously, in a tragedy that not only pits tribes, valleys, clans, villages and families against one another, but, from at least the end of King Zahir Shah's reign, has violently and savagely pitted the urban, secular, educated and modern of Afghanistan against the rural, religious, illiterate and traditional. It is this latter group that composes and supports the Pashtun insurgency. The Pashtun insurgency, which is composed of multiple, seemingly infinite, local groups, is fed by what is perceived by the Pashtun people as a continued and sustained assault, going back centuries, on Pashtun land, culture, traditions and religion by internal and external enemies. The US and NATO presence and operations in Pashtun valleys and villages, as well as Afghan army and police units that are led and composed of non- Pashtun soldiers and police, provide an occupation force against which the insurgency is justified. In both RC East and South, I have observed that the bulk of the insurgency fights not for the white banner of the Taliban, but rather against the presence of foreign soldiers and taxes imposed by an unrepresentative government in Kabul.

The United States military presence in Afghanistan greatly contributes to the legitimacy and strategic message of the Pashtun insurgency. In a like manner our backing of the Afghan government in its current form continues to distance the government from the people. The Afghan government's failings, particularly when weighed against the sacrifice of American lives and dollars, appear legion and metastatic:

* Glaring corruption and unabashed graft;

* A President whose confidants and chief advisors comprise drug lords and war crimes villains, who mock our own rule of law and counter-narcotics efforts;

* A system of provincial and district leaders constituted of local power brokers, opportunists and strongmen allied to the United States solely for,

and limited by, the value of our USAID and CERP contracts and for whose own political and economic interests stand nothing to gain from any positive or genuine attempts at reconciliation; and

* The recent election process dominated by fraud and discredited by low voter turnout, which has created an enormous victory for our enemy who now claims a popular boycott and will call into question worldwide our government's military, economic and diplomatic support for an invalid and illegitimate Afghan government.

Our support for this kind of government, coupled with a misunderstanding of the insurgency's true nature, reminds me horribly of our involvement with South Vietnam; an unpopular and corrupt government we backed at the expense of our Nation's own internal peace, against an insurgency whose nationalism we arrogantly and ignorantly mistook as a rival to our own Cold War ideology.

I find specious the reasons we ask for bloodshed and sacrifice from our young men and women in Afghanistan. If honest, our stated strategy of securing Afghanistan to prevent al-Qaeda resurgence or regrouping would require us to additionally invade and occupy western Pakistan, Somalia, Sudan, Yemen, etc. Our presence in Afghanistan has only increased destabilization and insurgency in Pakistan where we rightly fear a toppled or weakened Pakistani government may lose control of its nuclear weapons. However, again, to follow the logic of our stated goals we should garrison Pakistan, not Afghanistan. More so, the September 11th attacks, as well as the Madrid and London bombings, were primarily planned and organized in Western Europe; a point that highlights the threat is not one tied to traditional geographic or political boundaries. Finally, if our concern is for a failed state crippled by corruption and poverty and under assault from criminal and drug lords, then if we bear our military and financial contributions to Afghanistan, we must reevaluate and increase our commitment to and involvement in Mexico.

Eight years into war, no nation has ever known a more dedicated, well trained, experienced and disciplined military as the US Armed Forces. I do not believe any military force has ever been tasked with such a complex, opaque and Sisyphean mission as the US military has received in Afghanistan. The tactical proficiency and performance of our Soldiers, Sailors, Airmen and Marines is unmatched and unquestioned. However, this is not the European or Pacific theaters of World War II, but rather is a war for which our leaders, uniformed, civilian and elected, have inadequately prepared and resourced our men and women. Our forces, devoted and faithful, have been committed to conflict in an indefinite and unplanned manner that has become a cavalier, politically expedient and Pollyannaish misadventure. Similarly, the United States has a dedicated and talented cadre of civilians, both US government employees and contractors, who believe in and sacrifice for their mission, but they have been ineffectually trained and led with guidance and intent shaped more by the political climate in Washington, DC than in Afghan cities, villages, mountains and valleys.

"We are spending ourselves into oblivion" a very talented and intelligent commander, one of America's best, briefs every visitor, staff delegation and senior officer. We are mortgaging our Nation's economy on a war, which, even with increased commitment, will remain a draw for years to come. Success and victory, whatever they may be, will be realized not in years, after billions more spent, but in decades and generations. The United States does not enjoy a national treasury for such success and victory.

I realize the emotion and tone of my letter and ask that you excuse any ill temper. I trust you understand the nature of this war and the sacrifices made by so many thousands of families who have been separated from loved ones deployed in defense of our Nation and whose homes bear the fractures, upheavals and scars of multiple and compounded deployments. Thousands of our men and women have returned home with physical and mental wounds, some that will never heal or will only worsen with time. The dead return only in bodily form to be received by families who must be reassured their dead have sacrificed for a purpose worthy of futures lost, loved vanished, and promised dreams unkept. I have lost confidence such assurances can anymore be made. As such, I submit my resignation.

Sincerely,

Matthew P. Hoh
Senior Civilian Representative
Zabul Province, Afghanistan
Cc: Mr. Frank Ruggiero
Ms. Dawn Liberi
Ambassador Anthony Wayne
Ambassador Karl Eikenberry

3

Obama Is Praised and Attacked for Winning the 2009 Nobel Peace Prize, the Third Sitting U.S. President Awarded the Honor

MR. PRESIDENT:

Congratulations for winning the 2009 Nobel Peace Prize. Condolence for being attacked for the coveted award and great honor.

You are the third sitting U.S. president in history to win the award after President Theodore Roosevelt who won in 1906 and President Woodrow Wilson who was awarded the prize in 1919.

Two other peace prize winners are former President Jimmy Carter (2002) for his humanitarian service and former Vice President Al Gore (2007) for his inconvenient truth on global warming. In four decades only President Clinton has not won such award.

Mr. President, in your case world public reaction is mixed. Even you yourself were surprised for winning the trophy. You woke up in the morning and learned from your daughter that you won.

In Oslo, when the Norwegian Nobel Committee announced you as the winner, there were gasps of surprise and cries of too much, too soon.

Chairman Thorbjørn Jagland said the group whittled down a record pool of 205 nominations and picked you because "we couldn't get around these deep changes that are taking place" under you. He said the decision was unanimous.

"The Nobel Peace Prize for 2009 is to be awarded to President Barack Obama for his extraordinary efforts to strengthen international diplomacy and cooperation between peoples," the Nobel committee said.

Mr. President, the Nobel committee said it paid special attention to your vision of a nuclear-free world laid out in your speech in Prague and in April and at the United Nations last month.

Former Peace Prize winner Mohamed ElBaradei, director general of the International Atomic Energy Agency in Vienna, said you have already provided outstanding leadership on nuclear non-proliferation.

Still, while Nobel judges hailed your "extraordinary" diplomatic efforts since your election last year, many ask what you have achieved to deserve such an honor.

Journalists at the press conference where the announcement was made questioned your concrete achievements and the wisdom of giving the prize to a sitting U.S. president.

On Afghanistan, Mr. President, where you face a growing dilemma over the course of action to follow, Taliban leaders criticized the decision.

"We have seen no change in his strategy for peace. He [Obama] has done nothing for peace in Afghanistan," Taliban spokesman Zabihullah Mujahid told French news agency *AFP*.

"He reinforces the war in Afghanistan, he sends more troops to Afghanistan and is considering sending yet more. He has shed Afghan blood and he continues to bleed Afghans and to boost the war here," he said of what you are doing.

In any event, Mr. President, the Nobel committee's decision awarding you the prize peace was a clear slap at your predecessor, George W. Bush, who carpet-and-napalm bombed the Muslims in his phony war on terror.

Bush was previously also nominated for the Nobel Peace Prize based on his war on terror but he didn't get it.

In contrast, Mr. President, who can forget your speeches in Berlin following in the footsteps of President Reagan who caused its wall to collapse and united Germany, and in Cairo where you extended the olive branch and reached out to the Muslim world in a peaceful diplomatic coup?

Mr. President, you said you were surprised and deeply humbled by the honor, and that you plan to travel to Oslo in December to accept the prize.

"Let me be clear: I do not view it as a recognition of my own accomplishments, but rather as an affirmation of American leadership on behalf of aspirations held by people in all nations," you said at the White House.

"To be honest, I do not feel that I deserve to be in the company of so many of the transformative figures who've been honored by this prize."

And your decision to donate the $1.4 million cash award that comes with the prize to charity, is truly charitable and admirable.

Nonetheless, Mr. President, filmmaker Michael Moore said it best, He said that since you have won the 2009 Nobel Peace Prize, "Now earn it!"

However, Republican Party Chairman Michael Steele said you won because of your "star power" rather than your meaningful accomplishments.

"The real question Americans are asking is, 'What has President Obama actually accomplished?'" Steele demanded to know.

Right-wing commentator Rush Limbaugh sided with the enemy and said, "Something has happened here that we all agree with the Taliban and Iran about, and that is he [Obama] doesn't deserve the award."

The *Los Angeles Times* in its editorial said, "Obama and the Nobel: He loses by winning. Giving the Peace Prize to the president so soon in his term embarrasses him and diminishes the honor." It continued:

"Excessive praise can be both unwelcome and embarrassing. Just ask President Obama, who awoke Friday to discover that he had been awarded the Nobel Peace Prize before he had completed even a year in office. Obama managed to be both abashed and appreciative in his response, but no amount of self-effacing spin can obscure the oddity of this award."

Mr. President, Jesse Berney of *Huffington Post* commented the Norwegian Nobel Committee made a grave mistake by awarding you a Nobel Peace Prize. and that you should have turned it down.

He emphasized that the Nobel Peace Prize should be more than simply a symbolic gesture of hope for the future. It should be a reward for extraordinary accomplishment and real-world results. It should be the culmination of a career devoted to the cause of building a better world.

Mr. President, former Polish President Lech Walesa, who won the peace prize in 1983, also expressed surprise. He said: "So soon? Too early. He has no contribution so far. He is only beginning to act."

Archbishop Desmond Tutu of South Africa, who won the prize in 1984, said the decision showed that great things are expected from you and "wonderful recognition" of your effort to reach out to the Arab world after years of hostility.

"It is an award that speaks to the promise of President Obama's message of hope," Tutu said.

Bobby Muller, who won the Nobel Prize as co-founder of the International Campaign to Ban Landmines, told *The Times of London*:

"I don't have the highest regard for the thinking or process of the Nobel committee. Maybe Norway should give it to Sweden so they can more properly handle the Peace Prize along with all the other Nobel prizes."

Mr. President, your former presidential rival Senator John McCain who lost the election to you last year, said he was proud of you.

Israel's President Shimon Peres congratulated you, saying that you have restored hope to the world. Under your leadership, he said that "peace has become a real and original agenda."

Mr. President, Palestinian leader Mahmud Abbas wished the prize will help you achieve your quest for peace throughout the Middle East by establishing an independent Palestinian state.

But Iranian Foreign Minister Manouchehr Mottaki called the Nobel decision awarding you the peace prize as "hasty." As this is written, we have yet to hear from President Amadinejad himself.

Mr. President, in retrospect, Norwegian Alfred Nobel in his 1895 will stipulated that the peace prize should go "to the person who shall have done the most or the best work for fraternity between the nations and the abolition or reduction of standing armies and the formation and spreading of peace congresses."

There is not enough space to include all the mixed world public reaction to your winning the 2009 Nobel Peace Prize.

So goodnight, Mr. President.

© Hermie Rotea/Philpress, October 9, 2009

4

Michael Moore's "Capitalism: A Love Story" is a Guerrilla Filmmaking at its Best and a Prescription for a Revolution

MR. PRESIDENT

Filmmaker Michael Moore is at it again. His new documentary film "Capitalism: A Love Story" is a call to arms and a prescription for a revolution, which is his trademark.

He is the writer, producer, director as well as the narrator and main actor all rolled into one in a film project that is cut out for him . He is also the consummate provocateur, agitator, rabble rouser and troublemaker.

Moore likewise is a rebel with a cause, civil rights activist, a self-style citizen police, and ironically a capitalist millionaire himself oddly fighting for the poor and the middle class.

That is the stuff Michael Moore is made of, Mr. President. In his film, he declares war on Wall Street, the financial center of America in New York City which he labels as the bastion of corporate greed and vultures that rob taxpayers' money and get away with murder.

The filmmaker denounces the giant corporations -- banks, insurance companies, auto manufacturers, and other favored businesses -- that secured billions of dollars in federal aid to rescue them from bankruptcy during the worst economic recession in years, and then misused millions of dollars in bonuses for their executives.

Mr. President, you took over from your predecessor George W. Bush in signing laws the U.S. Congress passed granting them $850 billions in taxpayer assistance to prevent the collapse of the financial markets and to spark economic recovery.

It was also with the expectation that the stimulus money would be used wisely to stop the business slide, promote growth, and that such federal aid would be repaid to taxpayers who, in effect, have become their part owners by 60 percent.

But what happened next, Mr. President? Behind your back and unknown to the Congress and the taxpayers, these giant corporations misused the federal grant money and shamelessly granted themselves millions of dollars in bonuses to their executives.

This is what angered Moore. To dramatize his righteous indignation, he uses guerrilla filmmaking at its best. Apparently without permit or prior warning, he pays an impromptu visit to the corporate headquarters of American International Group Inc. (AIG).

AIG is the biggest beneficiary of federal and taxpayer aid. The corporation gave out $165 million in bonuses to its executives after securing over $170 billion in stimulus money from the government.

So Moore, with camera rolling, brings a big roll of yellow tape that bona fide police usually employ to cordon off a crime scene from the public. He rolls it around the front of the building to discourage public entry. In fact, he is virtually trespassing on the premises.

Then with a bullhorn, Moore aims it upward to the windows and shouts: "I'm here to make a citizen's arrest on AIG! I'm declaring this building an official crime scene on behalf of the people of the United States."

To the public, he pleads: "Please don't cross the line!"

All the while AIG security guards who recognize Moore can only helplessly watch at his braggadocio while passersby are amused by what is happening.

This kind of guerrilla filmmaking continues throughout the documentary, thus adding drama, immediacy and authenticity to unscripted scenes that are filmed spontaneously.

In other scenes, Moore captures the plight of homeowners evicted from their properties for failure to pay their mortgages that led to bank foreclosures. In one instance victims of financial distress could only watch helplessly as police officers are called to enforce eviction.

But in another incident, homeowners facing eviction refuse to leave and invoke their right to have shelter over their heads. They defy sheriffs who responded to a bank call to evict them. The whole community rallies to their support. The officers leave to avoid trouble.

The evicted homeowners in this rare case take the law into their own hands and win -- for now at least. Of course what happens later, is not known.

But as Moore laments, capitalism has legalized robbery of the taxpayers' money and has made the rich richer and the poor poorer. He decries that the richest one percent of the U.S. population pyramid has more wealth than all the other 99 percent combined.

"That's insane!" he bewails.

Under such a vast inequity there cannot be a true democracy, which he says must be rooted in economic freedom. Without such liberty our way of life is a farce, Moore contends.

TIME newsmagazine calls Moore's documentary film his "magnum opus." To which he quips, "I only had a year of Latin when I was in high school, so I'm not quite sure what that means, but I think it's good."

Mr. President, Moore makes a good case against capitalism which he says has wiped out the middle class, beginning with the time of President Reagan whose Reaganomics favored the rich to the detriment of the poor.

The filmmaker puts in a "police lineup" the big guys he contends caused the current worst economic recession since the Great Depression.

He cites the case of a bank regulator who says why Timothy Geithner has no business being our Treasury Secretary. Moore also mentions the head of a congressional commission "charged with keeping an eye on the bailout money."

This witness reveals "how Alan Greenspan & Co. schemed and connived [with] the public into putting up their inflated valued homes as collateral -- thus causing the biggest foreclosure epidemic in our history."

According to Moore, there is now a home foreclosure filed in the United States once every seven-and-half seconds. He continues:

"None of this is an accident, and I name the names others seem to be afraid to name, the men who have ransacked the pensions of working people and plundered the future of our kids and grandkids.

"Somehow they thought they were going to get away with this, that we'd believe their Big Lie that this crash was caused by a bunch of low-income people who took out loans they couldn't afford.

"Much of the mainstream media bought this story line. No wonder Wall Street thought they could pull this off."

Moore stresses: "If you believe in democracy, democracy can't be being able to vote every two or four years. It has to be every part of every day of your life . . . When we remove money our political leaders will listen to us and not [to] Wall Street,"

Mr. President, while the Academy Award-winning documentary filmmaker attacks Wall Street for its corporate greed and robbery of the taxpayers' money, he refrains from criticizing you for the economic mess that you inherited from Bush.

Moore says that since you are only eight months in office, he is giving you the benefit of the doubt. However, he has serious misgivings about your trying to forge a bipartisan approach to Universal Healthcare reform with the Republicans.

He believes that is not going to happen because they are out to kill you politically in their scheme to recapture the White House in tho 2012 presidential election. They plot to make failure of Universal Healthcare Reform your political Waterloo.

So Moore strongly urges you to use the Democratic majority vote in Congress and ram through passage of the bill that includes the "Public Option" or "Single Payer" plan and make Universal Healthcare a fundamental right for all.

Mr. President. as you yourself said, the nation has waited too long for this moment. So now is the time to make it happen, even without Republican participation.

Capitalism, anyone?

Goodnight, Mr. President.

© Hermie Rotea/Philpress, September 30, 2009

5

Obama Tries to Corrupt Mainstream Media by Dangling Bills Before Congress Granting Them Nonprofit Status

MR. PRESIDENT:

Please stop corrupting the press as if you were dangling food to hungry dogs when you said Sunday that you are "happy to look at" bills before Congress granting starving news organizations tax breaks and status as nonprofit business.

You said, "I haven't seen detailed proposals yet, but I'll be happy to look at them." You told this to editors of the *Pittsburgh Post-Gazette* and the *Toledo Blade* in an interview.

To mainstream media, please stop acting like beggars by courting or expecting favors from the president or the government. You are now in a tremendous temptation to succumb to corruption that could lead to the death of press freedom in America, if it had not yet.

It is truly alarming that, in the guise of trying to help struggling mainstream media (newspaper, radio, TV and cable) survive the current recession, Senator Ben Cardin (D-Md.) has introduced a measure purportedly to help them out.

He filed Senate Bill 673, the so-called "Newspaper Revitalization Act," that is designed to give them lenient tax deals if they were to restructure as 501(c)(3) corporations to qualify for such favored status.

Already, the bill has attracted a cosponsor, fellow Democratic Senator Barbara Mikulski of Maryland. It would not be surprising if publicity-hungry lawmakers were to join them for "humanitarian reason."

Mr. President, there is no question as you said that good journalism is "critical to the health of our democracy." But at the same time you expressed alarm over growing trends in reporting especially in the blogosphere or Internet.

"I am concerned that at the direction of the news is all blogosphere, all opinions, with no serious fact-checking, no serious attempts to put stories in context, that what you will end up getting is [are] people shouting at each other [one another] across the void but not a lot of mutual understanding."

Now Mr. President, you are even lecturing the media on how to do their job. If what you said were a complaint, obviously it was a jab at *Fox News* of

Bill O'Reilly, Sean Hannity and Glenn Beck for consistently attacking you on vital issues on their cable TV programs.

They appear to be effective though in lowering your public approval rating below 50% as more and more people now don't trust you for breaking election campaign promises. Their news coverage of Tea Party rallies and tumultuous town hall meetings on healthcare reform issues have hurt you before the bar of public opinion.

During the time of war criminal President George W. Bush, *Fox News* was his propaganda attack dog. Hannity even received instruction and talking points direct from the White House for his radio and cable TV programs.

But truth be told, if there were no *Fox News* and its stalwarts O'Reilly, Hannity and Beck now, there would be no journalists and/or commentators who are probing for facts and truth or acting as public watchdog in the tradition of a free press.

Call it Republican propaganda if you must, but truth is truth and it hurts. The fact remains that their media public ratings are much higher than the rest or most of the captive mainstream media because people can see through the deception.

Mr. President, is that the reason why you support the bill pending in Congress granting them favored status as nonprofit business because you want to keep them in your pocket? That you are worried by the continued erosion of you rock-star popularity?

Now you are treating the mainstream media as though they were also Wall Street corporations like giant insurance, bank, healthcare providers, and auto manufacturers that badly need federal bailout money to survive from the brink of bankruptcy.

How kind and thoughtful of you, Mr. President. But wait a minute, you are killing them with kindness that could lead to death of journalism and press freedom in the United States of America for the first time in its history.

By the very nature of their job and duty as public watchdog to report wrongdoings in the corridors of power without fear or favor, the mainstream media are not supposed to expect or receive favors from the government.

The brutal truth is that a beholden press cannot be free. And where there is no press freedom, there cannot be a true democracy.

Goodnight, Mr. President.

© Hermie Rotea/Philpress, September 21, 2009

6

Congress Rebukes Rep. Wilson for Shouting the Truth at the Wrong Time and Wrong Place as If He Were a Member of the British House of Commons Where Heckling Is Normal

MR. PRESIDENT:

Republican Congressman Joe Wilson of South Carolina committed a political sin of shouting the truth at you at the wrong time, wrong place, and wrong occasion.

His punishment: The House of Speaker Nancy Pelosi passed a resolution 240-179 rebuking him. His reward: $1,005,021 from 18,859 political contributors.

Mr. President, your recent address on Universal Healthcare Reform before a joint session of Congress really provoked Wilson to shout "You Lie!" when you claimed that illegal aliens are not covered under your plan.

But although he is entitled to freedom of speech as guaranteed by the U.S. Constitution, his outburst was considered bad behavior unbecoming of a member of the Congress of the United States.

He must have gone through a senior moment and thus behaved as if he were a member of the British House of Commons where booing and shouting are normal, instead of a member of Speaker Pelosi's House of Majority Democrats.

The difference of course is that in England's parliament the Prime Minister is not considered the head of state. Thus when he speaks before the legislative body he could be booed or heckled as he is elected only by his peers, and not directly by the people.

In the Congress of the United States, however, when the President speaks before a joint session of the House and the Senate he is entitled to the respect due a head of state because he is directly elected by the people.

But getting back to what Rep. Wilson shouted about, Mr. President, he accused you of lying when you claimed that illegal aliens are not be covered under your healthcare reform package.

The fact though is that Democrat lawmakers had voted against two amendments in House Bill 3200 that would have required beneficiaries to first prove that they are not illegal aliens before receiving benefits. There are an estimated 12 million of them here.

Their reason is that such requirement would have put an undue burden on those in the United States legally.

So under the House measure, working undocumented aliens can use the loophole to buy insurance plans with government subsidy from health insurers in a marketplace designed to encourage competition and cushion the impact of "Public Option" plan.

Mr. President, you can't blame Rep. Wilson for accusing you of lying because what you said about non-healthcare coverage for illegal aliens was a statement that is not supported by facts.

At any rate, the congressman has already apologized to you for his misbehavior, not necessarily for telling the truth, but for shouting it at the wrong time, wrong place, and wrong occasion. You in turn has graciously accepted his apology.

After all, Mr. President, you do lie, flip flop, or change your mind yourself. Politicians do that all the time. It goes with the territory.

For example, what you promised during your 2008 campaign for the presidency and what you actually do now as president in 2009, are two different things.

Candidate Obama and President Obama are two different persons. They call that split personality.

Mr. President, you promised to change Washington and politics as usual. Instead, Washington has changed you.

You opposed the Iraq war, only to embrace it.

You attacked President Bush for his phony war on terror, only to continue it.

You vowed to ban lobbyists in Washington to avoid corruption, only to hire them.

You objected to imprisonment of detainees without trials, only to keep them.

You opposed rendition of detainees to avoid torture, only to follow the same policy.

You criticized health insurers and providers, but accepted $18.8 million from them in 2008

You said the Medicare benefits for the elderly will not be cut, but effective July 2009 they were already reduced.

And so on.

Not to be left out in the debate over Rep. Wilson's outburst in Congress, former President Jimmy Carter has weighed in by charging that his action was "dastardly" and "based on racism."

"There is an inherent feeling among many in this country that an African-American should not be president," the former president, a Democrat, said. He was responding to an audience question at a town hall meeting at his presidential center in Atlanta.

In response, the congressman's son Alan Wilson, who is running for state attorney general in South Carolina, defended his father, saying "There is not a racist bone in my dad's body. He doesn't even laugh at distasteful jokes."

Mr. President, to be sure the Wilson outburst in Congress against you has been a distraction. You have lost so much time already in your campaign to promote your Universal Healthcare Reform package.

The Rasmussen Reports daily Presidential Tracking Poll shows that only 32% of the nation's voters Strongly Approve of the way that you are performing as president, while 38% Strongly Disapprove.

Overall, 49% of voters say they at least Somewhat Approve of your performance, while 51% now Disapprove, despite your recent address before a joint session of Congress on the healthcare issue.

Mr. President, the moment of action is fast approaching. In the House of Representatives there is no problem because it takes only a simple majority of votes to approve your Universal Healthcare Reform package that includes the "Public Option" plan.

But in the Senate, the death of Edward Kennedy has left the Democrats with only 57 members. To overcome a filibuster that Republicans are sure to mount, 60 votes are needed.

Even if the two independent senators side with the Democrats, that is only 59 votes, one short of 60 to break a filibuster. A bipartisan deal with the Republican appears remote because they are ideologically and irreconcilably divided.

If the Democrats want to enact health care reform this year, they appear to have little choice but to adopt a high-risk, go-it-alone, majority-rules strategy as is the setup in the House of Representatives.

Mr. President, the brutal reality is the Republicans do not want a Universal Healthcare Reform this year as a political strategy to win in the 2010 midterm election as a steppingstone to recapture the White House in the 2012 presidential election.

As Republican Senator Jim DeMint of South Carolina put it: "If we're able to stop Obama on this, it will be his Waterloo. It will break him."

Goodnight, Mr. President.

© Hermie Rotea/Philpress, September 17, 2009

7

Facts Show That Bush, Cheney, Rice Neglected to Protect America from 9/11 Terrorist Attacks in Violation of the U.S. Constitution

MR. PRESIDENT:

The terrorist attacks on the United States on September 11, 2001 could have been prevented if only then President George W. Bush, Vice President Dick Cheney, and National Security Adviser Condoleezza Rice did their duty to protect America, but they criminally neglected to do so.

Under Article 1 of the U.S. Constitution, they were sworn in to faithfully execute the offices of president, vice president, and National Security Agency to the best of their ability, preserve, protect, and defend the nation's charter and the American people.

Yet Bush, Cheney and Rice all failed to perform their constitutional duties because they had ignored many early warnings of imminent Al Qaeda terrorist attacks relayed to the White House by 10 friendly nations, not to mention the CIA and the FBI, and did nothing to prevent the catastrophe.

Thus they violated the U.S. Constitution and committed both impeachable and criminal acts, including murder, for the death of nearly 3,000 victims who perished when suicide bombers hijacked four commercial planes, destroyed the World Trade Center in New York, and damaged the Pentagon.

Bush and Cheney are also culpable for murder for the death of over 5,000 in the Iraq and Afghanistan wars that they waged on the great deceptions that the two countries were allegedly involved in 9/11

Bush and Cheney, along with Rice, were to blame and responsible because they dismissed the many early intelligence warnings they had received long before 9/11, as "unreliable and incredible." So they did nothing to protect America.

The Seed and the Road to 9/11

Proof of their criminal culpability are documented and indisputable. A book *The Terror Timeline* by Paul Thompson and the Center for Cooperative Research based in California compiled a year by year, day by day, and minute by minute comprehensive chronicle of the Seed and the Road to 9/11. Other sources include en.wikipedia.org and rnc08report.org.

Simply put, Thompson said: "The Bush administration's continued secrecy in the name of 'national security' only exacerbates this problem, leading many to cry cover-up, others to charge criminal negligence, and still others to consider conspiracy."

Note the Time Frame

1980 -- The United States and Osama bin Laden actually were allied and together with the CIA they supported the Afghan Mujahideen rebels in the war against Soviet occupation of Afghanistan. With Saudi Arabia and U.S. backing, bin Laden led the successful fight against Soviet troops, who subsequently withdrew from Afghanistan in 1989.

Bin Laden became a hero and household name to the Muslim world. He worked with the CIA, at least indirectly. They built tunnels in Afghanistan against Soviet forces, although a CIA spokesperson later claimed, "For the record . . . the CIA never employed, paid or maintained any relationship whatsoever with bin Laden"

In fact, the CIA even trained Bin Laden's "Holy War" recruits from other countries in the United States to fight Soviet troops. Ironically, among them were 15 of the 19 hijackers who later carried out the 9/11 terrorist attacks that destroyed New York's World Trade Center and damaged the Pentagon.

The Blueprint of 9/11 that the White House Dismissed

1995 -- On January 20, the blueprint of the terrorist attacks on the United States code-named "Operation Bojinka" was discovered six years before they happened. It was based on the confession of mastermind plotter Abdul Hakim Murad who was captured in Manila, Philippines, where he operated. He was later turned over to the FBI.

Investigator Col. Rodolfo Mendoza revealed the plot to hijack commercial planes and crash them to the CIA headquarters, the Pentagon, World Trade Center in New York City, Sears Tower in Chicago, Transamerica Tower in San Francisco, and an unidentified nuclear power plant.

But when this early intelligence warning was relayed to the White House, Bush, Cheney and Rice dismissed it as "impossible and not credible." Frustrated investigators lamented: "We told the Americans everything about Operation Bojinka. Why didn't they pay attention?"

Clinton Rejects Bin Laden Turnover

1996 -- CIA Counter Terrorism Center created a Bin Laden Unit after he was linked to the 1993 World Trade Center bombing in New York. He was identified not just a financier but also the organizer of terrorist activity. Actually, the U.S. was too late in discovering the existence of Al Qaeda.

The United States under President Clinton and Britain under Prime Minister Tony Blair rejected the offer of Sudan to turn over to them voluminous files about bin Laden and Al Qaeda while he was living there and using it as his base of global operations and was under its jurisdiction.

Thus the United States and Britain at that time missed an opportunity to know more about Bin Laden and Al Qaeda and possibly prevent 9/11 from happening.

Sudan offered to turn over Bin Laden to the United States to get rid of him as a problem, but then President Clinton refused to accept him because the U.S. at the time had no evidence against him.

Later Bin Laden fled to Afghanistan along with many of his followers and his money resources. The U.S. knew of his plan beforehand but failed to stop him.

FBI Fumbles Its Investigation of Terrorists Training as Pilots in U.S. Flight Schools

Also in 1996, the FBI likewise missed a chance to know where the suicide hijackers had trained as pilots in U.S. flight schools. A business card was found from Murad, the mastermind plotter, that revealed where and what flight schools he had trained off and on starting in 1990.

But the FBI closed the investigation of "Operation Bojinka after they failed to find other potential suspects. What the FBI did not realize is that they already had the names of 10 other trainees in their files which Murad had already provided in his confession during the probe that it bungled.

Indonesia Warns U.S. of 9/11 "But Nobody Believe Us"

1998 -- Indonesia also warned the United States of 9/11. Hendropriyono, the chief of intelligence in Jakarta, said: "We had intelligence predicting the September 11 attacks three years ago before it happened, but nobody believed us."

He said Indonesian intelligence agents had identified Osama bin Laden as the leader of the group planning the attack but that the United States disregarded the warning. Indonesia has the largest Muslim population in the world.

FAA, FBI Dismiss CIA Warning of Flying Bomber

In August, the CIA warned that terrorists planned to fly bomb-laden aircraft from a foreign country and directly target the World Trade Center in New York City. But the FBI and the FAA did not take the warning seriously because of the poor state of aviation of the country which was not disclosed, although later the group was linked to Al Qaeda.

In September, Senior U.S. officials received information from U.S. intelligence that bin Laden's network might crash a plane loaded with explosives into a U.S. airport.

Britain Warns U.S. of "Flying Bombs"

1999 -- British intelligence warned the American Embassy in London that Al Qaeda planned to hijack commercial aircraft and use them as "flying bombs" at American targets.

At the same time, the FBI received reports that a terrorist organization planned to send students to the U.S. for aviation training, the purpose of which was unknown. No investigation was conducted.

A U.S. intelligence report revealed that suicide bombers belonging to Al Qaeda's Martyrdom Battalion could crash-land an aircraft packed with high explosives into the White House, the Pentagon, or the CIA headquarters.

The report was made by the National Intelligence Council which advises the President and U.S. intelligence on emerging threats. Bush, Cheney and Rice dismissed the early warning as "impossible." Later they claimed they never read the report until May 2002 although it had been publicly posted in the Internet.

Norad Stages 9/11 Exercises In Preparation for Attacks

2000 -- The North American Aerospace Defense Command (Norad) staged exercises similar to 9/11 terrorist attacks as part of U.S. preparedness program to protect America. It simulated hijacked airliners used as weapons to crash into targets and cause mass casualties and damages.

In another mock exercise, jets performed a shoot-down practice over the Atlantic Ocean of a jet laden with chemical poisons heading towards the U.S.

(Ironically and tragically, when 9/11 did happen, not a single U.S. military plane flew to intercept and thwart the suicide bombers who had hijacked commercial planes, destroyed the World Trade Center, and crash-damaged the Pentagon.)

YEAR 2001 -- THE COUNTDOWN BEGINS

The book *The Terror Timeline* by Paul Thompson intensified documentation of the many early warnings of imminent terrorist attacks on the United States by Bin Laden and Al Qaeda long before 9/11 which Bush, Cheney and Rice received but repeatedly dismissed as "unreliable and incredible" and did nothing to protect America.

On this Year of the 9/11 Attacks, Note Closely the Following Time Frame

January 10 -- Counterterrorism Tsar Richard Clarke briefed Rice as the National Security adviser and her deputy Steve Hadley about the expected strike by Al Qaeda. While presenting his plan to them, Clarke got the impression that she had never heard of Al Qaeda, which was odd.

February 7 -- CIA Director George Tenant warned Congress that "the threat from terrorism is real, it is immediate, and it is evolving." He testified that Bin Laden and his global network remained "the most immediate and serious threat" to the United States.

March -- Al Qaeda operatives plan to conduct unspecified attack inside the United States. An intelligence source said that one of the terrorists already resided in the U.S. Other reports said the planned attacks would target New York and California.

April -- The North American Aerospace Defense Command (Norad) planned to continue emergency exercise amidst persistent reports of Al Qaeda planned attacks on the U.S. Code-named "Positive Force", some Special Operations personnel would train to think like terrorists.

They added a scenario simulating "an event having a terrorist group hijack a commercial airliner and fly it into the Pentagon." But White House officials and military superiors rejected the emergency drill as either "too unrealistic" or too disconnected to the original intent of Norad exercise.

May -- Bush, Cheney and Rice received briefing papers titled: "Bin Laden Planning Multiple Operations, Bin Laden Public Profile May Presage Attack, Bin Ladin Network's Plans Advancing". The exact contents of the briefings were kept confidential.

U.S. intelligence reported to the White House that Al Qaeda planned to infiltrate the United States from Canada. It would carry out terrorist operation using high explosives. The information was shared with the FBI, INS, Custom Service, State Department, and the White House.

Bin Laden's Global Network prepared for martyrdom. The Defense Department received information that seven Al Qaeda operatives had departed from several locations for the United States and Canada. The CIA learned that key Al Qaeda operatives were disappearing as they prepare for martyrdom.

NSA Adviser Rice Repeatedly Ignores Attack Warnings

June -- National Security Adviser Rice dismissed chatters that were picked in spring and summer which said: "Big event -- there will be a very, very, very, very big uproar. There will be attacks in the near future." Reports also said that Bin Laden was mobilizing his forces.

But Rice said all the warnings were "red herrings" or merely a diversion."

June 28 -- CIA Director George Tenet warned the White House of imminent Al Qaeda attacks. He wrote and sent his intelligence summary to National Security Adviser Condoleezza Rice. He told her: "Based on a review of all sources reporting over the last five months, we believe that Bin Laden will launch a significant terrorist attack against the United States.

"The attack will be spectacular and designed to inflict mass casualties against U.S. facilities or interests. Attack preparations have been made. Attack will occur with little or no warning."

Bush, Cheney Told Attack Warnings Are Real

July -- President Bush and Vice President Dick Cheney and National Security Adviser Rice received more briefing papers as terrorist threat reports surged even higher, titled:
"Bin Laden Threats Are Real"
"Bin Laden Planning High Profile Attacks"
Again the exact contents of the new briefings remained classified. But it would be revealed later that the briefings consistently predicted upcoming terrorist attacks on the U.S.

Deputy CIA Director John McLaughlin was frustrated when inexperienced Bush officials questioned the validity of certain CIA intelligence findings. Two unnamed veteran Counter Terrorism Center officers involved in Bin Laden issues were so worried about the impending disaster that the White House repeatedly ignored that they even considered resigning in disgust and going public with their concerns.

Bin Laden Beats Drums of Imminent Al Qaeda Attacks on America, Pray for Martyrs

July -- Bin Laden recorded a speech at his Farug training camp in Afghanistan in which he urged trainees to pray for the success of an upcoming attack involving 20 "martyrs." His plot to attack the U.S. was now virtually an open secret to both the Muslim world and the United States.

But Bush, Cheney and Rice continued ignoring the many early warning of imminent terrorist attacks as "unreliable and incredible" and just a "diversion."

India Warns U.S. of Impending Attack

July -- The United States received intelligence alert from India that the White House would be hit by a terrorist attack, but no details were given. U.S. government officials confirmed that Indian intelligence got the tip from two Islamic radicals with ties to Bin Laden.

July 10 -- FBI agent Ken Williams in Phoenix, Arizona, warned that Muslims from the Middle East were taking flight training lessons in aviation school in Arizona and suspected they might be potential terrorists of Bin Laden.

July 15 -- CIA Director George Tenet again met with National Security Adviser Rice and her aides at the White House about the growing terrorist threat of Bin Laden and his Al Qaeda network. Tenet briefed Rice that "there was going to be a major attack. He displayed a huge wall chart showing a dozen possible targets.

Britain Receives Report that Al Qaeda Now Set to Attack U.S.

July 16 -- British Prime Minister Tony Blair received a report from British spy agencies warning that Al Qaeda was now in "the final stages" of preparing an attack on the United States. He reportedly relayed the information to the White House.

July 31 -- The FBI and the FAA issued similar warnings. The FAA warned commercial airlines: "Terror groups are known to be planning and training for hijacking, and we ask you therefore to use caution."

But later it would be known that pilots and flight attendants were never told about such warnings against hijacking.

Even the Taliban Warns America of Terrorist Strikes

August -- Little known is the fact that even the then de facto Taliban government in Kabul, Afghanistan, also warned the United States of imminent Al Qaeda attacks inside the U.S. Taliban Foreign Minister Wakil Ahmed Muttawakil relayed the warning to Washington and the United Nations.

He said that Bin Laden was planning a "huge attack" on targets inside America. He warned that the attack was imminent and would kill thousands. The Taliban foreign minister got the information from Tahir Yildash, leader of the rebel Islamic Movement of Uzbekistan which was allied with Al Qaeda at the time.

The Taliban de facto government in Kabul and the United States at the time had friendly relation.

Argentina, Jordan, Egypt Relay Warnings to U.S.

August -- Argentina warned the United States that an attack of "major proportion" on American targets would occur. The information came from reliable Jewish intelligence. The source said the U.S. was informed about the report.

At the same time, Egyptian intelligence in Cairo had received similar information from one of its agents in Afghanistan and relayed it to the CIA. Cairo expected the CIA to ask for more information. It never did.

Jordan also sent a top-secret message to the United States code-named "The Big Wedding" warning that a major attack inside the U.S. would occur with the use of planes. Jordanian intelligence deemed it so important that King Abdullah's own men relayed the warning to Washington through Arab and German intermediaries to avoid being intercepted.

Russia Warns America of Suicide Pilots

August -- Russia warned the Bush administration in Washington that suicide pilots were training for terrorist attacks inside the United States. President Vladimir Putin relayed the warning based on Russian intelligence findings.

It would be known later than Bush, Cheney and Rice took the warning lightly. The head of the Russian intelligence subsequently said: "We had clearly warning them on several occasions, but they did not pay the necessary attention."

Russian intelligence had solid information. Its agents knew the organizer and executors of the terrorist attacks, at least two of them being Muslim radicals from Russian-controlled Uzbekistan.

Egypt Again Warns Washington of Impending Al Qaeda Attacks

August 30 -- Egyptian President Hasni Mubarak said his government intelligence had warned Washington that Bin Laden's global network was in the advanced stages of unleashing attacks on the United States.

Mubarak said he got the information from an agent working inside Al Qaeda. However, U.S. officials later denied receiving any such warning from Egypt. In fact, U.S. intelligence was in disarray.

France Warns U.S. of Imminent Terrorist Attack

France warned the Bush administration of an impending terrorist attack inside the United States but provided no detail. French warning was similar to a previous Israeli warning. France has a Muslim population.

SEPTEMBER 2001

Bin Laden's telephone calls to the United States were intercepted. British insiders disclosed that the Al Qaeda leader contacted an associate thought to be in Pakistan. The conversation referred to an incident that would take place in the U.S. and discussed possible repercussions

In another call to an associate thought to be in Afghanistan, they discussed the scale and effect of the operation. The British government carefully referred to the intercepts: "There is evidence of a very specific nature relating to the guilt [plot] of Bin Laden and his associates that is too sensitive to release."

U.S. Skeptical on Bin Laden's Call to Stepmother Regarding 9/11

September 9 -- Bin Laden called his stepmother Al-Khalifa bin Laden using a satellite telephone and the signals were intercepted and sometimes recorded. He told her, "In two days you're going to hear big news and you're not going to hear from me for a while."

He called to cancel their meeting in Damaoouo, Syria. Sincc it was already September 9, it was obvious that when he said "In two days" he meant the big news or attack would explode on September 11.

In any event, the next day a U.S. official dismissed Bin Laden's call without taking any action, saying "I would view those reports with skepticism." The White House was reportedly informed of his intercepted call but did nothing.

Alarm Bells Sound at Stock Market in Expectation of Extraordinary Event

September 10 -- Alarm bells sounded over unusual trading in the U.S. stock options market. CBS reported on the extraordinary event. It was observed that whenever such kind of unusual heavy trading activity occurs "something big" is about to happen.

The U.S. National Security Agency (NSA) intercepted two messages in Arabic. One stated, "The match is about to begin." The other said, "Tomorrow is zero hour." The messages were transmitted between someone in Saudi Arabia and someone in Afghanistan.

But despite the bad omen, the United States took no immediate action. The White House of Bush, Cheney and Rice was still neglectful of their duty to protect America or were still in self-denial that such "incredible or unreliable" diversion would ever occur.

U.S. Officials, White House Call Warning Signs as "Needles in Haystack"

September 10 -- U.S. intelligence intercepted more terrorist messages. Electronic intercepts from undercover agents planted in Al Qaeda cells in the United States were busy monitoring the now fast-developing catastrophe. They heard messages like, "Tomorrow will be a great day for us."

But as usual the Bush administration of President Bush, Vice President Cheney, and NSA Adviser Rice took no action to protect America from impending terrorist attacks. Yet U.S. military generals were warned not to fly on the morning of September 11 due to the high state of alert during the past two weeks.

To believe or not to believe -- that was the big question. And the White House of Bush, Cheney, and Rice chose not to believe that 9/11 would ever happen despite all the many early warnings they had received from 10 nations, not to mention the CIA and the FBI.

NSA, CIA and FBI Intercept Terrorist Messages But Do Nothing

Sometimes they do, sometimes they don't, act at all. On September 10, they all slept in their job. Although the NSA, CIA and FBI also intercepted terrorist messages, yet they didn't immediately analyze them despite the ominous signs of impending disaster. The messages included:

"This is a big thing!"

"We're ready to go!"

"They are going to pay the price!"

But despite such ominous signs of imminent terrorist attacks, the White House, NSA, CIA, FBI, FAA, NORAD, all were caught sleeping in their jobs and failed to do their duty to protect America!

9/11 EXPLODES!

Source: Philpress Columns   38

September 11, 2001 -- Osama bin Laden's Al Qaeda suicide terrorists attacked the United States by hijacking four commercial jetliners and used them as guided bombers to strike at their intended targets: the World Trade Center in New York City, the Pentagon in Arlington, Virginia, and the U.S. Congress on Capitol Hill in Washington, D.C.

The first plane, American Airlines Boeing 767 Flight 11, at 8:46 a.m. crashed into North Tower of the World Trade Center, killing all 76 passengers, 11 crew members, five hijackers, and 1,366 in the building and ground.

The second aircraft, United Airlines Boeing 767 Flight 175, at 9:03 a.m. bombed WTC South Tower 2, killing all 51 passengers, 11 crew members, five hijackers, and 600 building personnel.

Minutes later, both twin towers collapsed.

The third jetliner, American Airlines Boeing 757 Flight 77, at 9:37 a.m. smashed into The Pentagon, headquarters of the U.S. Department of Defense in Arlington, Virginia, killing 53 passengers, six crew members, five hijackers, and 125 Pentagon personnel.

The fourth plane, United Airlines Boeing 757 Flight 93, at 10:03 a.m. was forced down in Stonycreek Township at Somerset County in Pennsylvania, killing all 33 passengers, seven crew members, and four hijackers. Its intended target was the U.S. Congress on Capitol Hill.

Finally, Bin Laden made good his threats and warnings to bring Jihad or his Holy War to America.

Not One U.S. Plane Flies to Intercept Terrorist Attackers During 9/11

U.S. officials made a shocking revelation that the entire United States under its defense plan was to be defended only by 14 fighter planes, two each from seven military bases. Not one was used during the 9/11 terrorist attacks.

According to author Paul Thompson and the *Dallas Morning News*, none of the fighter planes were at "bases close to two obvious terrorist targets -- Washington, DC and New York City.

As a defense official explained, "I don't think anyone of us envisioned an internal air threat by big aircraft. I don't know of anybody that ever thought through that."

Even NORAD, which had held exercises simulating expected plane hijackings and terrorist attacks, did not have any plane in the air to fight the attackers.

Foregoing Evidence of Bush-Cheney-Rice Criminal Culpability for 9/11 Are Documented and Indisputable

As contented in the beginning, let it be restated that the terrorist attacks on the United States on September 11, 2001 could have been prevented if only then President Bush, Vice President Cheney, and NSA Adviser Rice did their duty to protect America, but they criminally neglected to do so.

Under Article 1 of the Constitution, they were sworn in to faithfully execute their high offices of government to the best of their ability, preserve, protect, and defend the Constitution and the American people, "so help me God."

Thus Bush, Cheney and Rice violated the Constitution with respect to 9/11 and are responsible for the nearly 3,000 deaths and billions of dollars in damages in the aftermath of the catastrophe.

In fairness, conspiracy -- no. But criminal neglect and violation of the U.S. Constitution, yes!

As famed California prosecutor Vincent Bugliosi argued in his best-selling book *The Prosecution of George W. Bush for Murder*, they can also be indicted for murder for the death of overe 5,000 who died in Iraq and Afghanistan wars that they waged in violation of the U.S. Constitution and international laws.

Bush, Cheney, Rice, CIA, FBI Official Explanations Before 9/11 Commission

President Bush -- "Never [in] anybody's thought process . . . about how to protect America did we ever think that the evil doers would fly not one but four commercial aircraft into precious U.S. targets . . . never."

Vice President Cheney -- "Incendiary suggestions . . . that the White House had advance information that would have prevented the tragic attacks of 9/11 are thoroughly irresponsible . . . in time of war" any serious investigation of 9/11 foreknowledge would be tantamount to giving "aid and comfort" to the enemy.

National Security Adviser Condoleezza Rice -- "I don't think anybody could have predicted that these people would take an airplane and slam it into the World Trade Center, take another one and slam it into the Pentagon, that they would try to use an airplane as a missile."

CIA Director George Tenet -- "We are proud of that [our] record . . . [The 9/11 plot was] "in the hands of three or four people" and thus was impossible to prevent.

FBI Director Robert Mueller -- "There was nothing the agency could have done to anticipate and prevent the [9/11] attacks."

"Press For Truth" Documentary Exposes Bush-Cheney Obstruction and Stonewalling

In 2006 a documentary, *Press For Truth*, may well serve as a counterpoint to the allegations of President Bush, Vice President Cheney, NSA Adviser Rice, CIA Director Tenet and FBI Director Mueller.

Based in part on the book *The Terror Timeline* by Paul Thompson, the documentary was produced by Ray Nowosielski, John Duffy and Kyle F. Hence; written by Ray Nowosielski and Kyle F. Hence; and directed by Ray Nowosielski.

The film follows the Jersey Girls led by Lorie Van Auken who were widowed by 9/11 and who hounded and forced Bush and Congress to create the 9/11 Commission despite his obstruction and stonewalling.

The Unanswered Questions Remain Unanswered

1. Why had NORAD whose duty is to protect American airspace and even held exercises simulating predicted 9/11 attacks failed to fly a single military plane to protect known terrorist U.S. targets, the World Trade Center in New York City and the Pentagon in Arlington, Virginia?

2. Why did the World Trade Center twin towers completely collapse when no other steel-framed skyscraper had ever totally collapsed before due to fire?

3. Why did President Bush stay in a Florida school classroom for over 10 minutes after being told by his aide that New York had been attacked?

4. Why did the White House refuse to release documents that the 9/11 Commission had requested?

5. Why did the 9/11 Commission, whose chairman was recommended to that position by the White House, allow Bush and Cheney to testify behind closed doors and not under oath, thereby making it difficult if not impossible to double-check the accuracy and truthfulness of their assertions?

Whistleblower Exposes FBI Failure to Help Prevent 9/11 Terrorist Attacks on U.S.

In a related event, FBI special agent Coleen Rowley who was assigned to the FBI New York Office, turned whistleblower in May 2002 after the 9/11 terrorist attacks on the United States by testifying before the U.S. Senate Judiciary Committee that the FBI had neglected to help prevent the catastrophe.

After the September 11, 2001, Rowley wrote a paper for FBI Director Robert Mueller documenting how FBI HQ personnel in Washington, DC had mishandled and failed to take action on information provided by the Minneapolis, Minnesota Field Office where she was formerly stationed, regarding its investigation of suspected terrorist Zacarias Moussaoui.

Moussaoui had been suspected of being involved in preparations for a suicide-hijacking similar to the December 1994, "Eiffel Tower" hijacking of Air France 8969. Failures identified by Rowley might have left the U.S. vulnerable to the September 11, 2001 attacks.

Mueller and Senator Chuck Grassley (R-IA) pushed for and got a major reorganization, focused on creation of the new Office of Intelligence at the FBI. This reorganization was supported with a significant expansion of FBI personnel with counterterrorism and language skills.

As a result of Rowley's role as FBI whistleblower, she was named TIME "Person of the Year" award in 2002 along with two other women credited as whistleblowers, Sherron Watkins from Enron and Cynthia Cooper of WorldCom. Rowley also received the Sam Adams Award for 2002.

Mr. President, under the U.S. Constitution you are actually the top law enforcer of the United States, although the leg work is done by the U.S. Attorney General's Office and the U.S. Department of Justice.

Ironically you have done nothing about these constitutional violations related to 9/11, not to mention the illegal and immoral Iraq and Afghanistan wars that Bush and Cheney aggressively waged in violation of internatiuonal laws and based on great deceptions and their addiction to oil and profit.

You said you prefer to move forward instead of backward, which is a cop out. Explain that to famed California prosecutor Vincent Bugliosi, author of the best-sellling book *The Prosecution of George W. Bush For Murder*, who has already served notice that Bush will soon be indicted in California for murder related to 9/11 and Iraq.

Happy 9/11 anniversary? Forget it, Mr. President. Good night. (Excerpt from a book *Bush-Cheney War Crimes* by Hermie Rotea)

© Hermie Rotea/Philpress, September 11, 2009

8

Can Washington be Trusted to Reform a Broken System and Make Universal Healthcare a Fundamental Right for All?

MR. PRESIDENT:

Washington is captive of an "Invisible Government" dominated by lobbyists who work for the vested interests of vultures that rob the U.S. national treasury at the expense of taxpayers.

There is the Industrial-Military Complex that manufacture weapons of mass destruction to keep Iraq and Afghanistan wars and other conflicts going. Both President Lincoln and President Eisenhower warned the nation against this menace before.

It is not a dirty big secret anymore that America's addiction to war costs the government about 62 percent of its national budget. Currently the U.S. also owes Communist China about $1 trillion used to finance the phony wars on terror.

And at the rate things are going, Mr. President, you yourself have even projected a 10-year budgetary deficit of $9 trillion, which is unprecedented in American history. That is a lot of money.

Then there is the Industrial-Medical Complex composed of manufacturers of medicines, insurance corporations that control medical coverage, pharmaceutical group that dispense prescription drugs, and research agencies that conduct continuing studies to discover new treatment and promote the industry.

Both the Industrial-Military Complex and the Industrial-Medical Complex are the top political donors that "bribe" elected and appointed leaders of both the Democratic Party and the Republican Party with millions of dollars. That is how Washington elite from the president down have become captive of their "Invisible Government."

So when it comes to the question of Universal Healthcare for bona fide people of America as a matter of fundamental right, how can Washington be trusted to do the right thing? Despite White House's and Democratic

Congress' assurances that their Reform Package with the controversial "Public Option" plan is the right formula, how do the people really know that until it actually happens or proves itself? How do they know if there are hidden surprises?

Mr. President, sorry to sound skeptical. But it is hard to trust elected politicians when they do things after the election exactly the opposite of what they pledged as candidates. In your case, you have flipped flopped on Iraq war, Washington lobbyists, continued detention of Guantanamo Bay detainees without charges and trial, and rendition or sending detainees to other countries where they are tortured.

That is why the no-nonsense legal watchdog ACLU which supported your previous positions on these issues have filed cases against your flip-flopping.

And as the top law enforcer of the United States under the Constitution, Mr. President, you have also failed to do your constitutional duty with respect to war criminals.

Why is your U.S.Attorney General Eric Holder merely investigating water-boarding torture of detainees by CIA interrogators who are only "small fishes" who just followed orders from the White House and the Defense Department, which is laughable, instead of going after the real war criminals or "big fishes" like George W. Bush and Dick Cheney?

Common on, Mr. President, stop bullshitting the people with your alibi of preferring to move forward instead of backward. What you really mean is that you don't want any problem to disrupt legislation and your reelection in 2012.

But getting back to your Universal Healthcare Reform Package, how can we trust you and both the Democrats and the Republicans in Congress to institute real reform and repair a broken system when they are both "guilty" of receiving "bribes" disguised as "political contributions" from the Industrial-Medical Complex?

Here is the lowdown, Mr. President, take it or leave it.

The Center for Responsible Politics (CRP) has disclosed that you alone were in fact the very top recipient of political contribution from the Industrial-Medical Complex with a whopping $18.8 million during the 2008 election cycle, more than any other presidential candidate.

What more, CRP has also reported that the Democratic Party has already received 62 percent of the funds contributed so far for the forthcoming 2010 election cycle.

The top 10 U.S. senators who received political contributions from health providers, insurers and pharmaceutical corporations in the 2008 election cycle are:

1. John McCain (R-AZ) -- $7,436,673
2. Max Baucus (D-MT) -- $1,575,675
3. Mitch McConnell (R-KY) -- $1,497,235
4. John Cornyn (R-TX) -- $997,319
5. Arlen Specter (D-PA) -- $839,498
6. Saxby Chambliss (R-GA) -- $757,209

Source: Philpress Columns

7. Tom Harkin (D-IA) -- $727,248
8. Pat Roberts (R-KS) -- $718,949
9. Susan Collins (R-ME) -- $706,519
10. Harry Reid (D-NV) -- $671,900

The top 10 members of the U.S. House of Representatives who also received political contributions from health providers, insurers and pharmaceutical corporations in the 2008 election cycle are:

1. Charles B. Rangel (D-NY) -- $1,53,461
2. Frank Pallone Jr. (D-NJ) -- $985,345
3. Steny H. Hoyer (D-MD) -- $913,600
4. Ron Paul (R-TX) -- $880,544
5. John Boehner (R-OH) -- $731,000
6. Eric Cantor (R-VA) -- $711,050
7. Dave Camp (R-MI) -- $696,650
8. Tom Price (R-GA) -- 644,851
9. John D. Dingell (D-MI) -- $635,736
10. James E. Clyburn (D-SC) -- $593,098

Credit goes to author R.H. Sheldon of suite101.com for exposing this shenanigan behind the Universal Healthcare Reform debate.

These "political contributions" were just part of the $167 million the Industrial-Medical Complex donated during the 2008 election cycle. Because the Democrats are now the new majority in the U.S. Congress, they are expected to receive more "political contributions" this time around.

Now Mr. President, can you blame the people if they now find it hard to believe in politicians who promised them the moon and the stars during the election campaign? Of course not. They have good reason to be skeptical.

As the data above show, you and your fellow politicians in the U.S. Congress are beholden to health providers, insurers and pharmaceutical corporations for receiving "political contributions" from these vested interests that profit from cheating patients, especially the elderly.

So how can the people expect the White House and the U.S. Congress to really, truly, sincerely, honestly and without mental reservation, repair a broken system and deliver a no-nonsense healthcare reform that makes universal coverage a fundamental right for all?

Mr. President, don't just tell us. Show us. As the saying goes, action speaks louder than words. More on this hot topic later. Goodnight.

© Hermie Rotea/Philpress, September 2, 2009

9

Is Death of Senator Edward Kennedy the End of Camelot?

MR. PRESIDENT:

The Kennedy political dynasty may have faded into the sunset, but the dream lives on. The youngest and last of the three famous brothers of the Camelot has joined them in the world beyond. Here is their chronological order of departure at a glance:

Edward M. Kennedy, 1932-2009
John F. Kennedy Jr., 1960-1999
Robert F. Kennedy, 1925-1968
John F. Kennedy, 1917-1963
Joseph P. Kennedy Jr., 1915-1944
Joseph P. Kennedy Sr., 1888-1969

President Kennedy was assassinated in Dallas, Texas, while Senator Robert Kennedy was assassinated in Los Angeles, California. Now Senator Edward Kennedy has just died of brain cancer at his home on Cape Cod, Massachusetts. He was 77.

Long before them, U.S. Navy plane Commander John P. Kennedy Jr., older brother of President Kennedy and the oldest son of U.S. Ambassador to United Kingdom Joseph P. Kennedy Sr., in 1944 perished in action when his B-24 plane loaded with bombs exploded in midair after taking off from England enroute to a secret mission over Germany.

Who will now carry on the torch? Can the new generation of surviving Kennedys take over the political dynasty?

John F. Kennedy Jr., son of the 35th president of the United States, would have been the logical heir to the Camelot. But he died prematurely in July 1999 in a plane crash on the way to Martha's Vineyard where you are currently vacationing.

Rep. Patrick Joseph Kennedy, son of Edward Kennedy, is serving his 8th term in Congress representing Rhode Island. Robert Francis Kennedy Jr., son of Robert Kennedy, is an attorney and a radio talk show host of Air America. Joseph Kennedy III, also son of Robert Kennedy, has retired as a congressman. Can the torch be passed to them??

Mr. President, this is indeed a sad moment for the nation now that the last remaining survivor of the three brothers of the Camelot has passed away.

They will live long in our memory rich with beautiful thoughts and unforgettable experience. Legend has it that Camelot is a mythical name used to describe the administration of President Kennedy and his brothers Bobby and Ted in the good old days.

It is also the mythical capital of King Arthur's kingdom where, according to legend, truth and goodness and beauty reigned. It symbolized what is good and ideal in life and heaven. But it is also the name of the most famous castle and stronghold of King Arthur from which he fought many of the battles that marked his life.

And of course, Mr. President, not to be forgotten is the sight of John John playing under the desk of his father President Kennedy while he was at work at the White House Oval Office, and later when at the tender age of three he stood in attention alongside his widowed mother and First Lady Jacqueline Bouvier Kennedy, and smartly saluted his father' casket after it was carried down to the front steps of St. Matthew's Cathedral in Washington, DC on the final legal for burial at Arlington National Cemetery.

Yes, Mr. President, those were vivid and unforgettable moments in American history that will live long in our memory.

With Senator Kennedy's passing, you lost a supporter, a friend, and a leader who had worked for 1,000 bills that were enacted into laws of which 300 he had authored himself. He was among the first to support your candidacy for the first black president of the United States.

Like you he championed Universal Healthcare for all people of this country as a matter of fundamental right. Unfortunately he did not live long enough to cast his vote to make it a reality when the times comes.

With his demise, it may well be that the raging debate over your proposed "Option Plan" or so-called government takeover of Universal Healthcare (according to critics and the Republicans) is temporarily suspended as the nation mourns the death of one of the longest-serving senators in U.S. history.

Mr. President, that should cool off tempers and tensions that have marred town hall meetings held in different parts of the country over your controversial healthcare reform package. We do need a breather from the acrimonious debates lately.

But as Senator Ted Kennedy said, "The hopes rise again and the dream lives on. The dream shall never die!"

One thing about the famous Kennedy brothers is that they knew how to state their positions on the burning issues of the day with succinct words that are universally accepted and quoted through the ages.

Who can forget President Kennedy's words when he declared in his inaugural address, "Ask not what the country can do for you; ask what you can do for your country."?

Senator Bob Kennedy for his part said, "History belongs not to the many who are afraid to pursue new ideas in the face of a timid society, but rather to the few who dare seek to change a world that yields most painfully to change."

Mr. President, it is only appropriate that the nation pauses to lament the death of a political icon that was synonymous with public service. Ted Kennedy had been a United States senator from Massachusetts and a ranking member of the Democratic Party.

From 1962 he served nine terms in the Senate. At the time of his death, he was the second most senior member of the upper chamber of Congress after Robert Byrd of West Virginia, and the third-longest-serving senator in U.S. history.

Ted Kennedy was the youngest brother of President Kennedy and Senator Robert Kennedy, who were both assassinated, and the father of Rep. Patrick J. Kennedy.

Mr. President, because of the magic of the Kennedy name, supporters tried to groom him to follow in the footsteps of his older brothers and run for president. In 1968 no less than your Mayor of Chicago Richard J. Daley urged him to seek the Democratic Party presidential nomination as the natural heir to his famous older brothers.

More so in 1969 when Ted Kennedy defeated Louisiana Senator Russell B. Long by a 31–26 margin to become Senate Majority Whip, the youngest person to attain that position. That boosted his presidential image and made him the frontrunner for the presidency.

However, on the night of July 18, 1969, while Senator Kennedy was on Chappaquiddick Island of Martha's Vineyard where coincidentally you are now vacationing with your family, he left a party of young women who had worked for his brother Robert's presidential campaign the year before.

He was driving an Oldsmobile with one of the women, 28-year-old Mary Jo Kopechne, as his passenger, when he drove off Dike Bridge into the Poucha Pond inlet. Kennedy escaped the overturned vehicle and swam to safety, but Kopechne died in the car.

In his daze Kennedy left the scene of the accident without reporting it to the authorities. To make the long story short, he later explained in a national broadcast, "I regard as indefensible the fact that I did not report the accident to the police immediately," but denied driving under the influence of alcohol and any immoral conduct between him and Kopechne.

Kennedy then asked the Massachusetts electorate whether he should stay in office, and after getting a favorable response, he did. However, Chappaquiddick doomed his reluctant and conflicted quest for the presidency, although he bounced back and maintained his stature as an outstanding U.S. senator.

Mr. President, although Ted Kennedy did not make it for president, nevertheless later he said that he accomplished more as a senator, what with 300 bills that he had participated in enacting into laws, and his strong advocacy for Universal Healthcare for all people of the United States as a matter of fundamental right.

Senator Edward M. Kennedy will be greatly missed.

Goodnight, Mr. President.

© Hermie Rotea/Philpress, August 25, 2009

10

Is Obama Preparing for a Gen. Custer's Last Stand on Healthcare Reform as the "Sleeping Giant" is Awakened to Haunt Him in His "Public Option" Plan?

MR. PRESIDENT:

What's really going on in Obama la la land?

You are dancing around the controversial "public option" plan of your much debated Universal Healthcare Reform which has divided the nation. Now nobody knows for sure which way you are going. Are you caving in with a white flag of surrender to the Medical Industrial Complex that opposes your plan with its millions of dollars of lobby [aka bribe] money, or are you preparing for a proverbial General Custer's last stand in your own version of the 1876 Battle of Little Bighorn?

As your Republican detractors have put it, this burning issue could be your political Waterloo that will make you only a one-term president.

Already, as you walk through a tightrope of uncertainty, you have been attacked as Dictator Adolf Hitler of Germany with a mustache and swastika, and accused of trying to replace America's capitalism way of life with socialism, or with a system whose government is supposed to take care of the people from the cradle to the grave, which of course is easier said than done.

It is ironic that the more you talk about your Universal Healthcare Reform the more people know little about it. Even Congress' over 1,000-page bill to legislate your plan has not helped because even its members have no time to read it. Even Rep. John Conyers Jr. (D-Mich) has decried such a voluminous measure. So there is a move to "Kill the Bill!" But don't confuse that with director Quentin Tarantino's movie "Kill Bill".

A "SELLOUT" headline in *New York Post* is even being bruited about as appropriate in describing your enigmatic stance on Universal Healthcare Reform. A woman protester has also warned Congress during a tumultuous town hall meeting that your much-maligned plan has awakened the "Sleeping Giant," referring to the "revolt" against it which your people have dismissed as Republican-organized mobs.

That description was first heard in 1941 from a Japanese admiral after Japan had bombed Pearl Harbor, referring to the United States. As history goes, the "sleeping giant" did wake up and later dropped atomic bombs on Hiroshima and Nagasaki to end World War Two.

But getting back to your Universal Healthscare -- oops -- Universal Healthcare Reform -- the problem is that you have created the situation yourself. You and your team of so-called expert czars have said different and conflicting things about your plan. As a result, you have sent out mixed signals and confused the people.

Worse, you no longer smell like a rose. You have flipped flopped on vital issues like the Bush phony wars on terror and Washington lobbyists, which you pledged to outlaw but didn't. So although you promised to change Washington and politics as usual, instead Washington has changed you. Your credibility is sinking, and that is evidenced by the fact that current public opinion polls show more people now oppose your healthcare reform than favor it.

You blamed cable news networks, particularly Fox News of Bill O'Reilly, Sean Hannity and Glenn Beck who have consistently attacked you on the issue and boosted their channel's rating. But you need not worry about them because you always have Chris Matthews of MSNBC who adores you like a rock star.

Now let us get to specifics. You have repeatedly assured the nation that under your Universal Healthcare Reform and under your administration the senior citizens of this country will not be adversely affected. You promised that their Medicare and/or Medicaid benefits or services would not be cut.

Not true, Mr. President. In fact, in a previous column we stated that as "You have bailed out Wall Street giant corporations like banks, insurance companies, auto manufacturers and others who are the riches of the rich with billions of dollars of the taxpayers' money . . . you have neglected to rescue senior citizens who are the poorest of the poor whose Medi-Cal or Medicaid benefits have already been reduced effective July 2009."

That this has already happened under your administration does not speak well of you. If you didn't know about it or had nothing to do with it, then it merely showed that you don't really know what's going on.

You may be a good and articulate public speaker as well as a good community organizer and university lecturer, but your rhetoric in this case does not stand the test of truth.

You can't blame the people if they are puzzled by your true position on Universal Healthcare Reform. Your White House has not put its act together and appears to be in disarray. Your mixed messages on the administration's commitment to the "public option," for instance, have caused heads to spin.

Last Saturday you said during a town hall meeting in Grand Junction, Colorado: "All I'm saying, though, that the public option, whether we have it or we don't have it, is not the entirety of health care reform. This is just one sliver of it, one aspect of it."

Then on Sunday, your Health and Human Service Secretary Kathleen Sebelius told CNN's "State of the Nation" talk show that your government alternative to private health insurance is "not the essential element" of your administration's plan, and that the White House is open to health insurance cooperatives as an alternative to a government-run plan.

When CNN talk show host John King asked her, "So the public option is not a deal-breaker from the president's standpoint?", Sebelius without denying replied: "Well, I think there will be a competitor to private insurers. That's really the essential part, is you don't turn over the whole new marketplace to private insurance companies and trust them to do the right thing. We need some choices, we need more competition."

So what did your Press Secretary Robert Gibbs say to CBS anchor Harry Smith when asked if the government have to have government-sponsored insurance plan in order for him to sign off on it, "or is this a deal breaker?" Your spokesman was more emphatic for the public option:

"What the president has always talked about is that we inject some choice and competition into the private insurance market. There are places in this country, unfortunately, where if you don't get insurance through your job and you are seeking it on the the private insurance market, you don't have any choice but one health insurance company.

"What the president has said, in order to inject choice and competition, which will drive down costs and improve quality, that people ought to be able to have some competitor in that market. There ought to be a choice that they have. The president has thus far sided with the notion that that can best be done through a public option."

Your third spokesperson of the day, Linda Douglass, communications director for the White House Office of Health Reform, told *Politico:* "Nothing has changed. The president has always said that what is essential is that health insurance reform must lower costs, ensure that there are affordable options for all Americans and it must increase choice and competition in the health insurance market. He believes the public option is the best way to achieve those goals."

Then on the same Sunday night, Marc Ambinder of *The Atlantic* wrote that an administration official who requested anonymity told him that Secretary Sebelius "misspoke" in underplaying the importance of the "public option" although the White House acknowledged that this most important element of the reform package, while virtually assured of passage in the House, is a tough sell in the Senate.

You also claimed that the AARP with millions of members support the healthcare reform bill. But while the organization of seniors confirmed that it supports healthcare reform, it has not necessarily endorsed the bill. So except for the rebels who are adamantly against the "public option" plan, there is a lot of of semantics and political double talk going on. Naturally, the nation remains confused.

So there you are, Mr. President, you and your different spokespersons said vague, different and virtually conflicting statements on your Universal Healthcare Reform package. Because you have been put on the defensive, you even appeared to have already retreated or caved in from your original concept of a "public option."

Making matters worse, your chief adviser David Axelrod has been caught violating the privacy of people whose email addresses were included in your mailing list although they had not communicated with the White House. The excuse was to collect false information of your plan so that they could be corrected on the Internet. They call that invasion of privacy.

Are you trying to outdo your predecessor and war criminal George W. Bush who violated the privacy of countless Americans during his administration by tapping into their telephones without court order based on his flimsy excuse of national security?

And what about former Alaska Gov. Sarah Palin's accusation that your health reform plan is "downright evil" because of its so-called "death panel" that would put to death the grandmothers of America who have terminal illness to cut cost? The rationale is that they have already lived their lives, so it's time to go, goodbye.

Called euthanasia, it is supposed to be included in your Universal Healthcare Reform package whereby terminally ill seniors may opt to shorten their own lives during suggestive consultations with their doctors to stop skyrocketing cost of Medicare and Medicaid.

At first you denied such a provision ever existed in the bill. Later you admitted its existence but that it was already there and that it was a Republican idea. So Sarah Palin was right after all, but only after she was maligned for exposing the "death panel."

Finally, Mr. President, what about your secret internal memo that confirms big giveaways in a White House deal with the Big Pharmaceutical Lobby in Washington worth $80 billion? The lobby agrees to increase of Medicaid rebate worth $34 billion, get FOBs done worth $9 billion, sell drugs to patients at 50% discount worth $25 billion, and companies will be assessed a tax or fee worth $12 billion.

In return, the White House agrees to oppose importation [of medicines], oppose rebates in Medicare Part D, oppose repeal of non-interference, and oppose opening Medicare Part B.

Well, Mr. President. this secret memo is mind boggling. Interestingly, the Medical Industrial Complex composed of health providers, insurers, and pharmaceutical corporations contributed over $167 million for both Democratic and Republican candidates for the United States Congress in the 2008 general election.

But after all has been said and done, if you are really dead serious with your Universal Healthcare Reform package based on its most important element of "public option," and you may well be right, Arianna Huffington of *The Huffington Post* suggests that you stop dreaming of a bipartisan approval vote in Congress because it is not going to happen.

The Republicans are out to kill you politically in their determined bid to recapture the White House. So because right now the Democratic Party has the absolute majority vote in both houses of Congress, she likes you to just rally your troops and then go ahead and ram through the bill for floor vote by sheer force of number. So what are you in power for? Use it legislatively and legally!

Just food for thought, Mr. President. Good night.

© Hermie Rotea/Philpress, August 19, 2009

11

Bush, Cheney and Rice Will Be Indicted for Murder and Conspiracy to Commit Murder in California Related to 9/11 and Iraq War

MR. PRESIDENT.

"It's not over with."

Your predecessor former President George W. Bush, former Vice President Dick Cheney, and former Secretary of State Condoleezza Rice will soon be indicted for murder and conspiracy to commit murder related to 9/11 and the Iraq war.

This was revealed by Vincent Bugliosi, famed Charles Manson prosecutor and bestselling author of books, including *The Prosecution of George W. Bush for Murder*, in an interview August 12 with radio talk show host Nicole Sandler.

That's right, Mr. President, seriously.

Bugliosi disclosed this information in answer to a question by Sandler who pinch-hitted for Ron Reagan Jr. in his afternoon talk show on Air America. He said a local prosecutor will file the indictment in California.

The interview was conducted during the final segment of the radio talk show. Sandler ran out of time and could not follow up with a question of which local prosecutor would do the job considered "too hot to handle."

That is after Bugliosi also said that he is involved in a documentary on the controversial issue, which is already "95 per cent complete."

Mr. President, by the way Bugliosi sounded during the radio interview he means business. He also has a bone to pick with the mainstream media which blacked out his latest book.

They refused to review his book and also declined to run his publisher's advertisements promoting it. In so doing, they betrayed their lack of guts and interest for truth. Worse, they failed to perform their journalistic duty to probe for facts as a public watchdog.

But thanks to the foreign press, especially the militant ones in Great Britain and the Internet journalists, although the U.S. mainstream media had censored Bugliosi's book, it still landed in the *New York Times*' bestselling books list.

So, Mr. President, "It's not over with."

Not for Bush, Cheney and Rice and their accomplices as the famed California prosecutor has served notice. Although they are out of office now, there is no statute of limitation for the crime of murder. The long arm of justice awaits them.

Logically, they should be indicted for war crimes before the United Nations International Court of Justice at The Hague, Netherlands.

But because the UN is riddled with politics and the fact that the UN Security Council which has jurisdiction over war crimes is controlled by permanent members with veto power, particularly the United States, that is not possible.

However, the learned Bugliosi, whose record as a famed California prosecutor is exemplary and legendary, has laid out the legal road map for the criminal prosecution of Bush, et. al, in his book.

But which prosecutor in California will handle the case? Is it State Attorney General Edmund Brown Jr., former governor and former Democratic presidential candidate?

Not likely, because he is running for governor again, this time against Republican Governor Arnold Schwarzenegger who wants to keep his job despite his growing unpopularity over state bankruptcy. For Brown to handle such a case would surely disrupt his campaign.

So in all likelihood the prosecutor would be a county district attorney who is ready and willing to go for broke. This particular prosecutor can be catapulted to national and international prominence and the case can be his or her passport to fame.

Bugliosi and his publisher saw to it that copies of his book were sent to all states' attorneys general and county district attorneys to make them aware of his legal road map for the prosecution of Bush, Cheney and Rice for murder and conspiracy charges.

It needs only one state attorney general or one county district attorney to accept the challenge to indict them, and the case would become a legal fiat accompli.

Once the former White House crime trio were indicted for murder and conspiracy charges in California, this time the U.S. mainstream media can't black out such big news event unless they want to look ridiculous and embarrass themselves. The dam of media censorship would burst and end.

Mr. President, take note of what Bugliosi said in his legal road map for the prosecution of Bush [Cheney and Rice] for murder and conspiracy charges:

"The preferable venue for the prosecution of George W. Bush for murder and conspiracy to commit murder would be the nation's capital, with the prosecutor being the Attorney General of the United States acting through his Department of Justice.

"This book, however, establishes jurisdiction for any state attorney general (or any district attorney in any county of a state) to bring murder and conspiracy charges against Bush for any soldiers from that state or county who lost their lives fighting the Bush's war, which as you can see applies to every state in this nation . . ."

As of August 13, 2009, the total war fatalities in the Middle East war is 5,081. The breakdown is: Operation Iraqi Freedom -- 4,318. Operation Enduring Freedom (Afghanistan) -- 763.

In his legal road map for the criminal prosecution of Bush, Bugliosi said that Bush had perpetrated "the most serious crime ever committed in American history -- the president of this nation, George W. Bush, knowingly and deliberately taking the country to war in Iraq under false pretenses, a war that condemned 100,000 human beings, including [over] 4,000 young American soldiers, to horrible, violent deaths.

"That, of course, is the most serious consequences of Bush's monumentally criminal behavior. But let us not forget that, additionally, thousands upon thousands of people have suffered injuries that have disabled them for life, hundreds of thousands of humans have sustained psychic damage from the war, and literally hundreds upon hundreds of thousands of people will involuntarily re-create in their mind's eye, over and over again, what happened to their loved ones.

"Assuming Bush's guilt for the sake of argument at this point, if what he did is not the greatest crime ever committed by any public official or private citizen in this nation's history, then I ask you, what is?

"I am fully aware that the charge I have just made is an extremely serious one. But if there is one thing that I take pride in, it is the fact that I never, ever make a charge without offering a substantial amount of support for it. You may ultimately end up not agreeing with me, but you will have to concede that I offered much evidence in support of my position, something that people frequently do not do. How often, for instance, do you see an assertive, declarative caption or headline in a newspaper or magazine article, but when you read the article you find that either there is no support for the headline, or the evidence is very anemic? I don't do that. That's not my style.

"Before I get into the heart of this book, *The Prosecution of George W. Bush for Murder*, I want to discuss some preliminary matters in this and the following two chapters. Without your consideration of these matters, I believe that what I am urging -- the prosecution of the president of the United States, yes, the president of the United States, for murder -- would be much more of a shock to your sensibilities. That inevitable shock is a burden I know I have overcome. I am very confident, however, that I will be able to do so, and that open-minded people will agree that in this book I set forth the legal architecture that authorizes Bush's prosecution and, more importantly, I present evidence against Bush that proves, beyond all reasonable doubt, that he is guilty of murder."

Goodnight, Mr. President.

© Hermie Rotea/Philpress, August 13, 2009

12

Obama Gets Over 30 Death Threats a Day, 400 Per Cent More Than During GW Bush, That Over-Stretch His Under-Resourced Secret Service and Make Him the Most Threatened President in U.S. History

MR. PRESIDENT:

It is alarming to learn that you get over 30 death threats a day or 400 per cent more than during the time of George W. Bush. The US mainstream media generally have not reported on this bad news because your Secret Service fears it might increase the number of copycat attempts.

In effect, law enforcement officials say you are the most threatened president in United States history,

This sensitive information is based on a book, *In The President's Secret Service*, by Ronald Kessler. It is only the foreign press, particularly the *Telegraph* of UK, that have publicized the news and didn't consider inhibited or bound by White House secrecy.

Actually, Mr. President, news is news in any language. Back in journalism class, students are taught the simple definition of news. If dog bites man, that is not news. But if man bites dog, by golly, that is news. Similarly, if it snows during winter, that is not news. But if it snows during summer, that is news. And so on.

So in the spirit of free press and free speech, it is the duty of journalists or commentators to report or comment on news no matter who are affected. They are the watchdog of the people who have a right to know what is happening in and out of their government.

Just as it is the duty of your Secret Service to guard and protect you no matter what. That is your SS duty, nothing less and nothing more.

So let us get down to business, Mr. President.

You are to be admired and congratulated for doing your job under fire without fear of consequences. The American people certainly don't want a repetition of the assassinations of President John F. Kennedy in 1963 and his brother presidential candidate Senator Robert Kennedy in 1968.

Just as America cannot afford to see other assassination attempts as what happened to President Gerald Ford in 1975 and President Ronald Reagan in 1981.

The American people elected you as their first black president in U.S. history. They invested their votes, hopes and dreams for a better tomorrow in you. They expect you to serve your full term in the service of the nation. They wish you well.

But, Mr. President, we are bothered by what author Kessler has written about your Secret Service in his book, which may well serve as an eye-opener. Simply put, he said your SS agents are not doing a good job and there is big room for improvement.

For example, efforts to meet the growing threats against you which your Secret Service has codenamed "Renegade," have glaring loopholes in the security which have yet to be plugged. After your election and before your inauguration last January, intelligence officials received information that people associated with the Somalia-based Islamist group al-Shabaab might disrupt the ceremony.

Your Secret Service coordinated at least 40,000 agents and officers from 94 police, military and security agencies. More than a dozen counter-sniper teams were stationed along the parade route and the criminal records of employees and hotel guests in nearby buildings were scrutinized.

Despite all this, the book described how more than 100 VIPs and major campaign donors were screened by metal detectors but allowed to walk along a public pavement before boarding "secure" buses and were not checked again.

Kessler wrote that it could have been relatively easy and simple for an assassin to have mingled with them in order to get close enough to shoot President-elect Barack H. Obama.

As *Telegraph* reported in a bylined story by Toby Harnden, the Secret Service also turned its attention to the new First Lady Michelle Obama who was codenamed "Renaissance," and the First Children Malia, 11, codenamed "Radiance" and Sasha, eight, codenamed "Rosebud."

The Secret Service likewise started to protect Vice President Joe Biden's children, grandchildren, and mother.

But instead of bringing in more agents -- instantly identifiable because of their bulky suits worn over bullet-proof jackets and earpieces, the Secret

Service directed agents to work longer hours to cover the extra load and to miss firearms training, physical fitness sessions and tests.

"We have half the number of agents we need, but requests for more agents have fallen on deaf ears at headquarters," a Secret Service agent told Kessler. "Headquarters' mentality has always been, 'You can complete the mission with what you have. You're a USSS agent.'"

Mr. President, please take note!

In Vice President Biden's case, his constant travel, including back to his home state of Delaware, the burden has meant that all agents on his team have ceased training. However, according to Kessler, they fill in forms stating that they have "taken and passed all tests, when they have not, creating a dishonest culture."

When Biden threw the first pitch at the first Baltimore Orioles game of the 2009 season, the Secret Service did not even screen any of the more than 40,000 fans. That stunned his agents and the local Secret Service field office.

Mr. President, despite the over 30 death threats that you receive a day, the over-stretched and under-resourced Secret Service has increasingly cut corners after it was absorbed by the new Homeland Security Department under Bush.

Clearly, this is a serious problem with your Secret Service. Its loopholes in security must be plugged. The job of protecting you should not be taken lightly. If more agents are needed because of growing danger to your person, let's have them.

The death threats against you are real, or should be treated seriously. Well, maybe some are not. Regardless, there should be no unguarded moment in your security. Your Secret Service must do a better job. It must avoid one fatal mistake at all cost.

Remember what happened in Denver, Colorado, Mr. President? Four people were arrested after plotting to assassinate you. One of the group said he was "going to shoot Obama from a high vantage point using a rifle sighted at 750 yards."

Police said that one of the suspects "was directly asked if they had come to kill Obama. He responded in the affirmative."

In another plot by white supremacists in Tennessee late last year, the plan was to rob a gun store, shoot 88 black people, decapitate another 14, and then assassinate the first black president in American history.

Interestingly, Mr. President, your Secret Service has blamed resigned Governor Sarah Palin of Alaska over the death threats against you for attacking your patriotism during the final weeks of the presidential election campaign last year.

The then Republican vice presidential candidate accused you of "palling around with terrorists," citing your association with radical William Ayers of the 1960s who had bombed the Pentagon but who is now working as a university professor.

Palin's attacks against you in her campaign speeches provoked a near lynch mob atmosphere at her political rallies with supporters yelling "terrorist!" and "kill him!" until the McCain campaign ordered her to tone down the rhetoric.

But, Mr. President, you know damn well that in the heat of an election campaign, it is "fair game" to attack political opponents. Even then Senator Hillary R. Clinton attacked you and said: "Shame on you, Barack Obama!" But after the election, the rhetoric is forgiven and forgotten.

So it is with Sarah Palin. Your Secret Service should stop blaming her for the death threats against you. That's a cop-out. Instead, the SS should concentrate on plugging security loopholes and improving your protection.

Goodnight, Mr. President.

© Hermie Rotea/Philpress, August 9, 2009

13

Bill Clinton's Success in Securing the Release of Two U.S. Journalists from North Korea Prison Shows that Diplomacy with Leader Kim Jong-il Really Works

MR. PRESIDENT:

Two for the price of one gambit didn't work for Senator Hillary Clinton when she ran for the Democratic presidential nomination in 2008, but it has worked this time as your secretary of state when she sent her husband and former President Bill Clinton to North Korea to secure the release of two American journalists Laura Ling and Euna Lee from hard labor prison.

As this is written, they boarded the private jet plane of Bill Clinton at North Korean capital of Pyongyang on the way back to the United States. Later they arrived in Los Angeles.

Ling, 32, and Lee, 36, both of former Vice President Al Gore's Current TV media venture, on March 17 illegally strayed from China into North Korea where border guards arrested them. They were accused of "hostile acts" and the nation's top court sentenced them in June to 12 years of hard labor. Their release ended five months of detention.

Mr, President, North Korean leader Kim Jong-il granted them "special pardon" and ordered their freedom after he met with Bill Clinton who had flown to Pyongyang Tuesday in his private jet on an unannounced trip. North Korean's official news agency reported that their talks were "exhaustive."

Clinton was accorded honors typically reserved for heads of state. The reclusive and reportedly ailing Jong-il actually appeared healthy and, in an unprecedented gesture, even tendered Clinton with a state dinner.

The Korean Central News Agency stated that the release of the two American journalists was a sign of North Korea's "humanitarian and peace-loving policy."

State media said Clinton apologized on behalf of women and relayed President Obama's gratitude. The report said Clinton's visit would "contribute to deepening the understanding between North Korea and the United States."

Well, Mr. President, now that the ice has thawed, this good news may be what you need to improve U.S. relation with that rogue and economically poor nation in the hope that the impasse over its nuclear weapon program may be broken.

Like we have repeatedly contended in previous columns in this website and in blogs in Huffington Post, it is possible to improve relation with North Korea if the United States stopped disrespecting, belittling, and insulting that rogue nation and its leader Kim Jong-il.

There is nothing to be gained by pursuing the hardened policy of your predecessor George W. Bush who labeled North Korea as part of the "Axis of Evil" along with Iran and Iraq in the wake of 9/11 terrorist attacks on the United States.

What Bush and Dick Cheney later did in invading and occupying Iraq and Afghanistan based on great deceptions that Saddam Hussein had weapons of mass destruction and that Afghanistan was involved in 9/11, made them the worst war criminals in modern history.

United Nations' sanctions against North Korea, along with Iran, have not worked in persuading them to give up their nuclear programs. In North Korea's case, critics have called Kim Jong-il crazy and dying. Clinton saw how wrong they were.

Commenting on the release of Ling and Lee, Bush's former ambassador to the United Nations, John Bolton, said it was wrong for the U.S. to reward North Korea with respect and recognition for bad behavior after pardoning and ordering their freedom.

Mr. President, your Press Secretary Robert Gibbs has denied Clinton went to North Korea with a message from you. "That's not true," he told reporters. What is wrong with that?

U.S. Secretary of State Clinton urged North Korea last month to grant them amnesty, saying they were remorseful and their families were anguished by their detention.

Ling and Lee admitted guilt and expressed remorse for their illegal border crossing in an attempt to document the trafficking of women from North Korea to China in the wake of the rogue nation's food crisis and serious economic condition.

Mr. President, their release would not have been possible if they had not admitted their wrongdoing and expressed remorse, and if Secretary Clinton had not expressed the same feeling and requested their release on humanitarian reason.

That softened up Pyongyang and persuaded Kim Jong-il to grant Clinton's appeal for their freedom based on their expression of guilt and remorse. That proved that the "crazy" guy is still human contrary to what he had consistently and wrongly been described.

Mr. President, the bottom line is that diplomacy did work in the case of the two American journalists. If the U.S. played hardball with North Korea in their case, they would still be in hard labor prison.

Nothing is impossible under the sun. North Vietnam and South Vietnam reunited in the crucible of war. East Germany and West Germany became one after President Reagan told Soviet Premier Mikail Korbachev to tear down the Berlin wall. Sooner or later, it might also happen with North Korea and South Korea.

Right now what North Korea wants and needs are also humanitarian aid in addition to respect and recognition. More than that, Kim Jong-il prefers direct or bilateral talks with the United States instead of the on-and-off six-nation meeting. What is wrong with that?

Like it or not, Mr. President, North Korea although economically poor is already a nuclear power capable of producing eight atomic bombs by experts' estimation. Pyongyang's recent firing of guided missiles that can reach Hawaii attests to that.

In the past, North Korea had agreed to modify its nuclear program in exchange for humanitarian aid like food and energy for its starving people. But the United States reneged from its pledge to extend such economic assistance.

So North Korea boycotted the six-nation talks and resumed its hostile policy against Washington and violated repeated United Nations' sanctions. Thanks to support from China, Kim Jong-il so far has kept his sanity and survived despite U.S. broken promises of humanitarian aid.

As we wrote in a previous column, Mr. President, in the summer of 2008 it looked like there was finally a breakthrough in the negotiation with North Korea on its nuclear program. Believing that this time the United States was really sincere in its promise of humanitarian aid for its poor people, Jong-il finally opened its door to the world.

Before the very eyes of nuclear inspectors and the world media as eyewitnesses, North Korea destroyed a plutonium facility that is needed to produce nuclear weapon. It was proof that Pyongyang appeared ready to abandon its nuclear program in return for aid and diplomatic concessions.

In another heartwarming gesture, Jong-il even allowed a cultural exchange with the United States by inviting New York Philharmonic Orchestra to perform in Pyongyang. It was truly a historic event that touched the heart of the world. It shows that Jong-il was not that "crazy" but also human like you, Mr. President.

But negotiations at the six-nation talks stalled again after the promised shipments of humanitarian aid to the starving people of North Korea stopped — as usual. North Korea accused the United States and other participants of reneging on commitments. Jong il apparently had enough and decided never to trust the United States again. It was the last straw.

Mr. President, that was then. This is now. You have your opportunity to succeed with North Korea where your predecessors failed. Bill Clinton has opened the door for you. Tread carefully if you must.

In your election campaign speeches you welcomed direct talks with Fidel Castro or Raul Castro of Cuba and with Mahmoud Amadinejad of Iran without pre-condition. Why not also with Kim Jong-il of North Korea?

Think it over, Mr. President. Goodnight.

© Hermie Rotea/Philpress, August 4, 2009

14

Cop Calls Prof. Gates "Banana-Eating Jungle Monkey" as President Obama Acts as Mediator and Bartender-in-Chief During the Beer Summit at the White House

MR. PRESIDENT:

Your happy-hour beer peace summit at the White House Thursday with black Prof. Henry Louis Gates Jr. of Harvard and white police Sgt. James Crowley of the Cambridge, Massachusetts, Police Department along with Vice President Joe Biden was almost ruined by another white cop Justin Barrett who called Gates a "banana-eating jungle monkey."

The Boston officer. 36, a police for two years and a former captain in the National Guard, didn't like the news report of The Boston Globe on the Gates' arrest on July 16 for "disorderly conduct" that put the Cambridge police in a bad light over racial profiling after President Obama commented that the police "acted stupidly."

Barrett fired off an email globally to the newspaper and to his fellow officers in the force, calling the story "jungle monkey gibberish." He wrote that Gates' "first priority should get off the phone and comply with police."

Angered by how the police were treated badly over the incident that grabbed national attention, Barrett said that "if I was the officer he [Gates] verbally assaulted like a banana-eating jungle monkey, I would have sprayed him in the face with OC deserving of his belligerent non-compliance." (OC is pepper spray).

The angry cop even questioned Gates' credentials as a Harvard scholar and documentary filmmaker. He called the professor a "God damned fool" and challenged the Boston newspaper to "ax me" for what he thinks.

Barrett in his email wrote that "I am not a racist, but I am prejudice [sic] towards people who are stupid and pretend to stand up and preach for something they claim is freedom."

Mr. President, fortunately Barrett's fellow officers in the Cambridge police force disagreed with him and referred the matter to higher authority. In a swift move, Boston Police Commissioner Ed Davis immediately suspended him.

"This type of venomous rhetoric is severely damaging. We will not allow the unacceptable actions of one member to define who we are," Davis declared.

Boston Mayor Tom Menino said of Barrett: "He's gone. I don't care, it's like cancer. You don't keep those cancers around."

Following his suspension, Barrett insisted that he was not a racist. "I did not mean to offend anyone. I was just venting about the July 16 arrest of Gates by a white Cambridge cop that became a national discussion about race when President Obama said the officers acted 'stupidly.'

"People are making it about race. It is not about race." Barrett stressed. "The words were being used to characterize behavior, not describe anyone . . . I treat everyone with dignity and respect."

Officer Barrett did apologize to Prof. Gates. He conceded that his statement about the Harvard scholar was a "poor choice of words."

Mr. President, see what happens when you stir a hornet's nest or poke your nose on every thing that happens in America? But you are right though that the Gates-Crowley case has been a "teachable moment" or a talkable one.

Your beer diplomacy or brouhaha during happy hours at the White House Rose Garden worked all right, although you three Ps -- president, professor, and police -- still didn't agree on what beer to drink. Yours was Bud Light, Gates chose Sam Adams, and Crowley preferred a Blue Moon.

Mr. President, you said after your beer summit meeting with Prof. Gates and Sgt. Crowley in the Rose Garden outside the Oval Office that "I have always believed that what brings us together is stronger than what pulls us apart." Well said, Sir.

"I am confident that has happened here tonight, and I am hopeful that all of us are able to draw this positive lesson from this episode," you added.

For his part, Sgt. Crowley said: "I think what you had today was two gentlemen who agreed to disagree on a particular issue. I don't think that we spent too much time dwelling on the past. We spent a lot of time discussing the future."

Asked about the president's contribution to the meeting, Crowley said: "He provided the beer." That was nice of you, Mr. President or, shall we say, Mr. Bartender-in-Chief?

Gates said he and Crowley had been cast together "through an accident of time and place" and must use the opportunity "to foster greater sympathy among the American public for the daily perils of policing on the one hand, and for the genuine fears of racial profiling on the other hand."

Mr. President, your job approval rating has fallen from 61 percent in mid-June to 54 percent now, in part due to your handling of the Gates-Crowley case, a Pew Research Center poll found.

You said the White House had tried to lower expectations for the gathering, that there would be no big announcements, and that it was just three guys having a beer.

Well, now you know the peril of poking your nose in every teeny-weeny thing that happens in America. Of course, race happens to be a subject close to your heart.

Nice try though, Mr. President. Goodnight.

© Hermie Rotea/Philpress, July 31, 2009

15

Gates Had Right to be Angry for Being Wrongly Suspected as Burglar in Own Home. Instead of Apologizing for Error, Crowley Arrested Him and Committed Abuse of Authority

MR. PRESIDENT:

You would think that when the United States elected you as the first black president in history last year the racial divide has already been bridged, right? Nah.

The case of your friend black professor Henry Louis Gates Jr. of Harvard, and Cambridge white police Sgt. James Crowley who arrested him on July 16 for "disorderly conduct" after mistakenly suspected him of breaking into his own home, showed once again that racial profiling is still very much alive.

The acclaimed Harvard scholar and documentary filmmaker had just returned from a trip to China. Unable to find his keys, he broke into his own home.

At that point the Cambridge, Massachusetts, police received a report that two black men were attempting to break into Gates' home. Officer Carlos Figueroa who had responded to an ECC broadcast of a possible burglary filed this report [verbatim]:

"On July 16, 2009 at approximately 12:44 PM, I Officer Figueroa #509 responded for a possible break[in] at [blacked out] Ware St. When I arrived, I stepped into the residence and Sgt. Crowley had already entered and was speaking to a black male.

"As I stepped in, I heard Sgt. Crowley ask for the gentleman's information which he stated "NO I WILL NOT!" The gentleman was shouting out to the Sgt. that the Sgt. was a racist and yelled that "THIS IS WHAT HAPPENS TO BLACK MEN IN AMERICA!" As the Sgt. was trying to calm the gentleman, the gentleman shouted "You don't know who your messing with!"

"I stepped out to gather the information from the reporting person, [blacked out] stated to me that she saw a man wedging his shoulder into the front door as to pry the door open. As I returned to the residence, a group of onlookers were now on scene. The Sgt., along with the gentleman, were now on the porch of [blacked out] Ware St. and again he was shouting, now to the onlookers (about seven), "THIS IS WHAT HAPPENS TO BLACK MEN IN AMERICA"! The gentleman refused to listen as to why the Cambridge Police were there. While on the porch, the gentleman refused to be cooperative and continued shouting that the Sgt. is a racist police officer.["]

The "Statement of Facts in Support of Application for Criminal Complaint" stated: "On Thursday July 16, 2009, Henry Gates, Jr. [Blacked out] of [blacked out] Ware Street, Cambridge, MA) was placed under arrest at [blacked out] Ware Street, after being observed exhibiting loud and tumultuous behavior, in a public place, directed at a uniformed police officer who was present investigating a report of a crime in progress. These actions on the behalf of Gates served no legitimate purpose and caused citizens passing by this location to stop and take notice while appearing surprised and alarmed."

A neighbor took a front-view photo of Gates in handcuff with his mouth open apparently protesting his arrest as three police officers escorted him out of his house. The police mug shot of Gates shows him in front and side views. The Cambridge police subsequently dropped the charge against Gates.

The incident raised concerns among some Harvard faculty that Professor Gates was a victim of racial profiling. His friends said he was already in his home when the police arrived. He showed his driver's license and Harvard identification.

Boston Globe Metro Desk confirmed that Gates did tell Sgt. Crowley that he was being targeted because "I'm a black man in America." When contacted Gates, 58, declined to comment.

Staffer Tracy Jan reported that the arrest of such a prominent scholar under what some described as dubious circumstances shook some members of the black Harvard community.

"He and I both raised the question of if he had been a white professor, whether this kind of thing would have happened to him, that they arrested him without any corroborating evidence," said S. Allen Counter, a Harvard Medical School professor who spoke with Gates about the incident Friday. "I am deeply concerned about the way he was treated, and called him to express my deepest sadness and sympathy."

Counter, who had called Gates from the Nobel Institute in Sweden, where Counter is on sabbatical, said that Gates was "shaken" and "horrified" by his arrest.

Counter has faced a similar situation himself. The well-known neuroscience professor, who is also black, was stopped by two Harvard police officers in 2004 after being mistaken for a robbery suspect as he crossed Harvard Yard. They threatened to arrest him when he could not produce identification.

That incident was among several that ignited criticism from black students and faculty, highlighting the prejudices that many black students say they continue to face at Harvard.

"This is very disturbing that this could happen to anyone, and not just to a person of such distinction," Counter said. "He was just shocked that this had happened, at 12:44 in the afternoon, in broad daylight. It brings up the question of whether black males are being targeted by Cambridge police for harassment."

Now Mr. President, when the Cambridge police learned of Gates' identity and eventually dropped the charge of "disorderly conduct" against him, what did you do? You exacerbated the situation and stirred up a hornet's nest by commenting that the police had "acted stupidly" even before you knew what had really happened.

So instead of Prof. Gates and Sgt. Crowley consigning the incident to bad experience and to a lesson learned, in effect you re-ignited the debate of racial profiling between them and before the nation. Why did you have to bat in with such remark before the facts were in?

You are the President, Mr. Obama, and you don't have to poke your nose in everything that happens in America. You are overexposing yourself. In your 5th television press conference on healthcare, you deviated from the subject in response to a question on the incident you knew nothing about.

That same amount of time you faced the nation on TV equaled the period of time that your predecessor George W. Bush had over eight years in office. That is a lot, Mr. President, which shows that you are addicted to TV exposure and public adulation.

So what happened next, Mr. President? When the Cambridge Police Department held its own press conference and supported Sgt. Crowley's action as legitimate under police guidelines, contending that he was the victim and not the victimizer, you backtracked.

You also wade into Republican and conservative media critics who have mocked you for such equally "stupid" comment on the Gates-Crowley encounter. You made a surprise appearance at the daily White House press briefing to diffuse the escalating race explosion. Without apologizing, you said you should have chosen different words in commenting on the Gates' arrest.

"In my choice of words, I unfortunately gave the impression that I was maligning the Cambridge Police Department or Sergeant Crowley specifically," you corrected yourself. You also praised him to be "an outstanding police officer."

You also said that "I continue to believe, based on what I have heard, that there was an overreaction in pulling Prof. Gates out of his home and to the [police] station. I also continue to believe, based on what I heard, that Prof. Gates probably overreacted as well."

Mr. President, that sounded like political double talk in the tradition of a smooth politician as longtime White House journalist Helen Thomas has described you to be, during a recent radio interview on Air America by progressive talk show host Ron Reagan Jr., son of the late President Ronald Reagan.

In fact, if as you said Prof. Gates overreacted, he had valid reason for his behavior. He was mistakenly suspected of burglarizing his own home. Police version claimed that he refused to give information and accused Sgt. Crowley of racial profiling.

Conflicting version said Gates identified himself as the homeowner and produced his Harvard ID. At that point he had good reason to be angry and for shouting at the police officer. Who won't be insulted and feel mad for being suspected of breaking into his own home?

In any event, when Sgt. Crowley learned of Prof. Gates' identity and Harvard credentials, he should have just walked away and returned to his police station even if Gates followed him with accusatory remark. The guy was angry for being suspected as a burglar, what do you expect? It was a normal human reaction, especially for a man of his position.

Sure, Mr. President, Sgt. Crowley definitely overreacted himself, if not more and unjustifiably. He should have stayed cool under fire in the face of black anger that was provoked like an angry volcano that finally exploded in the face of continued racial profiling in the country.

If Sgt. Crowley really wanted Prof. Gates to calm down as the police report alleged, he should have apologized for the mistake even if it were caused by a 911 caller. But no, he was the guy with a badge of authority and power. Apologizing is not in his vocabulary and beneath his position. It would also dignify Gates at his expense.

Then adding injury to insult, the high and mighty Sgt. Crowley himself exploded and handcuffed Gates for "disorderly conduct" without reading his Miranda right, even though he practically waived his right to remain silent by shouting or screaming at the officer, if the police report is to be believed.

In effect Sgt. Crowley also violated the professor's right to free speech which he exercised under duress and provocation, by shutting him up and hauling him to the police station.

If that is not police abuse of power, what is it?

Interestingly, the caller identified as Lucia Whalen said there was no mention of black male or race in her police call. That contradicted earlier report that two black men were seen trying to break into Gates' house. If the Cambridge police tried to cover up something, that would be misconduct.

Anyway, Mr. President, you later did a wise move by acting like a referee and inviting both Prof. Gates and Sgt. Crowley to a "peace summit meeting" over beer at the White House on Thursday, July 30 at 6 p.m. Both of them have graciously accepted in the spirit of reconciliation. Just be sure you guys don't drink too much beer, okay?

That should shut up your Republican and conservative media critics like Fox News Bill O'Reilly, Sean Hannity and Glenn Beck who have mocked you on the Gates-Crowley encounter.

Finally, Mr. President, let us face it. Although you tried to diffuse the situation, and even as this column is written, at this very moment hundreds if not thousands of blacks, Latinos and other minorities are being disproportionately pulled over and arrested by white police officers in the streets and ghettos of America.

Naturally they are not reported and do not become news headlines because the victims are just common folks without big names, titles and positions of influence. They are only, as they say, small fishes who are not worth mentioning. Their cases land in the trash unnoticed, buried and forgotten.

Unfortunately, like it or not that is still a fact of life in the United States.

Have a nice day, Mr. President

© Hermie Rotea/Philpress, July 27, 2009

16

WALTER CRONKITE -- "THE MOST TRUSTED MAN IN AMERICA"

MR. PRESIDENT:

American journalism has just lost a legend when Walter Cronkite died today, July 17, 2009. He was 92.

Cronkite will be remembered as a great journalist in the tradition of Joseph Pulitzer. In 1972, an Oliver Quayle poll showed him as the "most trusted man in America." At the height of his career as anchor of CBS Evening News, he was even more popular than public figures in and out of government, including presidents of the United States from Lyndon Johnson to Richard Nixon during the Vietnam war.

He built on the legacy of Edward R. Murrow. Every evening he did not just broadcast news and commentary. He addressed the nation, and the people listened. Cronkite was their voice because he spoke from the heart.

Born in Saint Joseph, Missouri, and educated at the University of Texas in Austin, he started as a newspaper reporter and later as a radio announcer in Oklahoma City. Later he joined the United Press news agency where he improved his journalistic ability.

After Japanese planes bombed Pearl Harbor and World War Two broke out, in December 1941 Cronkite signed up as a war correspondent. He covered Europe, including the air war between England and Germany, the Allied invasion of North Africa, and the Battle of the Bulge.

A hardworking wire service reporter, Cronkite would ride on a bomber or glider into combat for an eyewitness coverage of the war. This impressed the legendary Edward R. Murrow of CBS Evening News who followed his career and liked what he saw.

After the war, Cronkite covered the war crimes trials at Nuremberg, Germany, and from Moscow, the beginnings of the Cold War between the Soviet Union and the United States.

The advent of television led Cronkite to work for CBS Evening News at Murrow's prodding. The new technology was still unknown but the prospect of growth looked good. The time was great and they developed together.

Since then Cronkite was thrust into the vortex of earthshaking events of the time. Along with the new challenge he improved the standard of broadcast and print journalism.

The camera captured the developments of the day while he added his authoritative voice on the CBS Evening News as no other could. He mastered the art of reporting, analysis, suspense, and narration.

His coverage of the Republican and Democratic parties conventions in the 1950s were classic example of his mastery of the craft. He would go live on the air and report or comment extemporaneously without notes or scripts.

As journalist and colleague Bill Moyers of PBS observed, "The camera either sees you as part of the environment or it rejects you as an alien body. And Walter had IT, whatever IT was."

By 1962, Cronkite succeeded Douglas Edwards as anchor of the CBS Evening News. He continued to build on the legacy of icon Edward Murrow who had been his ardent admirer and supporter.

In the turbulent decades of the 1960s and the 1970s, Cronkite's commanded national attention to his CBS Evening News with his mastery of the craft. He was the TV news anchor that the people looked up to everyday.

As Wikipedia stated online, Cronkite trained himself to speak at a rate of 124 words per minute in his newscast, so that the viewers could clearly understand him. In contrast, Americans average about 165 words per minute, and fast, difficult to understand talkers speak close to 200 words per minute.

Cronkite is well remembered for his dramatic announcement of the assassination of President John F. Kennedy on Nov. 22, 1963 in Dallas, Texas. As described by author Leslie Clark, co-producer of Witness to History: Walter Cronkite (2006) and published online by PBS.org:

"Throughout the morning, he [Cronkite] calmly filled the story, squelched any information that hadn't been verified, reduced speculation to certainty -- until he was handed a dispatch confirming that the President of the United States was indeed dead.

"He pulled off his glasses, looked to the clock to repeat the time, and seemed to subdue a sudden wave of emotion, before he continued with the broadcast.

"The assassination was on a Friday. All of America watched this event together. Whether in California, Nebraska, or Mississippi, the entire nation was seeing the same thing -- for three days.

"Saturday, Sunday, Monday . . . the networks ran nothing but coverage of the president's death, the return of his body to Washington, the funeral procession to the Capitol, and the final journey of President Kennedy to his burial in Arlington National Cemetery.

"There were no commercials for those three days. By today's standards, the coverage was simple and sedate. No emotion was added to the trauma of loss, nor was any needed.

"It was a show of dignity that America never forgot. And, as a result, Americans awarded Cronkite the honor of allowing him to give us the bad news about our world as well as the good.

The messenger was not condemned when he reported that America's deeply racist history had to change. And he was not punished in the ratings when he went to Vietnam and reported that he had seen the lies, corruption, and stalemate in that war and that it was time for us to go."

Indeed, Vietnam War was a dark page in American history. Cronkite plunged deep into the crisis and tangled with President Lyndon Johnson on the issue with dignity. He was not in to name-calling. He just stuck to the issue, contending that it was based on lies and not winnable.

He defended antiwar activities who demonstrated at the 1968 Democratic National Convention in Chicago, and denounced the local police for attacking them and violating their constitutional right to free speech and assembly.

President Johnson, who succeeded Kennedy and who had escalated the war in Vietnam, regularly followed up Cronkite's antiwar broadcasts on the CBS Evening News as he weighed their effect on his reelection bid that year.

As opposition to the war escalated and Johnson lost control of the Democratic Party that divided into different factions each with presidential aspiration, he listened to Cronkite's news and commentary broadcasts with sadness and apprehension.

In one of those listening sessions at the White House, President Johnson ruefully commended to an aide, "If I've lost Cronkite, I've lost America."

Then on March 31, 1968, the 36th president of the United States shocked the nation when he announced, "I shall not seek, and I will not accept the nomination of my party for another term as your president."

On October 31 Johnson followed with another announcement, saying that he had ordered a complete cessation of "all air, naval and artillery bombardment of North Vietnam."

In another surprise, the president also said that if the Hanoi government was up to it, he was receptive to the ideal of holding peace negotiations in Paris, the favorite site of signed treaties among warring nations in the history of the world.

That President Johnson's retreat from reelection and the Vietnam war was mainly attributed to Cronkite's tireless and persistent opposition to the "unwinnable" conflict, was a foregone public conclusion, which showed that even one man could make a difference.

Cronkite also took on Johnson's successor, President Richard Nixon, in the wake of the Watergate scandal. When the White House tried to stonewall the news media from getting information on the burglary of the Democratic Party's national committee offices at Watergate Hotel in Washington, DC, he made it national news.

In 1972 just before the election, Cronkite defended freedom of the press and emphasized "the important right of the people to know what their government is doing in their name."

He broadcast in the CBS Evening News a two-part story of the Watergate scandal based on an article by the Washington Post whose reporters Bob Woodward and Carl Bernstein exposed the burglary linking the White House to the break-in based on confidential tip from a secret source dubbed as "Deep Throat."

The White House dismissed Cronkite's broadcast and demanded a retraction, even as it threatened to retaliate by revoking CBS's station license. But Cronkite and CBS stuck by the story and called the bluff. The punishment did not happen.

For the next two years the Watergate scandal, the arrests and convictions of the burglars connected with the Republican Committee to Reelect Richard Nixon, including White House aides, and the subsequent Congress' investigation and impeachment of the president, consumed the nation.

Before Congress could conclude its investigation, in 1973 President Nixon was reelected. But his second term was short-lived. In 1974 the House Judiciary Committee impeached Nixon for abuse of power and obstruction of justice.

When he sensed that the Senate acting as the court could convict him based on incriminating evidence, included tapes, Nixon abruptly resigned.

Again, as in the case of President Johnson, it could be said without fear of contradiction that Cronkite, because of his forceful and authoritative broadcasts on CBS Evening News, played a major role that led to President Nixon's downfall.

Cronkite was saddened by the turn of events that befell Johnson and Nixon partly because of him, but he felt that he had a professional duty to uphold the truth and serve as the watchdog of the people no matter who was hurt or affected.

In 1981 he had a surprise of his own. Upon reaching a point in his life and career at 65, Cronkite resigned, which shocked his audience. But as he explained it, "This is my last broadcast as the anchorman of the CBS Evening News. For me it's a moment for which I have planned but which nevertheless comes with some sadness . . ."

Then sounding like General Douglas MacArthur when he addressed the U.S. Congress upon his return from the Korean War, Cronkite said:

"Old anchormen, you see, don't fade away, they just keep coming back for more. And that's the way it is, Friday, March 8, 1981 . . . Good night."

Mr. President, that was Walter Cronkite, 1916-2009.

Goodnight, Mr. President.

© Hermie Rotea/Philpress, July 17, 2009

17

AS OBAMA BAILS OUT THE RICHEST OF THE RICH, HE NEGLECTS TO HELP THE POOREST OF THE POOR

MR. PRESIDENT:

You have bailed out Wall Street giant corporations like banks, insurance companies, auto manufacturers and others who are the richest of the rich with billions of dollars of the taxpayer's money. Now as you push your universal healthcare plan for every American which is fine, at the same time you have neglected to rescue senior citizens who are the poorest of the poor whose Medi-Cal or Medicaid benefits have been reduced effective July 2009.

You are also too busy traveling and delivering speeches here and there so much so that you have failed to notice what is happening in your own backyard or, if you did, you don't give a damn about it. Despite surrounding yourself with so-called expert czars whose appointments don't need Senate confirmation or oversight, there appears to be disarray in your team that indicates that your priorities may not be in order.

For instance, Mr. President, states like New York and California which bear the brunt of the current economic recession suffer from budgetary deficits and badly need federal assistance. But you are not inclined to grant such aid because it would prompt other states to fall in line. Yet you extended billions of dollars in stimulus bailout to big financial and industrial complex whose executives give themselves huge bonuses from taxpayers' money.

In California, which used to enjoy the 6th biggest economy in the world, public services have been cut and employees have been laid off by 25 percent. With $26 billion budget deficit, the state government has reduced work days, enforced job furloughs, cut salaries, issued IOU vouchers for the first time in its history, closed school classes, and even limited operations of courts and state licensing agencies like the Motor Vehicles Office, not to mention the U.S. Postal Service.

Amid this crisis, Mr. President, the biggest casualty who suffer the most are senior citizens who have worked all their lives and earned their current social security pension and Medicare benefits, including Medi-Cal or Medicaid for the poor with special circumstances. To suddenly deprive them of some of these services and benefits under your administration, is ironic and unacceptable.

It is ironic and unacceptable because such situation did not happen during the eight years of the Bush administration, unless you are conceding this early that you are worse than President George W. Bush whom you always blame for the economic mess the country is in.

Put yourself in the place of senior citizens or the poorest of the poor, Mr. President. In June 2009 you received from the Department of Health Care Services in Sacramento a "Notice of Reduction of Medi-Cal Benefits" which reads:

"Dear Beneficiary:

"The California Department of Health Care Services has sent this notice to let you know of a change in the law contained in Welfare and Institutions Code section 14131.10. Starting July 1, 2009, Medi-Cal will no longer pay for some benefits. This change will affect only Medi-Cal beneficiaries age 21 and older. If you are age 21 and older, you can still get all of these benefits through June 30, 2009."

But, and here is the but, Mr. President:

"What benefits will Medi-Cal no longer pay for?

"Medic-Cal will no longer pay for the following benefits and services for most adults (there are some exceptions):

"• Dental services
"• Speech therapy services
"• Podiatric services
"• Audiology services

"• Chiropractic services
"• Acupuncture services . . .
"• Incontinence creams and washes"

Mr. President, to the average person this may not be important, but to senior citizens who have reached their golden years and who cannot afford to pay for these benefits and services, it is a big deal.

Just to cite one example, on dental services whose cost in the private dentistry sector is beyond the reach and affordability of retired seniors and the poor, how can they eat and enjoy their food if their teeth or denture need repair or replacement? Healthwise, it is disastrous. It is sheer cruelty to regard them as expendable.

That this is happening to the poorest of the poor while the riches of the rich like big banks, insurance corporations and car manufacturers of Wall Street have received billions of dollars in stimulus bailout grants from the Obama administration, is revolting. If this is not discrimination against the poor in favor of the rich, what is it?

Mr. President, you actually took over from your predecessor George W. Bush in bailing out Wall Street. You have even outbushed Bush by granting bigger bailout grants from taxpayers' money to big corporations to the extent of 60 percent ownership of these beneficiary firms. Yet taxpayers don't benefit from such action. On the contrary, they are adversely affected, like the seniors.

Take the case of American International Group. After AIG had received $182.5 billion in federal bailout grant from the taxpayer's money, it handed out $165 million in executive bonuses although it previously suffered financial loss. Your Treasury Secretary Timothy F. Geithner concluded the government could not stop AIG from running amuck with taxpayers' money.

What happened, Mr. President? Well, here the answer. Author Barry Ritholtz has written a book, Bailout Nation: How Greed and Easy Money Corrupted Wall Street and Shook the World Economy, which title is self-explanatory. It describes not only what happened and what went wrong, but also why.

Mr. President, some people criticize you for trying to do so much in less time and accomplishing little. After all, operating in a projected budgetary deficit of $1.8 trillion, and with your universal healthcare expected to cost $1.5 trillion, which you plan to raise by taxing the rich, is a gigantic problem and challenge.

No wonder your critics are now even touting your proposed Universal Healthcare as "Healthscare" and your government policy as "Socialism."

Have a nice day, Mr. President.

© Hermie Rotea/Philpress, July 16, 2009

18

It's Going to be Barack Obama Versus Sarah Palin in 2012 Presidential Election. Mainstream Media Will Continue Kicking Her Around. Who Will Have Last Laugh?

MR. PRESIDENT:

When you run for reelection in 2012 your Republican challenger will not be former Massachusetts governor Mitt Romney or ex-Arkansas governor Mike Huckabee, but Governor Sarah Palin of Alaska.

Palin has announced she will not seek reelection as governor but will in fact even resign on July 26 in order to "take a stand and effect change, not just hit our head against the wall and waste valuable state time and money."

In short, "No more politics as usual," the resigning governor said as she criticized your administration as going in the wrong direction.

Mr. President, you can laugh off or dismiss Palin as a political threat at your own peril. Like it or not, right now she is the brightest star of the battered and leaderless Republican Party. So her timing is right on target.

Announcing her resignation plan on the eve of the July 4 Independence Day anniversary has catapulted her to headline news and intense public speculation as to her plan and intention. The guessing game is over. She is running for president in 2012.

Palin's candidacy for vice president as the handpicked running mate of Senator John McCain of the Republican Party in the 2008 presidential election which they lost, has turned out to be just a dress rehearsal or steppingstone for her.

No doubt the *Vanity Fair*, the David Letterman (CBS), the Katie Couric (CBS), and the Charles Gibson (ABC) of the world will have an oversupply of fodder for their comedic or "Gotcha" commentaries in the next three years to increase their readership and TV ratings.

But who will have the last laugh, remains to be seen.

Mr. President, remember Richard Nixon? On November 7, 1962 after the former vice president lost the election for governor of California to reelectionist Governor Edmund (Pat) Brown, the embittered loser told a press conference:

"I leave you gentleman now and you will write it. You will interpret it. That's your right. But as I leave you I want you to know — just think how much you're going to be missing. *You won't have Nixon to kick around any more*, because, gentlemen, this is my last press conference and it will be one in which I have welcomed the opportunity to test wits with you."

But from private life with nothing much to do, Nixon resurrected himself and ultimately was elected president (1969-1974). Unfortunately, due to the Watergate scandal he was forced to resign the office.

Mr. President, of course there is no comparison between Nixon and Gov. Palin. Their only thing in common is that the mainstream media, rightly or wrongly, mercilessly used them as their punching bag.

This time though Sarah Palin appears raring to slug it out with her mainstream media critics who are cozy with the Obama administration. She can afford it now. She has the time.

She will disprove the public perception that she is not qualified to be president of the United States, that she doesn't have the resume for it, that she lacks knowledge in foreign and domestic affairs, which are unfounded.

So if the mainstream media want a slam bang or give-and-take slugfest with Sarah Palin, they got it. She is not to be underestimated. She is a fighter in her own right. That is why she is resigning as governor so that she can mix it up with her media critics in her own personal time, not official time.

As former mayor and then as outstanding governor of the nation's biggest state has qualified Palin to be president of the United States. That is a given. The office has provided her with enough executive experience and ability to run the White House, not to mention her expertise in oil and energy which are Alaska's top accomplishment.

Mr. President, underestimate Palin at your own risk. Right now you are still popular. Your public approval rating is still around 50-60 percent. But what counts more is your approval rating in 2012. When you are up, there is no other way but down.

In the meantime, Gov. Palin has a book deal which reports say gives her a seven-figure price. Again, the timing is good. When it comes out, who knows what it would detonate? Shocking disclosures? Maybe. Interesting read? You bet.

As a journalism graduate, former sportscaster, former beauty queen, former basketball player, exercise buff, outdoor hunter, Palin has a star quality that makes her truly the brightest star of the, repeat, battered and leaderless Republican Party.

The leadership of the opposition party has fallen to the ground in the aftermath of the Obama revolution. All Palin has to do is to pick it up from the ground and claim it.

Time might come when the same media "Gotcha" interviewers would beg Sarah Palin for interviews to boost their readership and TV ratings, and she would have the pleasure of telling them to get lost or go to hell and get away with it. She can afford it now and has virtually nothing to lose. Time and opportunity are on her side.

Interestingly, Mr. President, you campaigned for change and got it. Similarly, Sarah Palin is now also campaigning for change, and may get it.

And why not? With your election the United States has finally broken the racial barrier by electing the first black president in history. So next time around, the American electorate may be ready for another change -- the first woman president in history that Hillary Clinton had aspired for but failed.

Have a nice day, Mr. President.

© Hermie Rotea/Philpress, July 4, 2009

19

The Price of Oil Shoots Up, OPEC Sucks Blood Out of America, Laughs at Stupidity of U.S. Leaders [including Obama], and Nobody is Trying to Stop the Bleeding!

MR. PRESIDENT:

If you have been too busy to notice due to your continuing media blitz as the super pitcher for your government program, the price of gasoline has reached over $3 a gallon, which is outrageous. Of course you don't feel the pinch in your pocket because you ride in your No. 1 presidential limousine and Air Force One plane when traveling around.

But to the average guy, especially those who have lost their jobs and looking for work because of the current economic recession, the effect is devastating.

So Mr. President, why can't you solve this problem? Is it included in your agenda at all? If so, what do you plan to do? If not, why not?

Well, business tycoon Donald Trump -- you know him, of course -- has the answer that you don't have. Without mincing words, he has told Greta Van Susteren of Fox News in an interview what you don't like to hear, as follow:

"I can tell you this. OPEC is raising oil prices and absolutely draining and sucking the blood out of the country. There is no reason for $70 oil. That's very expensive. And OPEC is doing its thing. And as usual, nobody does anything about OPEC. So OPEC is draining the life blood of this country.

"We've been taken for years and nobody [including you, Mr. President] does anything about it. And you know why? Because they've hired every lobbyist in Washington. You don't even hear this! Other than from me and a couple of people, you don't even hear this.

"And then I watched one of the oil ministers the other day say -- and laughing to himself -- Oh, yes, it's the speculators. Let me tell you. The speculators are peanuts compared to the power of OPEC. The speculators don't have that kind of power.

"OPEC does because they tell everybody how much oil to sell and at what price. It's ridiculous. And yet there's so much oil right now. It's all over the world, you can't even -- the tankers are loaded with it.

"They don't know what to do with it. They'll end up dumping it in the ocean, which the environmentalists I'm sure will love. There's so much oil, and it's $70 a barrel, and that's ridiculous."

Mr. President, Trump was asked during the interview, if he were you, what would he do about the oil and OPEC problem.

Van Susteren to Trump: "So what -- if you were president, what would you do about the fact that OPEC -- the price of oil is shooting up -- and the second thing is that the banks aren't losing (sic) money? If you were President Trump today, what would you do?"

Trump answered: "Well, the first thing I'd do is get my biggest, smartest person, my toughest person, and have them negotiating, and I would try and divide OPEC because what they do -- any time anybody strikes oil -- they invited them to OPEC.

"If you have a store and I have a store and we set prices, we go to jail. OPEC is totally setting the price of oil and destroying many countries because of it! I mean, destroying this country, the biggest problem we have is OPEC.

"And it ultimately got us into a problem. We had $150 a barrel oil and it got us into a very big problem. Now oil that should be $20 a barrel is at $70 a barrel, and this country can't afford it. The other thing is, they gave billions and billions of dollars to the banks, and the banks aren't loaning the money!"

So what do you do, "President Trump"?

"You have to force the bank to loan money that you gave and the taxpayers gave. They are just sitting there, not loaning the money. They're building up their balance sheets, and it's disgraceful. That's number one."

And number two, "President Trump"?

"And you have to do something about OPEC. OPEC has to be destroyed in the sense -- in an economic sense. You have to do something about OPEC. They can't -- it really is an illegal situation what they are doing from any standpoint in most countries.

"But they are doing it and they laugh. The truth is, I know people involved with OPEC. They laugh at the stupidity of our country. They laugh at us. They laugh at the stupidity of our politicians in this country. They do whatever they want to do.

"There's oil all over the world in tankers. They can't even bring them in because there's so much oil. And OPEC has $70 a barrel oil. They are laughing at the stupidity of our leaders!"

Mr. President, back to you. What do you think of "President Trump" solution to the oil and OPEC problem? What he said is quite alarming, don't you think? OPEC sucking blood out of America, and laughing at the stupidity of American leaders? That includes you!

When you visited Saudi Arabia last April, you did bow before King Abdullah like a serf (not necessarily picking something from the floor that you dropped) but really bow before the Arabian king. Was that a sign of subservience or kowtowing?

Mr. President, you don't have to kowtow to anybody, not to King Abdullah or not to OPEC that he controls. You are the leader of the world's reputedly last remaining superpower. They may have the oil, but you or the United States has the power.

So Mr. President, why can't you use that power to "terrorize" OPEC, if need be, to stop selling oil to the United States at outrageous price of over $3 a gallon and laughing at the stupidity of American leaders, including you?

Or maybe you can even appoint Donald Trump as your oil czar. You need a tough guy to handle OPEC.

Have a nice day, Mr. President.   © Hermie Rotea/Philpress, 6/30/200

20

OBAMA IS LIKE DR. JEKYLL & MR. HYDE WITH SPLIT PERSONALITIES

MR. PRESIDENT:

Right now you are still popular and smell like a rose. But if you refuse to learn from history, you would be digging your own political grave and end up a one-term president just like Jimmy Carter.

You are committing the same mistakes of your predecessors. From anti-war, you have become pro-war. How times have changed. How you have changed, Mr. President.

Suddenly, you are no longer the candidate Barack H. Obama that the American people knew. As president, you have become like a Dr. Jekyll and Mr. Hyde with split personalities.

If you recall, that is a horror film about the strange tale of Dr. Jekyll who experiments with drug that turns him from a mild-mannered man of science into a crude homicidal maniac Mr. Hyde, and back. Which shows that within each man lurks impulses for both good and evil.

Pardon the analogy, Mr. President. It is hoped this jolts you a little, if at all.

Voters elected you president last year because you called the Iraq war "stupid" and promised to end it as soon as possible. But as this is written, the House just passed a $106 billion bill to further fund the wars in Iraq and Afghanistan. The Senate, of course, is expected to also approve such war funding.

Before the close 226-202 vote, you and Treasury Secretary Timothy F. Geithner forced some of 51 Democrats opposed to the bill to support it. Earlier Speaker Nancy Pelosi (D-Calif.) strongly pressured her colleagues to back the measure in a closed-door meeting. And voila, it is approved!

Sadly, as the new war president you are creating your own Vietnam in Iraq and Afghanistan. That can only lead to disaster. For like Vietnam, they are unwinnable wars. Four American presidents -- John Kennedy, Lyndon Johnson, Richard Nixon, and Gerald Ford -- all failed in that war.

Unless the U.S. pulled out without further delay, Iraq and Afghanistan might surpass Vietnam (1960-1975) as the longest and costliest wars in U.S. history.

Mr. President, what makes you think you can succeed where they failed? The United States is fighting the wrong wars for the wrong reasons in Iraq and Afghanistan where there is no end in sight. The Bush regime created fear of and defense against terrorism as the excuse, which is a great deception.

In Vietnam, the U.S. magnified the fear of communism to attack North Vietnam, which was also a great deception. In both wars, behind the great deceptions is the U.S. Military-Industrial Corporate Complex designed to expand imperialistic and business tentacles in foreign lands and profit from wars.

Mr. President, many wonder why you have changed and broken your pre-election promise to end the wars in Iraq and Afghanistan. That makes you no different from war criminals George W. Bush and Richard Cheney. Under your own war policy, more American soldiers have died and more will die.

In your hands are the blood of those victims of war crimes who had been misled that they were fighting to protect America from terrorist attack or to help Muslim nations gain their freedom from dictators, which of course is also a myth.

Mr. President, you have disregarded the warning of President Eisenhower who in his farewell address to the nation warned against the danger of allowing the U.S. Military-Industrial Corporate Complex to control Washington as some sort of "Invisible Government."

As you should very well know, this moneyed and powerful "Invisible Government" is composed of top lobbyists that contribute campaign funds to both Democratic and Republican leaders in and out of Congress, and influence the outcome of elections.

Mr. President, you should know that they are behind the wars in Iraq and Afghanistan where their hordes of war contractors -- 250,000 -- have even increased under your administration. What does that mean? It means, like during Bush's time, no-bid war contracts continue to make wars their milking cow, so to speak.

According to new statistics that the Pentagon has released, under your watch the number of mercenaries and armed contractors in Iraq and Afghanistan has increased. Under you as the new commander-in-chief, there is a 23% increase in the number of Private Security Contractors in Iraq.

In Afghanistan, in the second quarter of 2009 there is a 29% increase in the number of such Private Security Contractors working for the Department of Defense. Companies like Blackwater and its successor Triple Canopy work on State Department contracts.

According to the same statistics, there is no limit to the number of contractors that can be deployed in the war zone, Mr. President. This looks like war expansion, not reduction. So it is asked, is your stated 2010 timetable for pullout of Iraq for real, or just a big joke?

Or will the United States be stuck in the quagmire of Iraq and Afghanistan wars indefinitely? Hope not.

But have a nice day, Mr. President.

© Hermie Rotea/Philpress, June 16, 2009

21

OBAMA'S CAIRO SPEECH TO MUSLIM WORLD IS BEAUTIFUL, BUT BEHIND THE RHETORIC HE IS WRONG ON IRAQ AND AFGHANISTAN

Source: Philpress Columns   77

MR. PRESIDENT:

You delivered a beautiful speech in Cairo addressed to the Muslim world. Beautiful because your message sounded good, and powerful because listeners were swept away by your powerful rhetoric. Indeed, your mastery of the spoken word is unequaled and you really know how to move the world.

"I have come here to seek a new beginning between the United States and Muslims around the world; one based upon mutual interest and mutual respect; and one based upon the truth that America and Islam are not exclusive, and need not be in competition. Instead, they overlap, and share common principles -- principles of justice and progress, tolerance and the dignity of all human beings."

Very well said, Mr. President. What must have even sounded like music to 1.2 billion Muslims in the world was when you even spoke some Muslim words and quoted from the Holy Koran that drew applause from the audience in Cairo.

"There must be a sustained effort to listen to each other; to learn from each other; to respect one another; and to seek common ground. As the Holy Koran tells us, 'Be conscious of God and speak always the truth.'"

"That is what I will try to do -- to speak the truth as best I can, humbled by the task before us, and firm in my belief that the interests we share as human beings are far more powerful than the forces that drive us apart.

Mr. President, you even spoke like from one Muslim to another and sounded believable. And why not? You do look like one of them. You said: "Part of this conviction is rooted in my own experience. I am a Christian, but my father came from a Kenyan family that includes generations of Muslims. As a boy, I spent several years in Indonesia and heard the call of the azaan at the break of dawn and the fall of dust. As a young man, I worked in Chicago communities where many found dignity and peace in their Muslim faith."

Then you gave the Muslims world food for thought. "So let there be no doubt: Islam is a part of America. And I believe that America holds within her the truth that regardless of race, religion, or station in life, all of us share common aspirations -- to live in peace and security; to get an education and to work with dignity; to love our families, our communities, and our God. These things we share. That is the hope of humanity."

Gee, whiz, Mr. President, you really delivered home your message. If anything, you calmed the tension that your predecessor, that war criminal and fugitive from justice George W. Bush, created during his eight years of antagonizing the Muslim world with his illegal, immoral, and phony war on terror.

That trigger-happy cowboy and oil man from Texas never treated the Muslims right during his eight years as president. Instead, he carpet-bombed and demonized them. But in your case, you reached out to Muslims with respect and recognition of their worth as fellow human beings.

You are the first U.S. president who gave the Muslims such recognition and importance, and rightly so. You assured: "In Ankara, I made clear that America is not -- and never will be -- at war with Islam. We will, however, relentlessly confront violent extremists who pose a grave threat to our security."

But in the afterglow of your beautiful speech in Cairo, Mr. President, when the aura of your rock-star charisma disapates and the dusts settle, what is the real score? Are you able to deliver amid the harsh reality of truth?

You said that Afghanistan is a war of necessity and Iraq is a war of choice. Nothing is further from the truth, Mr. President. You either unknowingly misstated the facts or you deliberately lied.

On Afghanistan, you stated that "the United States pursued Al Qaeda and the Taliban with broad international support. We did not go by choice, we went because of necessity."

On 9/11, you said: "But let us be clear: Al Qaeda killed nearly 3,000 people on that day. . . Al Qaeda chose to ruthlessly murder these people, claimed credit for the attack, and even now states their determination to kill on a massive scale."

Correction, Mr. President. Although Al Qaeda attacked America, Bush and Cheney violated their constitutional oath and duty to protect the people from outside catastrophic attack because although 10 nations, the CIA and the FBI had repeatedly warned them of imminent Al Qaeda attacks long before 9/11, they dismissed the many early warnings as "not credible and impossible," and did nothing.

True, Al Qaeda perpetrated the 9/11 terrorist attacks on America. But Al Qaeda is not Afghanistan, and Afghanistan is not Al Qaeda. The Afghan people, and even the then Taliban de facto government in Kabul, had nothing to do with 9/11. Yet the Bush-Cheney criminal clique invaded and occupied Afghanistan,

In the aftermath of war, Mr. President, the U.S. military carpet-bombed cities, towns and villages with prohibited Depleted Uranium (DU) weapons, killed civilians, women and children, uprooted and displaced millions of refugees, destroyed their entire infrastructures, and caused famine, starvation and widespread radioactive contamination much greater than those caused by the atomic bombs dropped on Hiroshima and Nagasaki that ended World War Two.

If you studied your homework, Mr. President, or if you are just pretending not to know, you know damn well that Bush and Cheney attacked Afghanistan on great deception that it was involved in 9/11 less than a month after the catastrophe when nobody yet knew at the time who had really perpetrated it.

The reason for the great deception, Mr. President, is the involvement of oil and energy companies in the United States in the internal affairs of Afghanistan as the reason for this war. Public documents established that the California-based Oil Company, the Unocal, through a seven-member consortium Centgas, had commenced negotiations with various factions in the government of Afghanistan, for the pipeline project across Afghanistan, Pakistan, to the Indian Ocean, from the oil-rich Central Asiatic Republics of the former USSR; in reference to the old pipeline routes through Russia or an alternative route through Iran (Unocal Position Statement: Proposed Central Asian Pipeline Projects 1998).

"This project aimed at exercising monopoly control over the hydrocarbon resources of this region and distribution through pipelines, referred to in the Complaint/Petition lodged in 1998 by citizens groups to the Attorney General of California, under California Code of Civil Procedure 803 and the California Corporations Code 1801, for cancellation of the Charter of Unocal for violation of human rights within the USA, in Afghanistan and Myanmar . . ." it was disclosed.

"Unocal in these circumstances, increasingly frustrated, sought political/military alternatives by way of regime change . . . In 1997 prominent Republican Party members among them, Donald Rumsfeld, Dick Cheney, Jeb Bush, Paul Wolfowitz, John Bolton, Peter Rodham, Zalmay Khalilzad (an employee of Unocal), and 18 other prominent Americans, broadly known as the Neoconservatives, organized the Project for the New American Century . . . for the establishment of a New World Order . . .

So "on December 1, 2001, President Hamid Karzai, a resident of the United States over several years, a green card holder, the former official Representative of Unocal to the erstwhile Taliban militia's de facto government in Kabul, was sworn in as [U.S. puppet or] head of the interim government (officially called the Transitional Government of Afghanistan). Unocal now directly controls the government of Afghanistan."

So Mr. President, your statement that Afghanistan is a war of necessity, in a way you are right -- the necessity to finally install Unocal's oil pipeline project of the Bush-Cheney crime clique, who deliberately allowed Osama bin Ladin to escape from his mountain hideout in Kandahar and made him their bogey man, so that they could shift their attention to the invasion of Iraq.

On Iraq, you said in your Cairo speech: "Unlike Afghanistan, Iraq was a war of choice that provoked strong differences in my country and around the world. Although I believe that the Iraqi people are ultimately better off without the tyranny of Saddam Hussein, I also believe that events in Iraq have reminded America of the need for diplomacy . . ."

Mr. President, please be reminded that Bush and Cheney invaded and occupied Iraq based on their great deception that Saddam Hussein had weapons of mass destruction and link to Al Qaeda. He neither attacked nor threatened the United States. In fact, they were motivated by oil and war profits. They eventually controlled Iraq's oil and economy.

You stated: "Today, America has a dual responsibility: to help Iraq forge a better future — and to leave Iraq to Iraqis. I have made it clear to the Iraqi people that we pursue no bases, and no claim on their territory or resources. Iraq's sovereignty is its own."

Yes Mr. President, Iraq war is indeed a war of choice —the choice made by the Bush-Cheney criminal clique who privatized and plundered Iraq while they were in power. Now you have taken over. You have flip-flopped from your pre-election pledge that U.S. troop withdrawal would be done "as soon as possible." Now it is until 2012.

So instead of cutting losses, you are virtually creating your own Vietnam and pushing America deeper into the quagmire of unwinnable wars with all their inevitable consequences, and also deeper into the abyss of bankruptcy.

What are you going to do with the mesh that Bush and Cheney left you, Mr. President? They destroyed Iraq's and Afghanistan's entire infrastructures and then awarded secret no-bid contracts to their business cronies who made billions of dollars in reconstruction projects with no oversight, including the largest American Embassy in the world?

By overstaying in Iraq and Afghanistan, Mr. President, wittingly or unwittingly you are in effect acting like a captive of the U.S. Military Industrial Complex that has robbed the national treasury of unaccounted war weapons and construction costs and profited from wars.

You must know by now that the U.S. Military Industrial Complex is referred to as the "Invisible Government" that actually controls Washington, being the No. 1 lobbyist that contributes campaign funds to both Democratic and Republican members of Congress. In that sense, you are its figurehead.

Mr. President, follow the lesson of history. Otherwise, Iraq and Afghanistan could be your own Vietnam or political Waterloo. Have a nice day!

© Hermie Rotea/Philpress, June 5, 2009

22
U.S. IS TO BLAME FOR NORTH KOREA'S WARLIKE STAUNCH

MR. PRESIDENT:

Bad foreign policy of the United States has made North Korea into a suicide-like regime and battle-ready for war with America, South Korea, and other nations that interfere with its nuclear program. To dramatize its resolve, the rogue nation has detonated an underground nuclear device and fired three short-range missiles off its coast in two days. Experts say North Korea is now capable of producing eight atomic bombs.

But guess what, Mr. President? It is the fault of the United States.

For a long time now America has bullied, punished, warned, insulted, belittled, humiliated, ridiculed, and mocked North Korea. Worst, the U.S. has repeatedly broken its commitments made at the bargaining table to ship badly needed aid to its 23 million ill-fed people in exchange for cooperation. North Korea cooperated and honored its part of the deal, but the U.S. did not.

The United States treats North Korea like a dog. The U.S. is like a person who plays with the animal. He entices and dangles food over the dog. When the dog reaches for the food, he pulls it away and laughs. That is how America treats North Korea. Like a dog.

So Mr. President, if North Korea is "crazy," a "terrorist," or part of the "Axis of Evil" as war criminal and fugitive from justice George W. Bush called it, the U.S. created that monster and it is to blame.

It is a vicious cycle of history repeating itself. In the backdrop of the Korean War, the United States is committed to the defense of South Korea and Japan. They do not want North Korea to develop nuclear weapons they consider a threat to peace in the region. The United Nations supports that goal.

So what happened? A six-nation panel was formed to discuss and solve the problem. North Korea wanted direct or bilateral talk with the United States. But the U.S. refused because it did not want to dignify the poor nation with such importance. In any event, North Korea reluctantly attended the meeting and got promises of humanitarian aid in exchange for cooperation. But the shipments did not come. If they did, they were short.

Feeling double crossed, North Korea naturally returned to its belligerent stance and went ahead with its nuclear program. The United States ran to the United Nations and secured sanctions against North Korea from the UN Security Council that is controlled by five permanent members composed of Russia, Britain, France, China and the U.S., all with veto power.

Mr. President, this scenario has been repeated several times with sequence of events that is all too familiar. The United States would again titillate North Korea with humanitarian aid, North Korea would reluctantly go back to the bargaining table. agree to cooperate and secure new pledge of aid. And as usual, promises of aid would be broken.

So North Korea would again boycott the meeting. The United States would again ran back to the United Nations and once more secure stricter sanctions against North Korea for violating UN resolutions. Ailing North Korean leader Kim Jong-il would again engage in saber rattling like an amok, and the U.S. would again warn North Korea of "serious consequences." The vicious cycle continues.

At the United Nations, Steven Edwards of Canwest News Service reports on the legal limits of a global, U.S.-led program aimed at halting atomic-weapons trafficking face scrutiny in closed-door UN talks over North Korea's nuclear weapon test.

Wrangling over the Proliferation Security Initiative, which involves stopping and searching ships suspected of illegally carrying weapons of mass destruction, has unfolded as North Korea responded with anger to its southern neighbor's decision to join the program.

Mr. President, Pyongyang said it was tearing up the armistice agreement that ended the Korean war of the 1950s, and threatened to retaliate against any attempt to search North Korean ships. North Korea also accused South Korea of being a "puppet" of the United States for agreeing to join the program, which the administration of George W. Bush launched in 2003 as part of its global "war on terror."

"Any minor hostile acts, including cracking down on or searching our peaceful vessels, will be an unacceptable infringement of our republic's sovereignty," North Korea's military said in a statement broadcast by the state media. "Our military will no longer be bound by the armistice."

North Korea also renounced the armistice in August 2006 to protest joint military exercises conducted annually by U.S. and South Korean forces.

But if you care to remember, Mr. President, in the summer of 2008 it looked like there was finally a breakthrough in the negotiation with North Korea on its nuclear program. Believing that this time the United States was really sincere in its promise of humanitarian aid for its poor people, Jong-il finally opened its door to the world.

Before the very eyes of nuclear inspectors and the world media as eyewitnesses, North Korea destroyed a plutonium facility that is needed to produce nuclear weapon. It was proof thatPyongyang appeared ready to abandon its nuclear program in return for aid and diplomatic concessions.

In another heartwarming gesture, Jong-il even allowed a cultural exchange with the United States by inviting New York Philharmonic Orchestra to perform in Pyongyang. It was truly a historic event that touched the heart of the world. It shows that Jong-il was not that "crazy" but also human like you, Mr. President.

But negotiations at the six-nation talks stalled again after the promised shipments of humanitarian aid to the starving people of North Korea stopped — as usual. North Korea accused the United States and other participants of reneging on commitments. Jong il apparently had enough and decided never to trust the United States again. It was the last straw.

Now Mr. President, you said before that you were ready to talk even with Fidel Castro of Cuba and Mahmoud Ahmadinejad of Iran without precondition. You stated that talking with the enemy is the right thing to do because diplomacy is better than military solution.

Yet that does not seem to apply to North Korean leader Kim Jong-il. But like it or not, you cannot deny the reality of a nuclear power that North Korea has become. If the United States keeps treating North Korea like a dog as we said earlier, or bully it around like a cornered animal, what do you expect?

Think it over, Mr. President. Have a nice day!

© Hermie Rotea/Philpress, May 28, 2009

23

TRICKY DICK CHENEY HAS NO BUSINESS LECTURING OBAMA ON SECURITY ISSUES

MR. PRESIDENT:

Tricky Dick Cheney has been attacking you lately on national security issues, particularly on how to make America safe from another 9/11 terrorist attack, your projected closure of Guantanamo Bay prison camp for captured "enemy combatants," and the CIA disclosure of waterboarding torture of detainees.

This shameless war criminal and fugitive from justice has the audacity to criticize your effort to undo seven years of injury and damage he and fellow criminal and fugitive George W. Bush have caused the United States and the American people. These two oil guys are addicted to wars in the same way that other people are addicted to drugs.

Mr. President, on this long Memorial Day observance let the nation and the world be reminded that because of their illegal, immoral and phony global war on terror, the U.S. military invaded and occupied Iraq and Afghanistan based on great deceptions that they were involved in 9/11, and that Saddam Hussein had weapons of mass destruction. In truth, they were motivated by oil and profit.

Their reckless aggressions violated the U.S. Constitution, the United Nations Charter according to then UN Secretary General Kofi Annan, the Geneva Convention, and the Nuremberg Convention relating to war crimes and crimes against humanity reminiscent of Dictator Adolph Hitler of Germany and Admiral Hideki Tojo of Japan during World War Two.

Because of Cheney and Bush, as of May 23, 2009 over 4300 Americans died in Iraq and another over 686 in Afghanistan. Contractor employee deaths include 1,306. Some 138 journalists were killed in Iraq. Total wounded include 31,285, with 320,000 veterans suffering from brain injuries, based on data from U.S. Department of Defense, Antiwar.com, and iCasualties.org.

Mr. President, as you well know the human and financial costs of Iraq and Afghanistan invasions and occupations are staggering. As of May 7, 2009 they top $900 billion but could hit $1.7 trillion. Iraqi deaths due to U.S. invasion have reached over 1,3 million. In addition, 1.2 million Iraqi refugees have been displaced.

Afghanistan is even worst. It is projected that the cost could surpass that of Iraq. Over 2.1 million have fled amid decades of civil war and insurgencies. The nation's entire infrastructure were destroyed like in Iraq due to American carpet napalm bombing of cities and villages that killed countless women and children from radioactive contamination not different from U.S. atomic bombings of Hiroshima and Nagasaki that ended World War Two.

Who else but Cheney and Bush are responsible for the horrific tragedy that they have caused not only in Iraq and Afghanistan but also in the United States. The 9/11 terrorists attacks by Osama bin Laden and his Al Qaeda suicide plane bombers could have been prevented if only these two war criminals had done their duty under the Constitution to protect America from outside attacks.

Mr. President, 10 other nations along with the CIA and the FBI long before 9/11 had repeatedly warned the White House that terrorist attacks inside the United States were imminent based on intercepted satellite messages by Bin Laden and Al Qaeda. But Cheney and Bush dismissed the many early warning relayed to them as "not credible and unbelievable."

Three thousand died when terrorists hijacked four commercial planes, destroyed the World Trade Center in New York City and bombed the Pentagon. The attacks cost billions of dollars in damage to properties. All because Cheney and Bush criminally neglected to perform their duties to protect America.

In fact, so serious were their violations of U.S. and international laws that at least four antiwar citizen groups formally accused Cheney and Bush of war crimes and crimes against humanity and found them guilty in public hearings held in Tokyo, Brussels and Tacoma. International legal luminaries, scientists, and victims testified and heard indisputable evidence against them. They ruled that their use of preemptive strike and self-defense to invade Iraq and Afghanistan violated international laws, and that their real motive was for oil and profit.

Mr. President, in Vermont the towns of Brattleboro and Marlboro voted to indict and impeach Bush and Cheney for their war crimes. They issued outstanding warrants for their arrest if they ever set foot on Vermont, which of course they won't do.

In the United Nations, several international antiwar organizations have filed petitions to indict Bush and Cheney and try them for war crimes and crimes against humanity at The Hague for their invasions and occupations of Iraq and Afghanistan in violation of international laws.

So Mr. President, this guy Tricky Dick Cheney has no business lecturing you on national security issues. He is like the proverbial wolf boy who cries "Wolf! Wolf!" although there is no wolf. He is fear-mongering again, maybe because he misses his old job as vice president when he and Bush used fear against new 9/11 terrorist attack to achieve their imperialistic addiction to war, oil and profit.

Have a nice Memorial Day observance, Mr. President.

© Hermie Rotea/Philpress, May 25, 2009

24

GOVERNING AS PRESIDENT AND CAMPAIGNING FOR PRESIDENT ARE TWO DIFFERENT ANIMALS

MR. PRESIDENT:

By now you must have already realized that campaigning for president and governing as president are two different animals. What you said then and what you say now contradict each other. You have flip-flopped.

For example, you stated during the 2007 campaign that Iraq was a "stupid war" that should not have been waged. Now you have embraced it and thus legitimized war criminal George W. Bush's illegal, immoral and phony war on terrorism.

Of course you have set an elastic timetable for withdrawal. But what the heck, you are now the leader of discredited Washington gang of old.

In fact, you are already even creating your own Vietnam with the U.S. military surge in Afghanistan and Pakistan. When will the United States ever learn a lesson from history?

The tragedy is that America is addicted to war in the same way that some people are addicted to drugs. Presidents Kennedy, Johnson and Nixon failed in the Vietnam war. Yet U.S. military bases are still all over the world.

Mr. President, what makes you think that the United States can win the war in Afghanistan where the former Soviet Union with more troops involved miserably failed in the 1980s? Wake up and stop playing politics or political expediency!

MEET YOUR FELLOW FLIP-FLOPPER

Former Speaker Newt Gingrich has demanded the resignation or ouster of current Speaker Nancy Pelosi for charging that the CIA had misled her about the waterboarding torture of suspected foreign terrorist prisoners. CIA Director Leon Panetta has contradicted her by stating that the CIA does not condone torture of detainees.

Mr. President, political sharks who smell blood are now circling your ship of state and maneuvering to sink it. Already Michael Steele, chairman of the Republican National Committee, has declared that the \'d2honeymoon\'d3 (what honeymoon?) is over and the opposition party is set for the kill. They see the Pelosi-Panetta dispute as a good opening for the attack.

Who better than Gingrich can lead such political offensive? The architect of the "Contract with America" revolution and now a Republican presidential aspirant, said that Pelosi should resign or be ousted because she had lied that the CIA had not actually briefed her, just informed her, about the waterboarding torture of suspected terrorists, which is illegal.

As Gingrich put it, Pelosi had committed a crime because "it is illegal to lie to Congress." Well said, Mr. ex-speaker.

But wait a minute. did not Gingrich himself accuse former President Bush, the notorious unindicted war criminal and fugitive from justice, of lying to the American people about his phony war on terror? Yes he did. That is a direct quote from him early in the 2007 presidential campaign when he was testing the political waters.

If Bush had lied about his imperialistic global war on terror, the CIA during his 8-year administration must have also lied or just kept quiet about waterboarding torture of prisoners to please the boss. After all, Bush was their commander-in-chief who who had tried but failed to prove that Saddam Hussein had weapons of mass destruction or that he had link to Osama bin Laden or Al Qaeda who had masterminded 9/11.

So Mr. ex-Speaker, your slip is showing. But nice try though.

YOU ARE A CHANGED MAN

Mr. President, doubting Thomases now say that they don't recognize you anymore. Are you the same Barack H. Obama who had campaigned for president to change Washington and politics as usual?

At first everybody thought you were a far-left guy who had associated with such radicals as Bill Ayers, a 1960s leader of the homegrown terrorist group Weatherman who had bombed the Pentagon, and with Rev. Jeremiah

Wright who had "God Damn America" repeatedly in his church sermons, and who was your own pastor who had performed your marriage with your wife Michelle, and whom you later you disowned.

Now you are being labeled as a pragmatic leader or moderate, a middle of the road guy. Whatever you really are, Mr. President, you have in fact already embraced some conservative policies of your cowboy predecessor from Texas, where there is a current movement to secede from the United States, now otherwise known as the Obama Union because they don't like your tax-and-spent "socialistic" policy.

The case of California which Tuesday rejected Gov. Arnold Schwarzenegger's five propositions to permanently fix its "broken budget system" in a special election, may well also serve as a warning to you, Mr. President. People need to survive the current economic recession, or you can say goodbye to your reelection chances.

WATCH OUT FOR O'REILLY AND HANNITY

Fox Cable News led by talk show hosts Bill O'Reilly and Sean Hannity have been consistently attacking you for remaking America as a socialist nation patterned after European countries that take care of their peoples from the cradle to the grave with their socialistic policies. Americans are beginning to wonder if you are really charting the ship of state in that same direction.

Mr. President, you are acting like Donald Trump in his TV Apprentice series. You have in fact already fired some CEOs at Wall Street with the government takeover of some giant banking, insurance and auto corporations as the majority owner. Your "socialistic" policy has even provoked the birth of the modern "Tea Party Movement" in protest against your taxation reminiscent of the historic Boston Tea Party of 1773 that ignited the events that led to American independence from England.

As Thomas Jefferson said, when the people fear the government, that is tyranny. When the government fears the people, that is liberty.

Have a nice day, Mr. President!

25
Jesse Ventura's Book Is a Portrait of Evil America

MR. PRESIDENT:

A new book *American Conspiracies* by former Minnesota Gov. Jesse Ventura with Dick Russell is a shocking portrait of evil America. The kicker says: "Lies, Lies, and More Lies that the Government Tells Us."

Indeed, few people of the United States know the truth or, if they do, prefer to ignore it or are in self-denial because it is too ugly, scary and shameful.

The former professional wrestler this time has wrestled with the hidden truth about this nation that makes one wonder why he is not a career investigative journalist in the mold of Joseph Pulitzer or Walter Cronkite, because he has exposed what the mainstream media are afraid or have failed to do.

Mr. President, although you have been in office only a little over a year, you are not exempted from his criticisms because you are now the new leader of the Washington Establishment that are addicted to war for oil, big business, and dirty politics.

Ventura's bestselling bombshell of a book includes, in chronological order, the following earthshaking events and virtual unsolved crimes:

• The conspiracy behind the assassination of President Abraham Lincoln.
• The big money plot to overthrow President Franklin Delano Roosevelt.
• The cover-up in the assassination of President John F. Kennedy.
• The CIA and FBI involvement in the assassination of Malcolm X.
• The Mob, Military, and Right Wing role in the assassination of Dr. Martin Luther King Jr.
• Did the CIA hypnotically program Sirhan Sirhan to assassinate Senator Robert   Kennedy?
• The CIA's War against President Richard Nixon that forced him to resign due to Watergate.
• "October Surprise": Ronald Reagan's Stolen Election of President Jimmy Carter.
• The Iran-Contra Scandal exposes U.S. government's involvement in global drug trade.
• How President George W. Bush stole the elections of 2000 and 2004.
• What really happened on September 11, 2001? Massive government cover-up exposed.
• The Wall Street Conspiracy and the scams that cheat American taxpayers.
• The Secret Plan to impose Martial Law and destroy American Democracy.

Mr. President, the Washington powers that be that now include you can thank the inept and cowardly mainstream media that have abdicated their role as public watchdog and have become complicit in government shenanigans, for making it possible for politicians and big business to get away with murder.

In effect, press freedom and free speech are virtually dead in the United States. The Internet has virtually taken over the task of upholding them.

It is a shame that it took a non-journalist like Jesse Ventura to write what the traditional media should be probing for facts and truth about earthshaking events that affect the future and destiny of America, but have instead reneged from their duty to probe for facts and truth about the government.

As CNN's Larry King put it, "If you're talking outspoken, unconventional, and no-holds-barred, you're talking Jesse Ventura."

Ventura tells it like it is: "As I got older and started looking back at the Sixties, where every assassin was supposedly a 'lone nut,' I began thinking how could that be?. These nuts who never told anybody anything or planned with anyone else, but just felt the need to go out and commit murders of prominent individuals – John and Robert Kennedy, Martin Luther King . . . the odds of that simply defied all logic. It made me wonder who's really running the show."

Also worth quoting is that in this explosive account of wrongful acts and ensuing cover-ups, the author offers a different side to the stories we've all heard about and read about in the history books. He takes a look at the wide gap between what the government knows and what is revealed to the American people.

The media is complicit in these acts of deception, often refusing to consider alternate possibilities and dismissing voices that diverge from public opinion. Ventura looks closely at the theories that have been presented over the years and examine the truth as well as the lies.

Here is how former Gov. Jesse Ventura, who is now a bestselling book author and host of the new television reality show *Conspiracy Theory* (TruTV), summarizes his book *American Conspiracies* and gives his take on each earthshaking event:

President Abraham Lincoln – *The Incident:* Lincoln was assassinated on April 14, 1865 at Ford's Theatre in Washington. *The Official Word:* He was shot in the back by prominent actor John Wilkes Booth who escaped and then was killed. Eight conspirators were also caught and found guilty by a military court. *Ventura's Take:* Besides leaders of the Confederacy, the conspiracy to kill Lincoln included people within his own Cabinet.

President Franklin Delano Roosevelt – *The Incident:* Roosevelt in 1934 was targeted by a coup to overthrow him from power by Wall Street titans who plotted to put the United States under military control. *The Official Word:* The plotters were foiled when the man they selected, Major General Butler, blew the whistle to Congress. *Ventura's Take:* This was an attempt to turn America into a fascist country run by corporate power, but it was ignored in most official histories of the Great Depression.

"*The liberty of a democracy is not safe if the people tolerate the growth of private power to a point where it becomes stronger than their democratic State itself. That, in essence, is Fascism -- ownership of government by an individual, by a group or by any controlling private power.*" – President Franklin Delano Roosevelt.

President John F. Kennedy – *The Incident:* Kennedy was assassinated on November 22, 1963 while riding in his limousine with First Lady Jacqueline in Dallas, Texas. *The Official Word:* Lee Harvey Oswald shot the president twice from behind with a rifle from a window of the Texas School Book Depository. He was captured the same day and killed two days later by Jack Ruby. *Ventura's Take:* The cover-up of what really happened starts with the Warren Commission's "lone assassin" conclusion and continues to this day with the big media. JFK was said to have been shot from behind when it is clear his head was thrust violently backward by the bullet. Thus a second gunman assassinated JFK from a grassy knoll, while Oswald was set up as the fall guy. The perpetrators behind Oswald are linked to the CIA, the Pentagon, and the Mob, along with right-wing extremists who tried to make it look like Cuba's Fidel Castro was behind it.

   "*In the councils of government, we must guard against the acquisition of unwarranted influence, whether sought or unsought, by the military-industrial complex. The potential for the disastrous rise of misplaced power exists and will persist. We must never let the weight of this combination endanger our liberties or democratic processes. We should take nothing for granted.*" – President Dwight Eisenhower in his Farewell Address in 1961.

   Malcolm X – *The Incident:* Gunned down, execution-style, while delivering a speech on February 21, 1965 inside the Audubon Ballroom in Harlem. *The Official Word:* His killers were Black Muslims loyal to Elijah Muhammad who was involved in a power struggle with Malcolm X. *Ventura's Take:* Malcolm X was set up by the CIA and the FBI who had him under constant surveillance and were afraid that he and Dr. Martin Luther King Jr. might form an alliance.

   Dr. Martin Luther King Jr. – *The Incident:* King was shot and killed on April 4, 1968 while standing on the balcony of the Lorraine Motel in Memphis. *The Official Word:* A racist and escaped convict James Earl Ray fired the shot from the window of a rooming home across the street, fled the scene, and was arrested two months later in London, after which he pleaded guilty to the murder. *Ventura's Take:* Ray was another fall guy like Oswald who had evidence planted to incriminate him while the real killer fired from behind some shrubs. The links to King's assassination trace to people in the Mob, the Military, and the Right Wing.

   Senator Robert Kennedy – *The Incident:* Kennedy was assassinated on June 5, 1968 in the pantry of the Ambassador Hotel in Los Angeles after winning the California primary and seeming to clinch the Democratic nomination for president. *The Official Word:* A Palestinian Sirhan Bishara Sirhan opposed to Kennedy's policy toward Israel fired a pistol eight times just a few feet from him, was arrested immediately and later pleaded guilty to the murder. *Ventura's Take:* Sirhan didn't have enough rounds in his gun to make all the bullet holes found by the police, so there was a second gunman firing from behind. Sirhan was hypnotically "programmed," using methods the CIA had developed, to take part in the assassination.

   President Richard Nixon – *The Incident:* The Watergate burglars on June 17, 1972 broke into the Democratic National Committee headquarters in Washington, were taken into custody by police, and discovered to have ties to the Nixon White House. *The Official Word:* President Nixon authorized the break-in, along with other dirty tricks, and then covered this up, leading to his resignation on August 9, 1974, before he could be impeached. *Ventura's Take:* Nixon was involved in a power struggle with the CIA, trying to pry loose what their files contained on President John F. Kennedy's assassination. He was taken down by "double agents" who actually worked for the CIA and who intentionally got themselves caught. Many of the Watergate cast track back to who killed JFK.

President Ronald Reagan – *The Incident:* On the same day that Reagan was inaugurated as president on January 20, 1981, Iran released 51 American hostages it had been holding for 444 days in the U.S. Embassy in Tehran. *The Official Word:* The timing was coincidental. *Ventura's Take:* Reagan's people had cut out a deal with Iran to keep the hostages beyond the presidential election, to ensure that President Jimmy Carter's negotiations with Iran failed and that he lost to Reagan in his reelection bid.

"*Concentrated power has always been the enemy of liberty.*" – Ronald Reagan

"*How can a president not be an actor?*" – Ronald Reagan

The Iran-Contra Scandal – *The Incident:* This scandal of 1986-1988 involved members of the Reagan administration breaking an arms embargo and selling weapons to Iran, in order to secure the release of six U.S. hostages and to fund the Nicaraguan Contras. *The Official Word:* Fourteen administration officials were charged with crimes, and 11 were convicted. Reagan eventually admitted "trading arms for hostages." *Ventura's Take:* Congress covered up the fact that illegal drug deals were at the heart of the Iran-Contra scandal, just as the CIA has been deeply involved in drug trafficking for decades.

The Stolen Elections of 2000 and 2004 – *The Incident:* In 2000 and again in 2004, George W. Bush won closely contested presidential elections against Democratic candidates, Vice President Al Gore and Senator John Kerry. *The Official Word:* The U.S. Supreme Court stopped a recount in Florida in 2000, giving Bush an Electoral College victory on December 12. In 2004, Bush took the deciding state of Ohio by a 100,000-vote margin and was reelected. *Ventura's Take:* Both elections were stolen by Republican operatives through manipulation of the electronic voting machines in deciding states where votes were shifted from one candidate to the other. A guy who might have blown the whistle was mysteriously killed in a plane crash right after the 2008 election.

What Really Happened on 9/11? – *The Incident:* On September 11, 2001 four airplanes were hijacked on American soil and crashed into New York's World Trade Twin Towers, the Pentagon, and a field in Pennsylvania. *The Official Word:* The 19 hijackers were all fanatic Muslim terrorists linked to mastermind Osama bin Laden and his Al Qaeda network. *Ventura's Take:* The U.S. government engaged in a massive cover-up of what really happened, including its own ties with the hijackers. Unanswered questions remain about how the towers were brought down, and whether a plane really struck the Pentagon. The Bush Administration either knew about the plan and allowed it to proceed, or they had a hand in it themselves.

The Wall Street Conspiracy – *The Incident:* America's worst economic crisis since the Great Depression in the fall of 2008, brought on originally by the collapse of a housing bubble that damaged financial institutions and caused the stock market to plummet. *The Official Word:* Huge corporations like AIG and Goldman Sachs were considered "too big to fail" and thus received multibillion-dollar bailouts from the federal government to prevent economic collapse. *Ventura's Take:* The government has conspired to keep the "fat cats" in business while the American taxpayers are left holding the bag. CEOs that should go to jail for their scams are instead reaping the biggest bonuses ever. Corporations basically run the government, and the same players that caused the mess still have a stranglehold on our future.

The Secret Plans to End American Democracy – *The Incident:* The two terms of President George W. Bush saw passage of the Patriot Act, the Foreign Intelligence Surveillance Act, and other similar laws in the wake of 9/11. Afghanistan and Iraq were invaded, and detention centers for terrorists established. *The Official Word:* The erosion of civil liberties, including wiretapping, torture, and the suspension of the writ of habeas corpus, is necessary to prevent the spread of terrorism on our shores. *Ventura's Take:* The federal government and elements of the military have used 9/11 as an excuse to put in place the means to impose martial law and lock up dissenters in "camps" if they deem it necessary. Our Constitution and Bill of Rights have never been in greater peril than now. The technology exists to further erode our democracy, and basically make slaves of those who won't go along with the program.

"With a fascist the problem is never how best to present the truth to the public but how best to use the news to deceive the public into giving the fascist and his group more money or more power. American fascism will not be really dangerous until there is a purposeful coalition among the cartelists, the deliberate poisoners of public information . . . They claim to be super-patriot, but they would destroy every liberty guaranteed by the Constitution." – U.S. Vice President Henry Wallace, 1944.

Mr. President, are you still there? If you are, it is hoped that author Jesse Ventura and his book *American Conspiracies* do not give you a nightmare.

As the most threatened president in the history of the United States, please be careful yourself. Well-meaning critics may disagree with you, but they do still wish you well. Good night, Mr. President.

© Hermie Rotea, April 11, 2010

26
Obama is a Captive of
the "Invisible Government"

MR. PRESIDENT:

The truth is out. You are really captive of the Military-Industrial Complex, aka, the "Invisible Government" in Washington that President Abraham Lincoln, President Franklin Delano Roosevelt, and President Dwight Eisenhower warned against its control of the government.

This shadowy power is behind the manufacture of U.S. weapons of mass destruction and the sponsorship of foreign wars that they benefit from, big time.

They are the bankers, industrialists, oil tycoons, businessmen, and lobbyists of Wall Street who thrive in international conflicts dating back to World War One through World War Two, the Korean War, the Vietnam War, now Iraq and Afghanistan wars, and others in-between.

They decide Presidential and U.S. Congress elections through political donations or bribery and thus control the national government and the destiny of the United States.

To them, that is big business.

So welcome to the ole old club, Mr. President. You have assured yourself of huge political contribution and campaign fund for your 2012 reelection bid. All you do is simply follow in the footsteps of your predecessor George W. Bush and Dick Cheney, the notorious war criminals who had the U.S. invade and occupy Iraq and Afghanistan without legal justification.

In your case, unfortunately, history repeats itself. In fact, whoever sits at the Oval Office in the White House has been, or will always be, captive of the "Invisible Government." It goes with the territory. This addiction to war is like a chronic and seemingly incurable disease.

Never mind what you said while campaigning for president in 2008 that Iraq was a "stupid" war that America should not have waged. Never mind what you said that terrorist suspects are entitled to a lawyer and a day in court. Why do you think that Amnesty International and the Civil Liberties Union are mad at you now?

Mr. President, one doesn't have to be a rocket scientist to understand. You have already exposed yourself. You are even trying to outdo Bush and Cheney in Afghanistan by sending 30,000 American soldiers in a new military surge to fight the Taliban and Al Qaeda there.

But after all has been said and done, what really is the reason why the United States still occupies Afghanistan, not to mention Iraq?

The Taliban are Afghan citizens who oppose foreign domination and occupiers. That is why they fought the Soviet Union in the 1980s and won. Now they are fighting American soldiers in defense of their sovereignty. They are branded as "insurgents" because they hate and even punish fellow Afghans who collaborate with foreign occupiers led by the United States. What is wrong with fighting for freedom and independence?

During your secret and surprise trip to Afghanistan today, Mr. President, you vowed to wipe out the Al Qaeda. Big talk. There are no more Al Qaeda in Afghanistan. Even the Taliban do not want them there because they attract more attacks from American forces.

In any case, Mr. President, your trip to Afghanistan merely shows that you are really a new good follower, disciple and captive of Washington's "Invisible Government", aka, the Military-Industrial Complex. Here is what

President Lincoln, President Roosevelt and President Eisenhower warned against its control of the government:

In 1864 President Abraham Lincoln noted the increasing interference of arms corporations in the political life of the United States. In a letter to Colonel Williams Elkins, he noted:

"I see in the near future a crisis approaching that unnerves me and causes me to tremble for the safety of my country. Corporations have been enthroned and an era of high corporation will follow and the money power of the country will endeavor to prolong its reign by working on the prejudice of the people until all wealth is aggregated in a few hands and the Republic is destroyed . . ."

Lincoln identified this strategy back in 1848 before he became president. He attacked President James Polk for his policy on Mexico. "Trusting to escape scrutiny, by fixing the public gaze upon the exceeding brightness of military glory -- that attracted rainbow that rises in shadows of blood -- that serpent's eye, that charms to destroy -- he plunged into war."

He added: "Kings had always been involving and impoverishing their people in wars, pretending generally, if not always, that the good of the people was the object."

Lincoln said this was "the most oppressive of all kingly oppressions" and that it was important that the United States should make surer that "no one man should hold the power of bringing this oppression upon us."

President Roosevelt, after he was elected in 1932 during the Great Depression, launched his New Deal to solve the country's economic problem that involved increasing taxes. Wall Street did not like it and plotted to stage a coup and overthrow him. That prompted Roosevelt to issue this prophetic public statement:

"The liberty of democracy is not safe if the people tolerate the growth of private power to a point where it becomes stronger than their democratic State itself. That, in essence, is Fascism -- ownership of government by an individual, by a group or by any controlling private power."

President Eisenhower emphasized the same concern in his Farewell Address to the nation on January 17, 1961. He sounded an alarm against the Military-Industrial Complex that had plunged the United States into foreign wars and robbed the national treasury of public funds.

"Until the latest of our world conflicts, the United States had no armament industry. American makers of plowshares could, in time and as required, make swords as well. But now we can no longer risk emergency improvisation of national defense;

"We have been compelled to create a permanent armaments industry of vast proportions. Added to this, three and a half million men and women are directly engaged in the defense establishment. We annually spend on military security more than the net income of all United States corporations.

"This conjunction of an immense military establishment and a large arms industry is new in the American experience. The local influence -- economic, political, even spiritual -- is felt in every city, every State house, every office of the Federal government.

"We recognize the imperative need for this development. Yet we must not fail to comprehend its grave implications. Our toil, resources and livelihood are all involved; so is the structure of our society.

"In the councils of government, we must guard against the acquisition of unwarranted influence, whether sought or unsought, by the military-industrial complex. The potential for the disastrous rise of misplaced power exists and will persist.

"We must never let the weight of this combination endanger our liberties or democratic processes. We should take nothing for granted. Only an alert and knowledgeable citizenry can compel the proper meshing of the huge industrial and military machinery of defense with our peaceful methods and goals, so that security and liberty may prosper together."

Eisenhower said: "Every gun that is made, every worship launched, every rocket fired signifies in the final sense, a theft from those who hunger and are not fed; those who are cold and not clothed. This World in Arms is not spending alone. It is spending the sweat of its laborers, the genius of its scientists, and the hopes of its children."

Mr. President, the shameful fact is that the United States still occupies Afghanistan and Iraq because of oil and profit. Yes, it is all about oil. Laws were passed in Baghdad to allow the U.S. access to and control of oil. In Afghanistan, U.S. oil companies have pipeline projects that can produce 200 billion barrels of oil worth billions of dollars. They need to be protected.

Yet the true reason behind the Iraq and Afghanistan wars and occupations is buried in the news and official government propaganda. The hypocrisy and cover-up are brazen with the cooperation of the mainstream media that have abandoned their role as public watchdog.

It is always to help Iraq and Afghanistan achieve peace, progress and democracy, when in fact they are better taught by showing good examples not through wars but by peaceful means.

Have a nice day, Mr. President.

© Hermie Rotea, March 29, 2010

27
Lawsuits Test President's Persistence
And Obamacare

MR. PRESIDENT:

> *Nothing in the world can take the place of persistence.*
> *Talent will not; nothing is more common than*
> *unsuccessful men with talent.*
> *Genius will not; unrewarded genius is almost a proverb.*
> *Education will not; the world is full of educated derelicts.*
> *Persistence and determination alone are omnipotent.*
> *So goes a quotable quote.*

Mr. President, it is a tribute to your persistence that you have resurrected the Healthcare Reform Bill from the grave.

After Republican Scott Brown shocked the nation with his win as an "Independent" in last January's U.S. Senate special election in Massachusetts and tilted the balance of power in the Senate, people thought that the bill was dead.

You even skipped the subject in your State of the Union Address before Congress out of shame to avoid embarrassment.

But now, bingo, it is a new law. So henceforth such monumental legislation, thanks to Speaker Nancy Pelosi and Senate Majority Leader Harry Reid in particular, will be known as the Healthcare Reform Act of 2010 – or simply Obamacare.

It is a remarkable feat that such new landmark law had not been enacted in the last half century comparable to President Lyndon Johnson's and the Reverend Martin Luther King's legacy in the Civil Rights Act of 1964, and to the enactment of Medicare in 1966.

Actually the battle for national healthcare reform dates back to 1912 when former Republican President Theodore Roosevelt, who was then running as a Progressive Party candidate for what would have been his third term, advocated national health insurance in its platform. He lost.

But that is now water under the bridge, so to speak. Congratulations, Mr. President. You have succeeded where President Bill Clinton and First Lady Hillary Rodham Clinton failed in 1993-1994 from which you apparently learned your lesson from their inaction and incrementalism.

But wait a minute. The issue is not really dead yet. As Senator John McCain whom you defeated for president in the 2008 election has served notice during an interview by ABC News, "You go against the will of the people, you pay the price."

He was referring to public opinion polls which consistently showed majority public disapproval of your Obamacare, your own low approval rating of 43 percent, and the much lower approval rating of your Democratic U.S. Congress at 19 percent despite its passage, with Pelosi at 11 percent, and Reid at 8 percent.

The opposition Republican Party and the Tea Party Movement have in fact made Obamacare their political battle cry in this year's midterm election. They hope to recapture control of the U.S. Congress reminiscent of Speaker Newt Gingrich's "Contract With America" Republican Revolution of 1994.

In that event, they vow to repeal your Healthcare Reform Act of 2010 and start all over again to repair a broken system their own way without new and increased taxes and skyrocketing budgetary deficit that is projected to reach $8 trillion in eight years.

Of course, Mr. President, that is like promising the moon and the stars as you members of the ole old club of professional politicians in Washington are wont to do to titillate the voters.

But what is on the record is the fact that the passage of your 2,700-page Obamacare which is 60 percent of the national economy, was passed strictly on Democratic Party line without participation of Republican lawmakers, many of whom had complained that such voluminous measure was not or could not have been read by all members of Congress before its enactment.

Mr. President, never in the history of the U.S. Congress that such a landmark law was enacted without bipartisan collaboration. You did invite the Republicans to join you in passing the bill. But of course they refused because they don't want you to be reelected in 2012. It was politics as usual.

So, rightly or wrongly, whether or not your historic Obamacare achievement would cause the Democratic Party's defeat in the coming November midterm election, or be your own political waterloo in your 2012 presidential reelection bid, remains to be seen.

Then, Mr. President, there is also the legal challenge to the constitutionality of your Obamacare. As this is written, already attorneys general of Florida and 12 other states have filed a lawsuit to block enforcement of your new federal healthcare reform law even before the ink was dry on your signature. They are just among 37 states taking such legal action.

Almost simultaneously, the attorney general of Virginia has filed a second lawsuit also alleging that the U.S. Congress has abused its authority mandating that uninsured Americans buy health insurance whether they are sick or not, or need it or not, or face fines and penalties from the dreaded Internal Revenue Service.

Under your plan, Mr. President, 18,000 so-called IRS czars will be added and deputized to police 42 million more people who are covered by medical insurance to see to it that they comply with the enrollment requirement -- or else.

That is scary, Mr. President.

Haven't the people have enough problem already with the IRS that sometimes acts like gestapo? Remember that guy whom the IRS had hounded and who last February went into a rampage, flew his small private plane and crashed it into the IRS office in Austin, Texas?

So much so that even right-wing radio commentator Rush Limbaugh said he would evacuate to Costa Rica if Obamacare passed. He told a caller: "I will tell you this, if this passes and it's five years from now and all that stuff gets implemented -- I am leaving the country. I'll go to Costa Rica."

A commenter Maureen S. told Limbaugh, "Don't forget to take your Viagra with you." As far as we know, Rush Limbaugh is still around and shows no sign of leaving.

But getting back to Obamacare, there are of course two sides to the issue that refuses to die. This year 2010, it is allegedly assured that:

1. Insurance plans are required, with the poor eligible for government subsidy.

2. Small companies will get tax break to help them enroll employees in healthcare insurance.

3. People with pre-existing condition will be covered and not be refused coverage.

4. Benefits for seniors will continue and not be cut. (In fact, they are already cut effective last July.)

5. The patients themselves control their own healthcare, not the insurance companies.

Some provisions of Obamacare will not be implemented until 2014, including the controversial requirement to buy health insurance. The main dispute stated in the lawsuits is whether or not such mandate is constitutional or has exceeded Congress' power to regulate interstate commerce.

The complaints argue that the new federal healthcare law is a violation of the individual's liberty to take care of himself without government interference, even at a time when the new federal law requires implementation of universal healthcare.

It is suggested that such lawsuits questioning the constitutionality of Obamacare, even if it may have criminalized noncompliance, be deferred or rejected because no such violation, if at all, has yet been committed.

Such lawsuits may also be deemed merely a political statement designed to influence the result of the 2010 midterm election in the opposition's bid by Republican Party and the Tea Party Movement to recapture control of the U.S. Congress from the White House and the Democratic Party.

Assuming for the sake of argument that they succeeded, their battle cry to Repeal and Reform Obamacare may just be an exercise in futility because you, President Obama, could just veto a replacement law, and any move to override your veto is unlikely for as long as you are the president.

Mr. President, as for your assertion that the cost of prescription drugs will be lowered, how can you expect the people to believe you when in June 2009 behind closed door at the White House you approved the request of the Pharmaceutical Lobby to block a proposal to import low-cost drugs from Canada that would have really lowered their cost in the United States?

As for the charge of rabid Republican conservatives that you are establishing Socialism in the United States with your Obamacare patterned after European welfare or nanny states, purportedly to take care of people from the cradle to the grave, may be a debatable question.

But in the case of U.S. government-run general hospitals and public health centers all over the country, they are doing such a good job of treating the needed and the poor. Is that necessarily Socialism? Let the people be the judge.

Good night, Mr. President.

© Hermie Rotea, March 28, 2010

28
Broken Promises and More Lies
Hurt Obama's Credibility

MR. PRESIDENT:

It is hard to trust you again.

The aura of your rock-star popularity is gone. Now people are agonizing whether or not they should trust you again. You have repeatedly made and broken promises as 2008 presidential candidate and now as the president.

You pledged to change Washington and politics as usual. Instead, Washington has changed you. Now you are the new leader of the old ole club of professional politicians or oligarchy. The right-wing conservatives have even accused you of plotting to convert the United States into a socialist country.

Your political foes try to equate Socialism with Communism. They make people believe that any ideology that spells, rhymes and ends in *ism* is bad and scary. The Cold War seems to have returned not between America and the Soviet Union, but between the Republican and Democratic parties.

Rightly or wrongly, many people are bothered by that. They don't know whom to believe. But what is now clear is that public opinion polls consistently show, as this is written, that your approval rating is now lowest at 46 percent. It is even worse for your Democratic Congress with a record low of 29 percent.

Mr. President, it is because of your now questionable honesty and credibility that your much touted Healthcare Reform Package in Congress is having a hard time getting the required votes for approval? House Speaker Nancy Pelosi as of now has not yet scheduled a vote.

Which means that you and she are still cracking the whip to force recalcitrant Democratic lawmakers to toe the party line and commit to vote for your so-called healthcare reform bill. Of course it is likely to be approved through bribery disguised as pork barrel earmarks a la Louisiana Purchase.

What is embarrassing for you and Speaker Pelosi, though, is the case of resigned Democratic Rep. Eric Massa of New York who charged that he was forced to quit last Tuesday because of his previous vote against your health care reform bill in the House and continued refusal to cooperate with you.

In an interview on Fox News "Glenn Beck Program," Massa turned whistle blower and accused your White House Chief of Staff Rahm Emanuel of confronting him while naked in the congressional shower in a dispute over your budget, pointing a finger at him and allegedly threatening him.

Massa minced no words and called Emanuel "the son of the devil's spawn."

Of course, Mr. President, your White House chief of staff is your point man or attack dog in Congress, being a former member of the U.S. House of Representatives, a role that is cut out for him.

Speaker Pelosi and your White House Press Secretary Robert Gibbs have fired back at Massa. Pelosi said that Massa was under investigation by the House Ethics Committee for sexually groping a male staffer. Gibbs alleged that Massa did commit sexual harassment, a charge that Massa denied.

In the Senate, Mr. President, the expectation is that you are pushing for a reconciliation vote on your healthcare measure, which needs only a 51-majority vote. It appears that, happen what may, it would ultimately be approved despite Republican opposition and reported public disapproval.

To prepare the public mind, you scolded healthcare providers for arbitrarily increasing drug prices and dropping or rejecting patients with pre-existing conditions from medical coverage. Is this merely theatrics or the real McCoy?

This is asked because not so long ago in a closed-door meeting at the White House with the big Pharmaceutical Lobby you approved its opposition to a proposal that would have allowed importation of low-cost medical drugs from Canada.

And also, Mr. President, if you are not really that cozy with U.S. pharmaceutical and medical providers, how do you explain the fact that you are the No. 1 recipient of political contribution from such lobbyists who are now also donating campaign funds for the Democratic Party in the 2010 midterm election?

To refresh your memory, Mr. President, here is the lowdown, take it or leave it.

The Center for Responsible Politics (CRP) has disclosed that you alone were in fact the very top recipient of political contribution from the Industrial-Medical Complex with a whopping $18.8 million during the 2008 election cycle, more than any other presidential candidate.

What more, CRP has also reported that the Democratic Party has already received 62 percent of the funds contributed so far for the forthcoming 2010 election cycle.

The top 10 U.S. senators who received political contributions from health providers, insurers and pharmaceutical corporations in the 2008 election cycle are:

1. John McCain (R-AZ) – $7,436,673
2. Max Baucus (D-MT) – $1,575,675
3. Mitch McConnell (R-KY) – $1,497,235
4. John Cornyn (R-TX) – $997,319
5. Arlen Specter (D-PA) – $839,498
6. Saxby Chambliss (R-GA) – $757,209
7. Tom Harkin (D-IA) – $727,248
8. Pat Roberts (R-KS) – $718,949
9. Susan Collins (R-ME) – $706,519
10. Harry Reid (D-NV) – $671,900

The top 10 members of the U.S. House of Representatives who also received political contributions from health providers, insurers and pharmaceutical corporations in the 2008 election cycle are:

1. Charles B. Rangel (D-NY) – $1,53,461
2. Frank Pallone Jr. (D-NJ) – $985,345
3. Steny H. Hoyer (D-MD) – $913,600

4. Ron Paul (R-TX) – $880,544
5. John Boehner (R-OH) – $731,000
6. Eric Cantor (R-VA) – $711,050
7. Dave Camp (R-MI) – $696,650
8. Tom Price (R-GA) – 644,851
9. John D. Dingell (D-MI) – $635,736
10. James E. Clyburn (D-SC) – $593,098

Credit goes to author R.H. Sheldon of suite101.com for exposing this shenanigan behind the Universal Healthcare Reform debate.

Mr. President, this is why it is hard to believe and trust you in the face of truth. Good night.

© Hermie Rotea, March 12, 2010

29

Despite Suicide Bombings in Pakistan, U.S. Should Avoid the Great Temptation of Crossing its Border in Pursuit of Al Qaeda and/or Taliban Without Permission

Mr. President,

The massive truck bombing of the Marriott Hotel in Islamabad, Pakistan, that killed 53 including two U.S. Defense Department employees and the Czech ambassador, is being investigated by Pakistani authorities who have rejected American help in the probe.

Pakistan's reluctance to accept such assistance is first, its intelligence network can handle the problem thank you, and second, the new government in Islamabad is weary of U.S. poking its nose in its internal affairs, because of previous American incursion inside the country in the manhunt for Osama bin Laden without Pakistani prior knowledge and permission.

In fact, Pakistan has issued a "shoot to kill" order to its soldiers in case U.S. special forces further trespass or perform airstrikes on suspected Al Qaeda and/or Taliban hideouts on Pakistani soil absent authority, saying that as a nuclear power it knows its responsibility.

Pakistan of course is a close ally of Washington in the war on terror, but it doen't want its sovereignty to be violated. Senator Barack Obama, take note. During the primary campaign he had advocated such Pakistani incursion. Careful guys.

@hermie, 21 Sep 2008

30
Bush-Cheney War Crimes
THE WORLD MUST NOT FORGET

Mr. President,

Former President George W. Bush and former Vice President Dick Cheney are the worst war criminals in modern history. They should be indicted, arrested, tried in court, convicted, and imprisoned for their war crimes. Their illegal and immoral invasions and occupations of Iraq and Afghanistan violated the U.S. Constitution, the United Nations Charter, Geneva Convention, Nuremberg Convention, and The Hague Convention relating to war crimes and crimes against humanity.

Because of their reckless U.S. military aggressions, thousands of Iraqis, Afghans, Americans, and other peoples dragged into the Bush-Cheney phony war on terror have died, while millions of refugees have been uprooted and displaced from their homes after American planes carpet-bombed cities, towns and villages of Iraq and Afghanistan with prohibited Depleted Uranium (DU) weapons, killed civilians, women and children, destroyed their entire infrastructures, and caused famine, starvation and widespread radioactive contamination much greater than those caused by the atomic bombs dropped on Hiroshima and Nagasaki that ended World War Two.

Bush and Cheney justified their military offensive as "self-defense" and "preemptive war" because Afghanistan was involved in the 9/11 terrorist attacks on the United States, while President Saddam Hussein of Iraq had weapons of mass destruction that threatened America and had link to Osama bin Laden and Al Qaeda that masterminded 9/11. But later they were disproved as great deceptions and Bush and Cheney were found to be motivated only by oil and profit.

The enormity and gravity of their war crimes are staggering. What Bush and Cheney committed during their eight years in power at the White House may be compared to what Dictator Adolf Hitler of Germany and Admiral Hideki Tojo of Japan committed during World War Two. Hitler exterminated the Jews and overrun Europe, while Tojo's imperial military bombed Pearl Harbor and butchered conquered nations of Southeast Asia.

Now out of office, Bush and Cheney are still only fugitives from justice, Why they have not yet been prosecuted is mind-boggling. Eyewitnesses, documented and scientific evidence are available to convict them if they were indicted before the United Nations International Court of Justice at The Hague, Netherlands, or in the United States as famed California prosecutor Vincent Bugliosi has advocated in his book, "The Prosecution of George W. Bush for Murder". This is no exaggeration. Facts are facts and truth is truth. Consider the following related events:

- Tokyo War Crimes Trial Finds Bush "Guilty" of Genocide in Afghanistan
- Brussels War Crimes Trial Rules that Bush Privatized the Iraq War for Oil and Profit
- Bush's Addiction to War Dates Back to Grandfather's Support of Hitler
- The Prosecution of George W. Bush for Murders in United States Courts
- Arrest Warrants for Bush and Cheney Issued in Vermont
- Government Drops Case Against First War Resister Who Called Iraq War Illegal
- UN Secretary General Declares that Bush-Cheney Wars Violated UN Charter
- Petitions Filed With United Nations to Indict Bush and Cheney for War Crimes
- Bush, Cheney Fail to Do Duty Under Constitution to Protect America from 9/11
- Human and Financial Costs of 9/11, Iraq and Afghanistan Wars By The Numbers
- Eisenhower, Lincoln Warn Against Military-Industrial Complex Control of Government
- Senator McCaskill Takes on Military-Industrial Complex for Scandal
- Democrats in Congress Break Pledge to Impeach Bush and Cheney
- U.S. Mainstream Media Abdicate Duty to Crusade for Truth as Public Watchdog
- Obama Vowed to Change Washington. Instead, Washington Has Changed Him
- Summing Up: Will Bush and Cheney Get Away with War Crimes?

• TOKYO WAR CRIMES TRIAL FINDS BUSH "GUILTY" OF GENOCIDE IN AFGHANISTAN

An International Criminal Tribunal for Afghanistan (ICTA) in 2004 convened in Tokyo and tried the case of "The People v. George Walker Bush, President of the United States," for war crimes. Nineteen prosecutors from Japan, Germany, and the United States presented evidence and eyewitnesses against the defendant before an international panel of judges from England, India, Japan, and the United States.

Bush in his defense was represented by amicus curiae during the trial after he failed to appear. Earlier he was served with the indictment and summons through the American Embassy in Tokyo. But the United States boycotted the public trial attended by antiwar celebrities and activists from around the world.

Chief Judge Niloufer Bhagwat of India on March 16 announced the ICTA verdict finding Bush and his accomplices "guilty" of war crimes, genocide, and crimes against humanity. The other jurists concurred with the decision, including Dr. R.I. Akroyd of England; Peter Erlinder, United States; Osamu Niikura and Asaho Mizushima of Japan. The ruling was published by Japan Times and posted online by GlobalResearch.ca.

The Prosecution presented a formidable indictment against Bush as Commander-in-Chief of U.S. military forces for waging a war of aggression on Afghanistan, war crimes and crimes against humanity against the Afghan people.

In announcing the verdict, Chief Judge Bhagwat declared: "I believe that 'Truth' is a weapon on the side of humanity. If truth is known, tyranny and injustice will be defeated. The Tribunal has performed its judicial task. It is now for the people to ensure the implementation of this verdict."

Tribunal Spells Out Seven Violations of ICTA Statute and International Laws

In the verdict, Chief Judge Bhagwat declared that Bush and his accomplices had committed the following:

1. Violated Article 1 of the ICTA statute and under the International Criminal Law, for "waging a war of aggression against Afghanistan and the Afghan people" in October-November 2001 after the 9/11 terrorist attacks on the United States "although Afghanistan was not involved and not the enemy."

2. Violated Article 2 of the ICTA statute, and under the International Criminal Law and the International Humanitarian Law, for committing genocide by carpet-bombing cities, towns and villages with prohibited Depleted Uranium (DU) weapons of mass destruction, napalm and cluster bombs that killed thousands of people including civilians, women and children, and destroyed the country's infrastructure, causing famine, starvation and widespread radioactive contamination much greater than those caused by the atomic bombs dropped on Hiroshima and Nagasaki that ended the Second World War.

3. Violated Article 4 of the ICTA statute and under the International Criminal Law, "for Crimes Against Humanity committed against the people of Afghanistan, resulting in inhumane acts, affecting large sections of the population caused by the [U.S.] military invasion, bombing, and lack of humanitarian aid.

4. Violated Article 3 of the ICTA statute and under the International Criminal Law, The Hague Convention, and the Geneva Convention of 1949, with respect to "the torture and killings of Taliban and other prisoners of war who had surrendered, and the inhumane conditions of detention and deportation of innocent civilians."

5. Violated Article 3 and Article 4 of the ICTA statute, for the adverse effect of the continuous U.S. military bombings of the civilian population that sparked a mass exodus of refugees causing "death . . . hunger, displacement, disease, and absence of humanitarian aid."

6. Violated Article 3 and Article 4 of the ICTA statute, and under the International Criminal Law, and the International Humanitarian Law, for using Depleted Uranium Weapons "on the people of Afghanistan to exterminate the population; and for the crime of Omnicide [or] the extermination of life, contamination of air, water and food resources . . ."

7. Violated Article 3 and Article 4 of the DICTA statute and under the International Criminal Court, "for exposing soldiers and other personnel of the United States, UK and other soldiers of coalition forces to radioactive

contamination by the use of DU [depleted uranium] weapons, hazarding their lives . . ."

Self-Defense Excuse Rejected, Oil Reason for War

The prosecution at Tokyo war crimes trial debunked Bush's and Cheney's excuse for attacking Afghanistan as "self-defense" and "preventive war" against global terrorism, and the panel agreed. "The war on Afghanistan was not in conformity with the Charter of the United Nations, customary International Law and the decisions of the International Court of Justice," the verdict stated.

The judgment concluded that the real reason why the United States military forces invaded and occupied Afghanistan was not really Al Qaeda leader Osama bin Laden, but President Bush's [and Cheney's] oil interests and connection with Unocal Corporation based in California and the Centgas consortium of oil and energy businesses.

Prosecutors noted Bush's involvement in oil business before he became president as founder of Arbusto Energy Inc., then as CEO of Spectrum 7 Energy of Ohio, and later as a consultant to Harken Energy.

Bush-Unocal Oil Pipeline Project Achieves Monopoly

The verdict stated: "The prosecution has referred in the indictment to the involvement of oil and energy Companies in the United States in the internal affairs of Afghanistan as the reason reason for this war, and relied on public documents establishing that the California-based Oil Company, the Unocal, through a seven-member consortium Centgas, had commenced negotiations with various factions in the government of Afghanistan, for the pipeline project across Afghanistan, Pakistan, to the Indian Ocean, from the oil-rich Central Asiatic Republics of the former USSR; in reference to the old pipeline routes through Russia or an alternative route through Iran (Unocal Position Statement: Proposed Central Asian Pipeline Projects 1998).

"This project aimed at exercising monopoly control over the hydrocarbon resources of this region and distribution through pipelines, referred to in the Complaint/Petition lodged in 1998 by citizens groups to the Attorney General of California, under California Code of Civil Procedure 803 and the California Corporations Code 1801, for cancellation of the Charter of Unocal for violation of human rights within the USA, in Afghanistan and Myanmar."

"Unocal in these circumstances, increasingly frustrated, sought political/military alternatives by way of regime change . . . In 1997 prominent Republican Party members among them, Donald Rumsfeld, Dick Cheney, Jeb Bush, Paul Wolfowitz, John Bolton, Peter Rodham, Zalmay Khalilzad (an employee of Unocal), and 18 other prominent Americans, broadly known as the Neoconservatives, organized the Project for the New American Century . . . for the establishment of a New World Order . .

Neocons Plot Regime Change to Benefit Bush, Unocal Project

"The PNAC document highlighted that . . . At present the United States faces no global rival. America's grand strategy should aim to preserve and extend this advantageous position so far into the future as possible . . . Further the process of transformation, even if it brings revolutionary change that is likely to be a long one, absent some catastrophic and catalyzing event -- like a new Pearl Harbor . . .

"The prosecution has conclusively proved its case, for the alternative reasons for the war of aggression waged by the Defendant [Bush], which was regime change in the interest of Unocal's pipeline, by inviting judicial notice of the Tribunal to established facts . . .

"That whereas Afghanistan was attacked on 7th October 2001, a conference was convened by the government of the United States and NATO on 27th November 2001, acquiesced to by the Secretary General of the United Nations to form a transitional government, not in Afghanistan but in Bonn [Germany] where the four non-Taliban Northern Alliance group remained. The Cabinet was nominated on 5th December 2001 by the United States . . . and other occupying powers, not by these [Afghan] groups.

"Even earlier, on 1st December 1, 2001, President Hamid Karzai, a resident of the United States over several years, a green card holder, the former official Representative of Unocal to the erstwhile Taliban militia's de facto government in Kabul, was sworn in as head of the interim government (officially called the Transitional Government of Afghanistan). Unocal now directly controls the government of Afghanistan."

• BRUSSELS WAR CRIMES TRIAL RULES THAT BUSH PRIVATIZED IRAQ WAR FOR OIL AND PROFIT

Antiwar and peace advocates on June 28, 2005 held a "World Tribunal on Iraq" in Brussels, Belgium, headquarters of the North Atlantic Treaty Organization (NATO). International legal jurists led by Professor Niloufer Bhagwat of India also participated in the event that focused on the Iraq war.

Her address to the Jury and Citizens of the World titled "The Privatization of War" drew universal acclaim for its direct attack on the United States' brutal invasion and occupation of Iraq for oil, war profits, and economic benefits in conspiracy with the military-industrial complex.

Concerned citizens of Turkey and other nations attended the trial of then President Bush at which Judge Bhagwat presented the Prosecution's indictment of Bush on the "criminalized and privatized nature of this brutal war which is the corporate invasion and occupation of Iraq." Findings included:

1. Judge Bhagwat said the war in Iraq was a private war of aggression declared by an oligarchy of financial and corporate conglomerates of the United States and its coalition partners using the soldiers to gather the economic surpluses and raw materials of other countries.

Evidence surfaced after the British media exposed 10 Downing Street Memoranda dated in July 2002 by the head of MI 6 Richard Dearlove which recorded the year before the invasion for Prime Minister Tony Blair that facts were "fixed around policy" at the White House in Washington to justify the war. "War itself has been dictated by a conspiracy of the predatory financial and corporate oligarchy of the United States, controlling both the Republican and Democratic parties."

The war of economic aggression was a "continuation of the policy dictated by Oil and Energy Companies, finance capital on Wall Street, and the Military Industries and Defense Contractors prior to, during and after the Gulf War of 1991 to attack Iraq despite withdrawal of Iraq forces [from Kuwait], to impose war and sanctions on Iraq, manipulating the [UN] Security Council, leading to the genocide of half a million Iraqi children, more than the number who died in Hiroshima, denied nutrition and medical care as a consequence of sanctions imposed on Iraq, with a view to prevent the Iraqi government and people from extracting and using petroleum resources for their own development and welfare, to bring the people of Iraq to their knees, to preserve the oil resources of Iraq for future use for the Oil Majors to subsidize the survival of US UK and other corporations of the Coalition of the Willing, and to control hydrocarbon regions of the world to ensure capital inflow into the United States and the primacy of the dollar."

Corporate Interests Dictate Decision to Wage Iraq War

2. Judge Bhagwat stated that Thomas Friedman, a vocal propagandist of this phase of privatized military globalization, articulated the use of the armed forces of the United States to achieve the objectives of Corporate America, supported by the evidence of the secret role played by the Energy Task Force constituted by President Bush and Vice President Cheney in 2001, in the decision that led to the Corporate invasion of Iraq, whose members included the major Oil and Energy Corporation with their names and recommendations concealed from Congress.

This is the first time in the history of the United States that the decision to launch a military invasion or carry out a coup has been taken by and dictated by oligarchies and corporate interests The difference between the earlier decision-making and the Iraq war of 2003 is that the nature of the incestuous relationship between the United States and its dominant corporations can no longer [be] camouflaged or concealed from the world, the identification is absolute and complete.

It is "Corporate Rule" using as its political base the born-again Christian Evangelical religious fascist movement as a diversion from policy, with homeland security and the Patriotic Act required to secure the political system against internal revolt.

On July 17, 2003 after the military aggression and occupation of Iraq was an accomplished fact, the Commerce Department of the United States turned over to Judicial Watch, the public interest group, under a court order as a result of a lawsuit filed by Judicial Watch . . . under the Freedom of Information Act, some documents dated March 2001, relating to the activities of the Cheney Energy Task Force, containing a map of Iraqi oil fields, pipelines, refineries and terminals, as well as two charts detailing Iraqi oil and gas projects, and the list of "Foreign Suitors for Iraq Oil Field

Contracts" including documents relating to oil fields of Saudi Arabia and the United Arab Emirates.

The concealment of the members, recommendations and documents of this Energy Task Force by the Bush Administration and Vice President Cheney from Congress upheld by the U.S. Supreme Court, establishes the undisputed control of the dominant corporations over the political and economic system of the United States.

With No Enemy Army, U.S. Military Targets Iraqil Civilians

3. Judge Bhagwat stressed two distinct features of this Privatized War: It is not waged against a standing army or combatants. The civilian non-military infrastructure are deliberately targeted for widespread destruction to award "Reconstruction" contracts to U.S. corporations in the immediate aftermath of the bombing.

The distinct and barbaric feature of the privatized Iraq war is that it has not been waged against a standing army or combatants. The shock and awe campaign against all established rules of warfare, to the knowledge of President Bush and Prime Minister Blair, and heads of the Coalition of the Willing governments and senior US and UK military leaders, targeted as the "enemy" the civilian population of Iraq under the continuing military occupation.

It is not an aberration that 90% of victims of the US and UK military forces are non-combatants, and those sympathizing with the Iraqi Resistance, deliberate and premeditated violations of the Geneva and The Hague conventions, the logical outcome of measures taken to depopulate Iraq, similar to the method Nazi Germany had used to exterminate people in occupied countries of East Europe during World War Two, were perpetrated in the economic interest of U.S. corporations,

Halliburton, Bechtel, Other Contractors Benefit From War

4. Judge Bhagwat disclosed that Lockheed Martin, Halliburton, Bechtel, Aegis, BKSH Associates, Bearing Point, Custer Battles, Local Satellite, Qualcom, CACI and Titan and several other US and UK companies apart from the Oil majors, are the top 10 direct beneficiaries of the Iraq war which include other corporations.

There is a direct historical continuity from the support extended by prominent US corporations and corporate players to the Corporate rule of the Nazi Party and its pillage of the occupying countries of Europe, and the role of the dominant US corporations in the decision to launch wars of aggression.

From 1939 to 1942 Ford Motor Company produced 1,000 combat vehicles for Nazi Germany, central to the military strategy of blitzkrieg, and special fuels were supplied by US Oil majors to the Nazi Army. Of the 35,000 trucks used by the motorized Germany Army in 1942, one-third were Ford products.

Several other U.S. firms had business with Nazi Germany, including

President Bush's grandfather Prescott Bush who had helped Hitler rise to power. through his bank. Halliburton, Cheney's old company from which he received deferred salary while serving as vice president, is now one of the largest oil services companies that benefited from secret no-bid contracts in Iraq.

Bush's Order Cancels Funds Accountability and Rule of Law

5. Judge Bhagwat said that the extraordinary presidential Executive Order No. 13303 signed by President Bush eliminated the judicial process in respect to the Development Fund for Iraq to which the revenues from the Oil for Food Program are credited including all commercial operations relating to Iraq oil.

Tom Devine, legal director for the Government Accountability Project (GAP), a nonprofit legal firm, stated that: "In terms of legal liability . . . the Executive Order cancels the concept of corporate accountability and abandons the rule of law."

6. Judge Bhagwat found pillage of the Development Fund of Iraq constituted from the revenues of the Oil for Food Program and its use to pay among other Halliburton by the CPA. The jurist said "It has been reported by Christian Aid, a charity organization in the UK, that the occupying powers have failed to account for $20 million of Iraqi oil revenues."

"These were oil revenues from Iraqi oil and gas exports permitted to be deposited by the UN Security Council into the Development Fund for Iraq," the jurist said. But according to an independent audit by the Multilateral International Advisory and Monitoring Board for Development in Iraq, billions of dollars have disappeared from the fund and they are not subject to judicial scrutiny because of President Bush's Executive Order 13303.

Bush-Cheney Crime Family Controls Iraq Economy

7. The military objective of the war to privatize the entire economy of Iraq was evidenced by Paul Bremer's 100 orders issued in June 2003 and renewed in 2004 to maintain varying degrees of economic and political control over the entire economy including the state-owned oil companies for the benefit of US, UK, Australia and other companies of the coalition partners, Judge Bhagwat stated,

The real policy by the Bush and Blair administrations was to transform Iraq's economy into one acceptable to US and UK corporations while eliminating local industries and businesses, public and private, and for that purpose Iraq's legal system was to be transformed.

Bremer's Order 58 creates and appoints an inspector within every Iraqi government ministry with five-year term who can perform audits, write policies and have full access to all offices, materials and employees to help insure control.

8. Judge Bhagwat noted privatized violence perpetrated on the people of Iraq using mercenaries and private companies outsourcing military functions of the US and UK armed forces, with no accountability to any

authority in occupied Iraq except that the private companies are not liable to any military chain of command.

The hiring of private military companies and outsourcing of several functions including training, logistics and supply operations traditionally performed by the armed forces is not unique to the Iraq war. What was once a function of mercenaries is now being performed by private military companies under the direction of allied forces.

U.S. Funds Private Armies and Death Squads to Sow Civil War

9. Judge Bhagwat also revealed the use of private militias of thugs and mercenaries being funded, trained and used as private armies and death squads by the U.S. against the people of Iraq and the Resistance, to fan fratricidal civil war among the Shiites, Sunnis, Turks and Kurds to criminally balkanize Iraq recalling the partition of countries under colonial rule.

The Bush and Blair administrations have failed to subdue the national resistance of the people of Iraq despite resorting to criminalized tactics and the use of private militias of thugs and mercenaries referred to by various names.

10. Judge Bhagwat cited the deficiencies of the Nuremberg and Tokyo war crime trials — camouflage of the economic and political systems of the Allied and Axis powers which had led to the rivalry for economic dominations and seizure of resources with certain exceptions; failure to convict some conglomerates for conspiracy to wage war of aggression, to regard the nuclear bombings of Hiroshima and Nagasaki, and the bombings of undefended cities like Dresden as war crimes.

11. Democracy is not compatible with economic systems which allow dominant corporations to control the economic and political space within and across nations. It is a contradiction that corporate oligarchies could just control the economic and political life of a country, Judge Bhagwat emphasized. She concluded:

"We are before the Board of Humanity. Let it not be said that we lacked the courage, honesty or the perspective to speak the truth. In conclusion, I submit that the Resistance of the people of Iraq to the tyranny described in the indictments before this World Tribunal, is sanctioned by a constitutional document maintained in archives of the United States — the Declaration of the Independence of the United States from British Colonial Rule."

• BUSH'S ADDICTION TO WAR DATES BACK TO GRANDFATHER'S SUPPORT OF HITLER

The Bushes or Bushism, like Nazism, have the same addiction to wars. George W. Bush had his Iraq and Afghanistan wars which are still ongoing. He bequeathed the mess to his successor President Barack H. Obama who is now trying to undo eight years of Bush's government mismanagement.

His father, former President George H.W. Bush, had the first Gulf War also known as Desert Storm in 1990. His grandfather, late Senator Prescott

Bush, had his World War Two when he helped Adolf Hitler rise to power in Nazi Germany in 1939.

Of the three Bushes, George W. Bush is the champion war addict because he not only invaded but also occupied Iraq and Afghanistan. Now they are Obama's problem.

The story behind his grandfather Prescott Bush's cozy relation with Nazi Dictator Adolf Hitler of Germany was reported in 2004 by The Guardian of UK as bylined by Ben Aris of Berlin and Duncan Campbell of Washington.

Rumors of a link between the Bush dynasty and the Nazi war machine have circulated for decades. Now The Guardian revealed how repercussions of world events culminated in action under the Trading with the Enemy Act affected the Bushes.

George Bush's grandfather, the late Senator Bush, was a director and shareholder of companies that profited from their involvement with the financial brokers of Nazi Germany.

The Guardian obtained information from newly discovered files in the U.S. National Archives that a firm which Prescott Bush was a director was involved with the financial architects of Nazism.

Prescott Bush's Company Assets Seized Under Trading With The Enemy Act

His business dealings, which continued until his company's assets were seized in 1942 under the Trading with the Enemy Act, has led more than 60 years later to a civil action for damages brought in Germany against the Bush family by two former slave laborers at Auschwitz and to a hum of pre-election controversy.

The evidence has also prompted one former U.S. Nazi war cronies prosecutor to argue that the late senator's action should have been grounds for prosecution for giving aid and comfort to the enemy. New declassified documents show that even after America had entered the war he worked for and profited from companies closely involved with the German business that financed Hitler's rise to power.

It has been suggested that the money he made from these dealings helped to establish the Bush family fortune and set up its political dynasty. Remarkably, little of Bush's dealings with Germany had received public scrutiny, partly because of the then secret status of the documentation involving him.

But now the multibillion dollar legal action for damages by two Holocaust survivors against the Bush family, and the imminent publication of three books on the subject threatened to make Prescott Bush's business history an uncomfortable issue for his grandson George W. who was then seeking reelection.

While there is no suggestion that Prescott Bush was sympathetic to the Nazi cause, documents reveal that the firm he worked for, Brown Brothers Harriman (BBH), acted as a U.S. base for the German industrialist, Fritz Thyssen, who helped finance Hitler in the 1930s before falling out with him at the end of the decade.

Bush Bank Continues Helping Hitler Even After America Entered War

The Guardian has seen evidence that shows Bush was the director of the New York-based Union Bank Corporation (UBC) that represented Thyssen's U.S. interests and he continued to work for the bank after America entered the war.

Bush was also on the board of at least one of the companies that formed part of a multinational network of front companies to allow Thyssen to move assets around the world. He owned the largest steel and coal company in Germany and grew rich from Hitler's efforts to re-arm between the two world wars.

One of the pillars in Thyssen's international corporate web, UBC, worked exclusively for, and was owned by, a Thyssen-controlled bank of the Netherlands. More tantalizing are Bush's link to the Consolidated Silesian Steel Company (ASSC) based in mineral-rich Silesia on the German-Polish border.

Two Holocaust Survivors Sue Bush Family, Government for $40 Billion

During the war, the company made use of Nazi slave labor from the concentration camps, including Auschwitz. The ownership of CSSC changed hands several times in the 1930s, but documents from the U.S. National Archive declassified last year link Bush to CSSC, although it is not clear if he and UBC were still involved in the company when Thyssen's American assets were seized in 1942.

Later two Holocaust survivors from Auschwitz concentration camp sued the U.S. government and the Bush family for $40 billion in compensation claim as they both materially benefited from the slave labor during World War Two.

Kurd Julius Goldstein, 87, and Peter Gingold, 85, bagan a class action in the United States in 2001, but Judge Rosemary Collier threw out the case on the grouind that the government could not be held liable under the principle of "state sovereignty."

One of their lawyers, Jan Lissmann, argued that genocide-related cases are covered by international law, which does hold government accountability for their actions. The attorneys filed a motion at The Hague asking for an opinion on whether sovereignty is a valid reason for refusing to hear their case.

Prescott Bush Files at National Archives Declassified

Three sets of archives spell out Prescott Bush's involvement. All three are readily available, thanks to the efficient U.S. archive system and a helpful and dedicated staff at both the Library of Congress in Washington and the National Archives at the University of Maryland.

The first set of files, the Harriman papers in the Library of Congress, show that Prescott Bush was a director and shareholder of a number of companies involved with Thyssen. The second set of papers in the National Archives are contained in vesting order under 248 which records the seizure of the company assets.

What these files show is that on October 20, 1942 the alien property custodian seized the assets of UBC of which Prescott Bush was a director. Having gone through the books of the banks, further seizures were made against two affiliates, the Holland-American Trading Corporation and the Seamless Steel Equipment Corporation.

But in November, the Silesian-American Company, another of Prescott Bush's ventures, had also been seized. The third set of documents, also at the National Archives, are contained in the files of IG Ferben, who was prosecuted for war crimes.

A report issued by the Office of Alien Property Custodian in 1942 stated of the companies that "since 1939, these (steel and mining) properties have been in possession of and have been operated by the German government and have undoubtedly been in considerable assistance to that country's war efforts."

Prescott Bush, a 6.4-foot charmer with a rich singing voice, was the founder of the Bush political dynasty and was once considered a potential presidential candidate himself.

• THE PROSECUTION OF GEORGE W. BUSH FOR MURDER

Famed California prosecutor Vincent Bugliosi said it best in his best-selling book, "The Prosecution of George W. Bush for Murder" whose title brutally speaks for itself. His powerful, explosive, and thought-provoking expose cannot but lead readers to believe that Bush and Cheney, if tried for murders, are likely candidates for the death penalty. There is no time limitation to file charges for murder.

"George Bush has gotten away with murder – thousands of murders," Bugliosi lamented. "And no one is doing anything about it." Although Bugliosi didn't mention Cheney, it was understood that he was linked to Bush as the war hawk behind the no-bid contracts that benefited their business buddies or war contractors with billions of dollars, particularly Halliburton of which Cheney was its CEO and chairman before his election as vice president.

The prosecutor said the indictment and trial of Bush [and Cheney] can be done outside of the United Nations. "I have set forth in my book the jurisdictional basis for the Attorney General in each of the fifty states – plus the hundreds upon hundreds of district attorneys in counties within the states – to prosecute George Bush for the murders of any soldier or soldiers from their state or county who were killed in Iraq fighting George Bush's war," Bugliosi said.

"I don't think it is too unreasonable to believe that at least one prosecutor out there in America – maybe many more – will be courageous enough to say – this is the United States of America. And in America no one is above the law."

In his book dedication, the famous prosecutor of Charles Manson for the murder of actress Sharon Tate and six others in the 1970s, stated: "To the thousands upon thousands of men, women, and children who have lost their precious lives in the senseless Iraq war and to all the loved ones they left behind whose suffering will never end, with the hope that this book will help bring those responsible to justice."

• ARREST WARRANTS FOR BUSH AND CHENEY ISSUED

In March 2008, voters in two Vermont towns of Brattleboro and Marlboro passed ballot measures in public referenda to prosecute President Bush and Vice President Cheney for committing war crimes and violatiing the U.S. Constitution and international laws.

The initiatives sought to have police arrest Bush and Cheney if they ever set foot on Vermont or to extradite them to appropriate venue for prosecution. The warrants for their arrest are said to be still valid and active even though they are now out of office, their terms of public service having expired.

Kurt Daims, 54, who had organized the petition that led to the Brattleboro vote, said: "I hope the one thing that people take from this is, 'Hey, it can be done.'" However, some observers consider the action more symbolic than substantive.

Another Brattleboro resident, Ellen Schwarz, said: "I voted in favor because I think that Bush and Cheney have committed high crimes and misdemeanors," which are grounds for impeachment.

Jeff Morris, who had voted against the indictment of Bush and Cheney, disagreed. He said: "I think it's outside the scope of town government. When history writes George Bush's story, he will be held in high record for going into Iraq."

• GOVERNMENT DROPS CASE VS. WAR RESISTER WHO REFUSED TO DEPLOY TO IRAQ

The government has dropped the case against Army Lt. Erhen Watada who was court-martialed for disobeying an order in 2006 to deploy to Iraq because the war is "illegal and immoral." As the first war resister, his case has generated international attention and galvanized the antiwar movement.

The Justice Department directed the U.S. Circuit Court of Appeals not to pursue a second court-martial of Watada, who is based in Fort Lewis, Washington, after his lawyers and supporters led by Courage to Resist had requested the U.S. solicitor general not to retry the case that cannot be won.

At the first court-martial, Military Judge John Head declared a mistrial after realizing that the government case was weak at the time, but later tried to subject Watada to a second court-martial. His lawyers protested the action on the ground of double jeopardy.

U.S. District Court Judge Benjamin Settle in Tacoma issued a preliminary injunction stating that Lt. Watada was likely to succeed in demonstrating that the military judge had acted "irresponsibly" and "abused his "discretion." He ruled that a Writ of Habeas Corpus sought in pretrial was rare but appropriate.

Court Victory Raises Questions on Legality of Bush-Cheney Wars on Terror

Watada's legal victory has raised questions about the legality of the Iraq war and the Army's order to deploy soldiers to the war zones. He said the Iraq war violated U.S. and international laws and therefore for him to deploy would make him complicit in the war crime.

He stated that the conduct of the U.S. occupation of Iraq that has led to "the wholesale slaughter and mistreatment of the Iraqi people" likewise violated the Army Field Manual, and thus for him to obey an order to deploy would make him vulnerable to charges of war crimes.

Watada's attorney James Lobsenz expects his client to be released from active duty. He said Watada plans to return to civilian life and attend law school. However, Army officials at Fort Lewis are considering whether or not to charge him for conduct unbecoming of an officer.

Case Attracts World Attention and Galvanizes Antiwar Movement

The war resister tried to resign from the military after he saw what was happening in Iraq. But Army authorities refused to let him go. They said he was taking advantage of legal technicality to avoid deployment. So they rejected his resignation and instead ordered him to deploy to Iraq.

After Watada was court-martialed, his supporters held citizens public hearing in Tacoma to dramatize their opposition to the Bush-Cheney so-called global war on terror. The tribunal attracted former war veterans, legal luminaries, eyewitnesses to U.S. military abuses, and celebrities who testified in support of the accused.

Among those who testified or provided moral support to Lt. Watada were Archibishop Desmond Tutu of South Africa, 1984 Nobel Peace Prize laureate; Rep. Dennis Kucinich, Rep. Mike Honda, former Rep. Cynthia McKinney, former UN Assistant Secretary General Denis Halliday, military analyst Daniel Ellsberg who released the controversial Pentagon Paper on the Vietnam war, Rev. Al Sharpton, former U.S. presidential candidate; Martin Sheen, Tim Robbins, Susan Sarandon, Ed Esner, Randi Rhodes, Willie Nelson, Harry Belafonte, Mike Farrell, and many others.

• UN SECRETARY GENERAL ABSOLVES AFGHANISTAN, CALLS U.S. IRAQ ATTACK ILLEGAL

On October 7, 2001, less than a month after 9/11, the United States military invaded Afghanistan. The next day, the secretary general of the United Natons, Kofi Annan, declared that Afghanistan had nothing to do with the Al Qaeda terrorist attacks on America, He said:

"The people of Afghanistan, who cannot be held responsible for the acts of the Taliban regime, are now in desperate need of aid. The United Nations had long played a vital role in providing humanitarian assistance to them, and it is my hope that we will be able to set up our humanitarian work as soon as possible."

Annan referred to Taliban's action allowing Osama bin Laden courtesy temporary stay in Afghanistan for his assistance in helping drive out Soviet troops from the country. But the then de facto Taliban government in Kabul had nothing to do with 9/11.

He added: "It is also vital that the international community now work harder than ever to encourage a political settlement to the conflict in Afghanistan."

When the United States next invaded Iraq in March 2003, the then UN secretary general called the U.S. invasion "a violation of the UN Charter" and therefore "illegal" as it was not a war in self-defense but a war of aggression.

At the United Nations, current Secretary General Ban Ki-moon of South Korea has been swamped with petitions from international antiwar movements urging that the UN indict Bush and Cheney for war crimes and crimes against humanity, calling for their prosecution at The Hague, Netherlands, where the International Court of Justice and UN jails are located.

• PETITIONS FILED WITH UNITED NATIONS TO INDICT BUSH, CHENEY

Antiwar organizations have petitioned the United Nations to indict George W. Bush and Dick Cheney for war crimes and crimes against humanity before the UN International Court of Justice at The Hague, Netherlands.

Petitions were submitted to current UN Secretary General Ban Ki-moon and to his predecessor Kofi Annan during whose term of office the United States invaded Afghanistan in October 2001 and Iraq in March 2003.

The Petition Online created and hosted by Donald Sevier addressed a petition to Annan titled, "A Call for a War Crimes Tribunal at the United Nations". It stated: "We, Citizens of the United States and of the World, the senders of this petition to you, urge you, as spokesman for the world's peoples, to investigate war crimes committed by the Bush Administration.

"President Bush and his Cabinet are guilty of crimes against humanity and violations of international laws." The petition cited: Preemptive war, torture of prisoners, destruction of religious temples, napalm bombing, killing of civilians, and use of radioactive weapons, which are all war crimes.

Evil May Triumph If Good Men Do Nothing

Sevier quoted from British statesman and philosopher Edmund Burke who said: "The only thing necessary for the triumph of evil is for good men to do nothing!" The petition bore 184 signatures.

In another petition submitted to the United Nations, a Bush Commission, also an online organization, on April 21, 2006 urged "Proposed Indictments Against George W. Bush".

"The Bush administration authorized a war of aggression against Iraq. The conduct of the war involved the commission of war crimes, crimes against humanity, and other illegal acts."

Still another petition sent to the United Nations by a War Crimes Group of New York City c/o Democrats.com is titled "Prosecute George Bush and Dick Cheney for War Crimes."

The declaration said: "We, the undersigned, believe that George Bush and Dick Cheney should be prosecuted for the following war crimes:"

War of Aggression, Torture and Indefinite Detention of Prisoners, Rendition of Prisoners, Illegal Detention, Murder, Destruction of the Global Environment, and Attacks on Global Public Health, The petition said:

"George Bush and Dick Cheney ordered a War of Aggression against Iraq. This constitutes a Crime Against Peace -- for which Nazi leaders were prosecuted at the Nuremberg Trials -- and violates the UN Charter.

"Iraq never attacked the United States or threatened an attack. So the U.S. was not acting legally in self-defense . . . Iraq played no role in the September 11, 2001 attack on the U.S. and never provided material support to any terrorist group that attacked the U.S. So even the non-legal Bush doctrine of preemptive attack did not apply."

Protester: "Evil Will Not Go Unpunished!"

A Dr. Glen Barry of Earth Meanders urged, "Indict Bush and and Friends on War Crimes", saying that their preemptive wars of aggression and torture of prisoners "are never justified, period."

Barry said, "This holds true whether you are an Islamic Jihadist or President of the United States." The time has come for war crime charges to be filed against Bush and his other top officials. He continued:

"The Bush administration has committed -- then covered up -- war crimes in Iraq, Guantanamo Bay and Afghanistan. President Bush and associates can be charged with violating the 1996 U.S. War Crimes Act, the Third Geneva Convention of 1949, and the 1987 United Nations Torture Convention."

Angered by Bush's war crimes, Dr. Barry swore: "Mark my words, those responsible in the United States for the crimes of preemptive war and torture will answer for their crimes. It may be soon, or it may take time, but such evil will not go unpunished!"

• BUSH, CHENEY NEGLECTED TO PROTECT AMERICA FROM 9/11 ATTACKS

The terrorist attacks on the United States on September 11, 2001 could have been prevented if only then President George W. Bush and Vice President Dick Cheney did their duty to protect America, but they criminally neglected to do so.

Under Article 1 of the Constitution, they were sworn in to faithfully execute the offices of president and vice president to the best of their ability, preserve, protect, and defend the nation's charter and the American people.

Yet Bush and Cheney both failed because they had ignored many early warnings of imminent Al Qaeda terrorist attacks relayed to the White House by 10 friendly nations, not to mention the CIA and the FBI, and did nothing to prevent the catastrophe.

Thus they violated the Constitution and committed both impeachable and criminal acts, including murder, for the death of nearly 3,000 victims who perished when suicide bombers hijacked four commercial planes, destroyed the World Trade Center in New York, and damaged the Pentagon.

Bush and Cheney are also culpable for murder for the death of 5,000 in the Iraq and Afghanistan wars that they waged on the great deception that the two countries were involved in 9/11

Bush and Cheney, along with then National Security Adviser Condoleezza Rice, were to blame and responsible because they dismissed the many early intelligence warnings they had received long before 9/11, as "unreliable and incredible." So they did nothing to protect America.

The Seed and the Road to 9/11

Proof of their criminal culpability are documented and indisputable. A book The Terror Timeline by Paul Thompson and the Center for Cooperative Research based in California compiled a year by year, day by day, and minute by minute comprehensive chronicle of the Seed and the Road to 9/11.

Simply put, Thompson said: "The Bush administration's continued secrecy in the name of 'national security' only exacerbates this problem, leading many to cry cover-up, others to charge criminal negligence, and still others to consider conspiracy."

Note the time frame:

1980 -- the United States and Osama bin Laden actually were allied and together with the CIA they supported the Afghan Mujahideen rebels in the war against Soviet occupation of Afghanistan. With Saudi Arabia and U.S. backing, bin Laden led the successful fight against Soviet troops, who subsequently withdrew from Afghanistan in 1989.

Bin Laden became a hero and household name to the Muslim world. He worked with the CIA, at least indirectly. They built tunnels in Afghanistan against Soviet forces, although a CIA spokesperson later claimed, "For the record . . . the CIA never employed, paid or maintained any relationship whatsoever with bin Laden"

In fact, the CIA even trained Bin Laden's "Holy War" recruits from other countries in the United States to fight Soviet troops. Ironically, among them were 15 of the 19 hijackers who later carried out the 9/11 terrorist attacks that destroyed New York's World Trade Center and damaged the Pentagon.

The Blueprint of 9/11 that the White House Dismissed

1995 -- On January 20, the blueprint of the terrorist attacks on the United States code-named "Operation Bojinka" was discovered six years before they happened. It was based on the confession of mastermind plotter Abdul

Hakim Murad who was captured in Manila, Philippines, where he operated. He was later turned over to the FBI.

Investigator Col. Rodolfo Mendoza revealed the plot to hijack commercial planes and crash them to the CIA headquarters, the Pentagon, World Trade Center in New York City, Sears Tower in Chicago, Transamerica Tower in San Francisco, and an unidentified nuclear power plant.

But when this early intelligence warning was relayed to the White House, Bush, Cheney and Rice dismissed it as "impossible and not credible." Frustrated investigators lamented: "We told the Americans everything about Operation Bojinka. Why didn't they pay attention?"

Clinton Rejects Bin Laden Turnover

1996 -- CIA Counter Terrorism Center created a Bin Laden Unit after he was linked to the 1993 World Trade Center bombing in New York. He was identified not just a financier but also the organizer of terrorist activity. Actually, the U.S. was too late in discovering the existence of Al Qaeda.

The United States under President Clinton and Britain under Prime Minister Tony Blair rejected the offer of Sudan to turn over to them voluminous files about bin Laden and Al Qaeda while he was living there and using it as his base of global operations and was under its jurisdiction.

Thus the United States and Britain at that time missed an opportunity to know more about Bin Laden and Al Qaeda and possibly prevent 9/11 from happening.

Sudan offered to turn over Bin Laden to the United States to get rid of him as a problem, but then President Clinton refused to accept him because the U.S. at the time had no evidence against him.

Later Bin Laden fled to Afghanistan along with many of his followers and his money resources. The U.S. knew of his plan beforehand but failed to stop him.

FBI Fumbles Its Investigation of Terrorists Training as Pilots in U.S. Flight Schools

Also in 1996, the FBI likewise missed a chance to know where the suicide hijackers had trained as pilots in U.S. flight schools. A business card was found from Murad, the mastermind plotter, that revealed where and what flight schools he had trained off and on starting in 1990.

But the FBI closed the investigation of "Operation Bojinka after they failed to find other potential suspects. What the FBI did not realize is that they already had the names of 10 other trainees in their files which Murad had already provided in his confession during the probe that it bungled.

Indonesia Warns U.S. of 9/11 "But Nobody Believe Us"

1998 -- Indonesia also warned the United States of 9/11. Hendropriyono, the chief of intelligence in Jakarta, said: "We had intelligence predicting the

September 11 attacks three years ago before it happened, but nobody believed us."

He said Indonesian intelligence agents had identified Osama bin Laden as the leader of the group planning the attack but that the United States disregarded the warning. Indonesia has the largest Muslim population in the world.

FAA, FBI Dismiss CIA Warning of Flying Bomber

In August, the CIA warned that terrorists planned to fly bomb-laden aircraft from a foreign country and directly target the World Trade Center in New York City. But the FBI and the FAA did not take the warning seriously because of the poor state of aviation of the country which was not disclosed, although later the group was linked to Al Qaeda.

In September, Senior U.S. officials received information from U.S. intelligence that bin Laden's network might crash a plane loaded with explosives into a U.S. airport.

Britain Warns U.S. of "Flying Bombs"

1999 -- British intelligence warned the American Embassy in London that Al Qaeda planned to hijack commercial aircraft and use them as "flying bombs" at American targets.

At the same time, the FBI received reports that a terrorist organization planned to send students to the U.S. for aviation training, the purpose of which was unknown. No investigation was conducted.

A U.S. intelligence report revealed that suicide bombers belonging to Al Qaeda's Martyrdom Battalion could crash-land an aircraft packed with high explosives into the White House, the Pentagon, or the CIA headquarters.

The report was made by the National Intelligence Council which advises the President and U.S. intelligence on emerging threats. Bush, Cheney and Rice dismissed the early warning as "impossible." Later they claimed they never read the report until May 2002 although it had been publicly posted in the Internet.

Norad Stages 9/11 Exercises In Preparation for Attacks

2000 -- The North American Aerospace Defense Command (Norad) staged exercises similar to 9/11 terrorist attacks as part of U.S. preparedness program to protect America. It simulated hijacked airliners used as weapons to crash into targets and cause mass casualties and damages.

In another mock exercise, jets performed a shoot-down practice over the Atlantic Ocean of a jet laden with chemical poisons heading towards the U.S.

(Ironically and tragically, when 9/11 did happen, not a single U.S. military plane flew to intercept and thwart the suicide bombers who had hijacked commercial planes, destroyed the World Trade Center, and crash-damaged the Pentagon.)

YEAR 2001 -- THE COUNTDOWN BEGINS

The book The Terror Timeline by Paul Thompson intensified documentation of the many early warnings of imminent terrorist attacks on the United States Bin Laden and Al Qaeda long before 9/11 which Bush, Cheney and Rice received but repeatedly dismissed as "unreliable and incredible" and did nothing to protect America.

On this year of the 9/11 attacks, note closely the following time frame:

January 10 -- Counterterrorism Tsar Richard Clarke briefed Rice as the National Security adviser and her deputy Steve Hadley about the expected strike by Al Qaeda. While presenting his plan to them, Clarke got the impression that she had never heard of Al Qaeda, which was odd.

February 7 -- CIA Director George Tenant warned Congress that "the threat from terrorism is real, it is immediate, and it is evolving." He testified that Bin Laden and his global network remained "the most immediate and serious threat" to the United States.

March -- Al Qaeda operatives plan to conduct unspecified attack inside the United States. An intelligence source said that one of the terrorists already resided in the U.S. Other reports said the planned attacks would target New York and California.

April -- The North American Aerospace Defense Command (Norad) planned to continue emergency exercise amidst persistent reports of Al Qaeda planned attacks on the U.S. Code-named Positive Force, some Special Operations personnel would train to think like terrorists.

They added a scenario simulating "an event having a terrorist group hijack a commercial airliner and fly it into the Pentagon." But White House officials and military superiors rejected the emergency drill as either "too unrealistic" or two disconnected to the original intent of Norad exercise.

May -- Bush, Cheney and Rice received briefing papers titled: Bin Laden Planning Multiple Operations, Bin Laden Public Profile May Presage Attack, Bin Ladin Network's Plans Advancing. The exact contents of the briefings were kept confidential.

U.S. intelligence reported to the White House that Al Qaeda planned to infiltrate the United States from Canada. It would carry out terrorist operation using high explosives. The information was shared with the FBI, INS, Custom Service, State Department, and the White House.

Bin Laden's Global Network prepared for martyrdom. The Defense Department received information that seven Al Qaeda operatives had departed from several locations for the United States and Canada. The CIA learned that key Al Qaeda operatives were disappearing as they prepare for martyrdom.

NSA Adviser Rice Repeatedly Ignores Attack Warnings

June -- National Security Adviser Rice dismissed chatters that were picked in spring and summer which said: "Big event -- there will be a very, very, very, very big uproar. There will be attacks in the near future." Reports also said that Bin Laden was mobilizing his forces.

But Rice said all the warnings were "red herrings" or merely a diversion."

June 28 -- CIA Director George Tenet warned the White House of imminent Al Qaeda attacks. He wrote and sent his intelligence summary to National Security Adviser Condoleezza Rice. He told her: "Based on a review of all sources reporting over the last five months, we believe that Bin Laden will launch a significant terrorist attack against the United States.

"The attack will be spectacular and designed to inflict mass casualties against U.S. facilities or interests. Attack preparations have been made. Attack will occur with little or no warning."

Bush, Cheney Told Attack Warnings Are Real

July -- President Bush and Vice President Dick Cheney and National Security Adviser Rice received more briefing papers as terrorist threat reports surged even higher, titled:

Bin Laden Threats Are Real.
Bin Laden Planning High Profile Attacks.

Again the exact contents of the new briefings remained classified. But it would be revealed later that the briefings consistently predicted upcoming terrorist attacks on the U.S.

Deputy CIA Director John McLaughlin was frustrated when inexperienced Bush officials questioned the validity of certain CIA intelligence findings. Two unnamed veteran Counter Terrorism Center officers involved in Bin Laden issues were so worried about the impending disaster that the White House repeated ignored that they even considered resigning in disgust and going public with their concerns.

Bin Laden Beats Drums of Imminent Al Qaeda Attacks on America, Pray for Martyrs

July -- Bin Laden recorded a speech at his Farug training camp in Afghanistan in which he urged trainees to pray for the success of an upcoming attack involving 20 "martyrs." His plot to attack the U.S. was now virtually an open secret to both the Muslim world and the United States.

But Bush, Cheney and Rice continued ignoring the many early warning of imminent terrorist attacks as "unreliable and incredible" and just a "diversion."

India Warns U.S. of Impending Attack

July -- The United States received intelligence alert from India that the White House would by hit by a terrorist attack, but no details were given.

U.S. government officials confirmed that Indian intelligence got the tip from two Islamic radicals with ties to Bin Laden.

July 10 -- FBI agent Ken Williams in Phoenix, Arizona, warned that Muslims from the Middle East were taking flight training lessons in aviation school in Arizona and suspected they might be potential terrorists of Bin Laden.

July 15 -- CIA Director George Tenet again met with National Security Adviser Rice and her aides at the White House about the growing terrorist threat of Bin Laden and his Al Qaeda network. Tenet briefed Rice that "there was going to be a major attack. He displayed a huge wall chart showing a dozen possible targets.

Britain Receives Report that Al Qaeda Now Set to Attack U.S.

July 16 -- British Prime Minister Tony Blair received a report from British spy agencies warning that Al Qaeda was now in "the final stages" of preparing an attack on the United States. He reportedly relayed the information to the White House.

July 31 -- The FBI and the FAA issued similar warnings. The FAA warned commercial airlines: "Terror groups are known to be planning and training for hijacking, and we ask you therefore to use caution.

But later it would be known that pilots and flight attendants were never told about such warnings against hijacking.

Even Taliban Warns America of Terrorist Strikes

August -- Little known is the fact that even the then de facto Taliban government in Kabul, Afghanistan, also warned the United States of imminent Al Qaeda attacks inside the U.S. Taliban Foreign Minister Wakil Ahmed Muttawakil relayed the warning to Washington and the United Nations.

He said that Bin Laden was planning a "huge attack" on targets inside America. He warned that the attack was imminent and would kill thousands. The Taliban foreign minister got the information from Tahir Yildash, leader of the rebel Islamic Movement of Uzbekistan which was allied with Al Qaeda at the time.

The Taliban de facto government in Kabul and the United States at the time had friendly relation.

Argentina, Jordan, Egypt Relay Warnings to U.S.

August   Argentina warned the United States that an attack of "major proportion" on American targets would occur. The information came from reliable Jewish intelligence. The source said the U.S. was informed about the report.

At the same time, Egyptian intelligence in Cairo had received similar information from one of its agents in Afghanistan and relayed it to the CIA. Cairo expected the CIA to ask for more information. It never did.

Jordan also sent a top-secret message to the United States code-named "The Big Wedding" warning that a major attack inside the U.S. would occur with the use of planes. Jordanian intelligence deemed it so important that King Abdullah's own men relayed the warning to Washington through Arab and German intermediaries to avoid being intercepted.

Russia Warns America of Suicide Pilots

August -- Russia warned the Bush administration in Washington that suicide pilots were training for terrorist attacks inside the United States. President Vladimir Putin relayed the warning based on Russian intelligence findings.

It would be known later than Bush, Cheney and Rice took the warning lightly. The head of the Russian intelligence subsequently said: "We had clearly warning them on several occasions, but they did not pay the necessary attention."

Russian intelligence had solid information. Its agents knew the organizer and executors of the terrorist attacks, at least two of them being Muslim radicals from Russian-controlled Uzbekistan.

Egypt Again Warns Washington of Impending Al Qaeda Attacks

August 30 -- Egyptian President Hasni Mubarak said his government intelligence had warned Washington that Bin Laden's global network was in the advanced stages of unleashing attacks on the United States.

Mubarak said he got the information from an agent working inside Al Qaeda. However, U.S. officials later denied receiving any such warning from Egypt. In fact, U.S. intelligence was in disarray.

France Warns U.S. of Imminent Terrorist Attack

France warned the Bush administration of an impending terrorist attack inside the United States but provided no detail. French warning was similar to a previous Israeli warning. France has a Muslim population.

SEPTEMBER 2001

Bin Laden's telephone calls to the United States were intercepted. British insiders disclosed that the Al Qaeda leader contacted an associate thought to be in Pakistan. The conversation referred to an incident that would take place in the U.S. and discussed possible repercussions

In another call to an associate thought to be in Afghanistan, they discussed the scale and effect of the operation. The British government carefully referred to the intercepts: "There is evidence of a very specific nature relating to the guilt [plot] of Bin Laden and his associates that is too sensitive to release."

U.S. Skeptical on Bin Laden's Call to Stepmother Regarding 9/11

September 9 -- Bin Laden called his stepmother Al-Khalifa bin Laden using a satellite telephone and the signals were intercepted and sometimes recorded. He told her, "In two days you're going to hear big news and you're not going to hear from me for a while."

He called to cancel their meeting in Damascus, Syria. Since it was already September 9, it was obvious that when he when he said "In two days" he meant the big news or attack would explode on September 11.

In any event, the next day a U.S. official dismissed Bin Laden's call without taking any action, saying "I would view those reports with skepticism." The White House was reportedly informed of his intercepted call but did nothing.

Alarm Bells Sound at Stock Market in Expectation of Extraordinary Event

September 10 -- Alarm bells sounded over unusual trading in the U.S. stock options market. CBS reported on the extraordinary event. It was observed that whenever such kind of unusual heavy trading activity occurs "something big" is about to happen.

The U.S. National Security Agency (NSA) intercepted two messages in Arabic. One stated, "The match is about to begin." The other said, "Tomorrow is zero hour." The messages were transmitted between someone in Saudi Arabia and someone in Afghanistan.

But despite the bad omen, the United States took no immediate action. The White House of Bush, Cheney and Rice was still neglectful of their duty to protect America or were still in self-denial that such "incredible or unreliable" diversion would ever occur.

U.S. Officials, White House Call Warning Signs as "Needles in Haystack"

September 10 -- U.S. intelligence intercepted more terrorist messages. Electronic intercepts from undercover agents planted in Al Qaeda cells in the United States were busy monitoring the now fast developing catastrophe. They heard messages like, "Tomorrow will be a great day for us."

But as usual the Bush administration of President Bush, Vice President Cheney, and NSA Adviser Rice took no action to protect America from impending terrorist attacks. Yet U.S. general were warned not to fly on the morning of September 11 due to the high state of alert during the past two weeks.

To believe or not to believe -- that was the big question. And the White House of Bush, Cheney, and Rice chose not to believe that 9/11 would ever happen despite all the many early warnings they had received from 10 nations, not to mention the CIA and the FBI.

NSA, CIA and FBI Intercept Terrorist Messages But Do Nothing

Sometimes they do, sometimes they don't, act at all. On September 10, they all slept in their job. Although the NSA, CIA and FBI also intercepted terrorist messages, yet they didn't immediately analyze them despite the ominous signs of impending disaster. The messages included:

"This is a big thing!"
"We're ready to go!"
"They are going to pay the price!"

But despite such ominous signs of imminent terrorist attacks, the White House, NSA, CIA, FBI, FAA, NORAD, all were caught sleeping in their jobs and failed to do their duty to protect America!

9/11 EXPLODES!

September 11, 2001 -- Osaka bin Laden's Al Qaeda suicide terrorists attacked the United States by hijacking four commercial jetliners and used them as guided bombers to strike at their intended targets: the World Trade Center in New York City, the Pentagon in Arlington, Virginia, and the U.S. Congress on Capitol Hill in Washington, D.C.

The first plane, American Airlines Boeing 767 Flight 11, at 8:46 a.m. crashed into North Tower of the World Trade Center, killing all 76 passengers, 11 crew members, five hijackers, and 1,366 in the building and ground.

The second aircraft, United Airlines Boeing 767 Flight 175, at 9:03 a.m. bombed WTC South Tower 2, killing all 51 passengers, 11 crew members, five hijackers, and 600 building personnel.

Minutes later, both twin towers collapsed.

The third jetliner, American Airlines Boeing 757 Flight 77, at 9:37 a.m. smashed into the Pentagon, headquarters of the U.S. Department of Defense in Arlington, Virginia, killing 53 passengers, six crew members, five hijackers, and 125 Pentagon personnel.

The fourth plane, United Airlines Boeing 757 Flight 93, at 10:03 a.m. was forced down in Stonycreek Township at Somerset County in Pennsylvania, killing all 33 passengers, seven crew members, and four hijackers. Its intended target was the U.S. Congress on Capitol Hill.

Finally, Bin Laden made good his treats and warnings to bring Jihad or his Holy War to America.

Not One U.S. Plane Flies to Intercept Terrorist Attackers During 9/11

U.S. officials made a shocking revelation that the entire United States under its defense plan was to be defended only by 14 fighter planes, two each from seven military bases. Not one was used during the 9/11 terrorist attacks.

According to author Paul Thompson and the Dallas Morning News, none of the fighter planes were at "bases close to two obvious terrorist targets -- Washington, DC and New York City.

As a defense official explained, "I don't think anyone of use envisioned an internal air threat by big aircraft. I don't know of anybody that ever thought through that."

Even NORAD, which had held exercises simulating expected plane hijackings and terrorist attacks, did not have any plane in the air to fight the attackers.

Foregoing Evidence of Bush-Cheney Criminal Culpability for 9/11 are Documented and Indisputable

As contented in the beginning, let it be restated that the terrorist attacks on the United States on September 11, 2001 could have been prevented if only then President George W. Bush and Vice President Dick Cheney did their duty to protect America, but they criminally neglected to do so.

Under Article 1 of the Constitution, they were sworn in to faithfully execute the offices of president and vice president to the best of their ability, preserve, protect, and defend the Constitution and the American people, "so help me God."

Thus Bush and Cheney violated the Constitution with respect to 9/11 and are responsible for the nearly 3,000 deaths and billions of dollars in damages in the aftermath of the catastrophe. And as famed California prosecutor Vincent Bugliosi contented, they can also be prosecuted for murder for the death of 5,000 who died in Iraq and Afghanistan wars that they waged in violation of the U.S. Constitution and international laws.

Bush, Cheney, Rice, CIA, FBI Official Explanations Before 9/11 Commission

President Bush -- "Never [in] anybody's thought process . . . about how to protect America did we ever think that the evil doers would fly not one but four commercial aircraft into precious U.S. targets . . . never."

Vice President Cheney -- "Incendiary suggestions . . . that the White House had advance information that would have prevented the tragic attacks of 9/11 are thoroughly irresponsible . . . in time of war" any serious investigation of 9/11 foreknowledge would be tantamount to giving "aid and comfort" to the enemy.

National Security Adviser Condoleezza Rice -- "I don't think anybody could have predicted that these people would take an airplane and slam it into the World Trade Center, take another one and slam it into the Pentagon, that they would try to use an airplane as a missile."

CIA Director George Tenet -- "We are proud of that [our] record . . . [The 9/11 plot was] "in the hands of three or four people" and thus was impossible to prevent.

FBI Director Robert Mueller -- "There was nothing the agency could have done to anticipate and prevent the [9/11] attacks."

"Press For Truth" Documentary Exposes Bush-Cheney Obstruction and Stonewalling

In 2006 a documentary, Press For Truth, may well serve as a counterpoint to the allegations of President Bush, Vice President Cheney, NSA Adviser Rice, CIA Director Tenet and FBI Director Mueller.

Based in part on the book The Terror Timeline by Paul Thompson, the documentary was produced by Ray Nowosielski, John Duffy and Kyle F. Hence; written by Ray Nowosielski and Kyle F. Hence; and directed by Ray Nowosielski.

The film follows the Jersey Girls led by Lorie Van Auken who were widowed by 9/11 and who hounded and forced Bush and Congress to create the 9/11 Commission despite his obstruction and stonewalling.

The Unanswered Questions Remain Unanswered

1. Why had NORAD whose duty is to protect American airspace and even held exercises simulating predicted 9/11 attacks failed to fly a single military plane to protect known terrorist U.S. targets, the World Trade Center in New York City and the Pentagon in Arlington, Virginia?

2. Why did the World Trade Center twin towers completely collapse when no other steel-framed skyscraper had ever totally collapsed before due to fire?

3. Why did President Bush stay in a Florida school classroom for over 10 minutes after being told by his aide that New York had been attacked?

4. Why did the White House refuse to release documents that the 9/11 Commission had requested?

5. Why did the 9/11 Commission, whose chairman was recommended to that position by the White House, allow Bush and Cheney to testify behind closed doors and not under oath, thereby making it difficult if not impossible to double-check the accuracy and truthfulness of their assertions?

Whistleblower Exposes FBI Failure to Help Prevent 9/11 Terrorist Attacks on U.S.

In a related event, FBI special agent Coleen Rowley who was assigned to the FBI New York Office, turned whistleblower in May 2002 after the 9/11 terrorist attacks on the United States by testifying before the U.S. Senate Judiciary Committee that the FBI had neglected to help prevent the catastrophe.

After the September 11, 2001, Rowley wrote a paper for FBI Director Robert Mueller documenting how FBI HQ personnel in Washington, DC, had mishandled and failed to take action on information provided by the Minneapolis, Minnesota Field Office where she was formerly stationed, regarding its investigation of suspected terrorist Zacarias Moussaoui.

Moussaoui had been suspected of being involved in preparations for a suicide-hijacking similar to the December 1994, "Eiffel Tower" hijacking of

Air France 8969. Failures identified by Rowley might have left the U.S. vulnerable to the September 11, 2001 attacks.

Mueller and Senator Chuck Grassley (R-IA) pushed for and got a major reorganization, focused on creation of the new Office of Intelligence at the FBI. This reorganization was supported with a significant expansion of FBI personnel with counterterrorism and language skills.

As a result of Rowley's role as FBI whistleblower, she was named TIME "Person of the Year" award in 2002 along with two other women credited as whistleblowers, Sherron Watkins from Enron and Cynthia Cooper of WorldCom. Rowley also received the Sam Adams Award for 2002.

Sources: en.wikipedia.org   and   rnc08report.org.

• HUMAN & FINANCIAL COSTS OF 9/11, IRAQ & AFGHANISTAN WARS BY THE NUMBERS

9/11 Terrorist Attacks:

Killed -- 2,973 (New York, Virginia and Pennsylvania)
Firemen -- 343
New York City Police -- 23
Port Authority Police -- 37
Other Nations' Citizens -- 115
Economic Loss to New York -- $105 Billion
Job Loss -- 146,100
People Who Lost Spouses or Partners -- 1,609
Children Who Lost Parents -- 3,051
Body Parts -- 19,858
Insurance Paid Worldwide -- $40.2 Billion
FEMA Emergency Fund Spent -- $970 Million
Charity Donation -- $1.4 Billion
New Yorkers with Post-Traumatic Stress Disorder -- 422,000
Government Sued for 9/11 Wrongful Deaths -- By Survivors of 2,880 Who Died
Paid to Complainants -- $7 Billion
Average Claim Paid -- $5 Million
Sources: New York Magazine, New York Times

Iraq War and Occupation

American Deaths Since War Began on March 19, 2003 -- 4311
In Combat -- 3455
American Wounded (Official) -- 31,327
American Wounded (Estimate) -- Over 100,000
Contractor Employee Deaths -- 1,306
Deaths of Other Coalition Troops -- 318
Journalists Killed -- 138

American Deaths since Obama Inauguration -- 83
War Veterans with Brain Injuries -- 320,000
War Veteran Patients -- 400,304
Iraqi Deaths -- 1.3 Million
Iraqi Women and Child Deaths -- Over 100,000
Iraqi Men Deaths -- Over 100,000
Iraqi Displaced Refugees -- 1.2 Million
Cost of War and Occupation -- Over $900 Billion
Projected Cost of War and Occupation -- $1.7 Trillion
Cost a Month -- $10 Billion
Owed to China for Financing War -- Almost $1.5 Trillion
American Troops Currently Deployed -- 143,000
Total Casualties -- 72 Times 9/11 Deaths
Updated -- June 6, 2009
Sources: U.S. Department of Defense, Antiwar.com, and Casualties.org

Afghanistan War and Occupation

U.S. Military Deaths -- 700
Other Coalition Troops -- 318
Other Military Deaths -- 474
Afghan Deaths --
American Troops Currently Deployed -- 31,000
Cost a Month -- $12 Billion
Afghans Fled and/or Displaced -- 2.1 million
Radioactive Contamination -- Greater than two Atomic Bombs U.S.
dropped on Japan during WWII
Sources: UN Assistance Mission in Afghanistan / Wikipedia,Org

Effect of Iraq and Afghanistan Combined

American Soldiers Who Died -- Now Over 5,000
Cost -- Has Exceeded Cost of 12-Year Vietnam War
Cost -- More than double the cost of the Korean War
Cost -- 10 times the cost of the first Gulf War in 1990-1991
Cost -- More than the cost of and longer than World War Two
VA Patients -- 400,000
War Veterans Diagnosed With Post-Traumatic Stressed Disorder
(PTSD) -- 105,000

• EISENHOWER, LINCOLN WARN AGAINST U.S. MILITARY-
INDUSTRIAL COMPLEX

President Dwight Eisenhower in his Farewell Address to the nation on January 17, 1961 sounded an alarm against the Military-Industrial Complex that had plunged the United States into foreign wars and robbed the national treasury of public funds.

"Until the latest of our world conflicts, the United States had no armament industry. American makers of plowshares could, in time and as required, make swords as well. But now we can no longer risk emergency improvisation of national defense;

"We have been compelled to create a permanent armaments industry of vast proportions. Added to this, three and a half million men and women are directly engaged in the defense establishment. We annually spend on military security more than the net income of all United States corporations.

"This conjunction of an immense military establishment and a large arms industry is new in the American experience. The local influence -- economic, political, even spiritual -- is felt in every city, every State house, every office of the Federal government.

"We recognize the imperative need for this development. Yet we must not fail to comprehend its grave implications. Our toil, resources and livelihood aare all involved; so is the structure of our society.

"In the councils of government, we must guard against the acquisition of unwarranted influence, whether sought or unsought, by the military-industrial complex. The potential for the disastrous rise of misplaced power exists and will persist.

"We must never let the weight of this combination endanger our liberties or democratic processes. We should take nothing for granted. Only an alert and knowledgeable citizenry can compel the proper meshing of the huge industrial and military machinery of defense with our peaceful methods and goals, so that security and liberty may prosper together."

Eisenhower said: "Every gun that is made, every worship launched, every rocket fired signifies in the final sense, a theft from those who hunger and are not fed; those who are cold and not clothed. This World in Arms is not spending alone. It is spending the sweat of its laborers, the genius of its scientists, and the hopes of its children."

Lincoln Warns Against Meddling of Corporations in Political Life of the Nation

In 1864 President Abraham Abraham Lincoln noted the increasing interference of arms corporations in the political life of the United States. In a letter to Colonel Williams Elkins, he noted:

"I see in the near future a crisis approaching that unnerves me and causes me to tremble for the safety of my country. Corporations have been enthroned and an era of high corporation will follow and the money power of the country will endeavor to prolong its reign by working on the prejudice of the people until all wealth is aggregated in a few hands and the Republic is destroyed . . ."

Lincoln identified this strategy back in 1848 before he became president. He attacked President James Polk for his policy on Mexico. "Trusting to escape scrutiny, by fixing the public gaze upon the exceeding brightness of military glory -- that attracted rainbow that rises in shadows of blood -- that serpent's eye, that charms to destroy -- he plunged into war."

He added: "Kings had always been involving and impoverishing their people in wars, pretending generally, if not always, that the good of the people was the object."

Lincoln said this was "the most oppressive of all kingly oppressions" and that it was important that the United States should make surer that "no one man should hold the power of bringing this oppression upon us."

• SENATOR McCASKILL TAKES ON MILITARY-INDUSTRIAL COMPLEX FOR SCANDAL

Just as President Eisenhower and President Lincoln had warned, Senator Claire McCaskill (D-Missouri) has disclosed in a speech on the Senate floor that the Military Industrial Complex is profiting from questionable war business with the government.

She reacted to a scathing report by the Government Accountability Office (GAO) that questioned whether or not the United States military gets what it pays from war contractors operating in Iraq and Afghanistan wars.

A former prosecutor and Missouri state senator, McCaskill outlined the findings of the GAO report which found that Defense Contract Audit Agency (DCAA) officials and major defense contractors had successfully pressured Pentagon auditors to hide damaging facts about the performance and costs of weapons systems.

The freshman senator said the DCAA has "gotten caught in what cold be the biggest auditing scandal in the history of this town, and I'm not exaggerating here. I will guarantee you, as auditors around the country learned about this, they're going to have disbelief and raw anger that this agency has impugned the integrity of government auditors everywhere by these kinds of irresponsible actions."

Matt Renner of Truthout reported that McCaskill fired off letters to Secretary of Defense Robert Gates and DCAA Director April G. Stephenson, demanding accountability and a full explanation of the issues the GAO raised. In a July 11 letter, Stephenson said that DCAA did not agree with the "totality" of the report but was addressing some of the issues raised.

The GAO, the top nonpartisan governmental investigative body in Washington, DC, looked at 14 audits performed by the 4,000-member DCAA, the internal government audit team that is supposed to oversee contracting for the Department of Defense and other government agencies.

• DEMOCRATS IN CONGRESS BREAK PLEDGE TO IMPEACH BUSH, CHENEY

NOTE: The Democrats regained control of the U.S. Congress on the strength of their 2006 pre-election promise to voters that they would impeach President George W. Bush and Vice President Richard (Dick) Cheney, and also stop the wars in Iraq and Afghanistan.

They broke that promise.

During the campaign, reelectionist Rep. John Conyers Jr. (D-MI) even staged a mock impeachment trial of Bush to dramatize his party's intent. The new Democratic majority in the 110th Congress in 2007 then elected Rep. Nancy Pelosi the new House speaker and made Conyers chairman of the House Judiciary Committee.

But after the euphoria of election victory, Speaker Pelosi put Bush's and Cheney's impeachment off the table and shoved Conyers aside, in favor of legislation. She also pigeonholed House Resolution 333 impeaching Cheney that Rep. Dennis Kucinich (D-NC) had filed.

But in so doing, the new Democratic majority in Congress not only broke their promise to the voters. They also violated the Constitution by refusing to prosecute Bush and Cheney for the high crimes and misdemeanors that they had committed that warrant impeachment and removal from office.

However, event like this should not be consigned to the trash can of history to be forgotten. It should be recorded for future reference so that lesson could be learned from it.

It is regrettable that the Democratic Congress reneged from their pledge and shrank from their constitutional duty. In any event, let it be recorded here for history's sake the Articles of Impeachment against Bush and Cheney that they should have honored and filed, but didn't, as follow:

THE IMPEACHMENT OF PRESIDENT GEORGE W. BUSH

(Draft by ImpeachBush.tv)

Articles of Impeachment
Resolved, that President George W. Bush be impeached for his crimes and misdemeanors, and that the following Articles of Impeachment be exhibited to the United States Senate.

Articles of Impeachment exhibited by the House of Representatives of the United States of America, in maintenance and support of its impeachment against President George W. Bush and his team for high crimes and misdemeanors.

Article I
In his conduct while President of the United States, George W. Bush, in violation of his constitutional oath faithfully to execute the office of President of the United States and, to the best of his ability, preserve, protect, and defend the Constitution of the United States, and in violation of his constitutional duty to take care that the laws be faithfully executed, has conspired to exceed his constitutional authority to wage war, in that: On March 10, 2003, George W. Bush invaded the sovereign country of Iraq

in direct defiance of the United Nations Security Council. This constitutes a violation of Chapter 1, Article 2 of the United Nations Charter and a violation of Principle VI of the Nuremberg Charter. According to Article to Article VI of the United States Constitution, "This Constitution, and the Laws of the United States which shall be made in Pursuance thereof; and all Treaties made, or which shall be made, under the Authority of the United States. shall be the supreme Law of the Land;" George W. Bush has thus acted in violation of the supreme Law of the Land by the following acts:

1. Invading Iraq with United States military forces.
2. Sacrificing the lives of thousands of American troops.
3. Killing tens of thousands of Iraqi civilians and Conscripts.
4. Rejecting possibilities for peaceful resolution of the conflict by rejecting acts of compliance by Saddam Hussein with the United Nations Resolutions, and ignoring the findings of Hans Blix that inspections were working to disarm Iraq.
5. Violating the Geneva Convention by abducting and transporting human beings to prisons in foreign countries where they can be tortured and subjected to inhuman treatment.

Article II

In his conduct while President of the United States, George W. Bush, in violation of his constitutional oath faithfully to execute the office of President of the United States and, to the best of his ability, preserve, protect, and defend the Constitution of the United States, and in violation of his constitutional duty to take care that the laws be faithfully executed, has subverted the principles of Democracy, by the following acts:

1. Providing misinformation to the United Nations Security Council, Congress and the American people overstating the offensive capabilities of Iraq, including weapons of mass destruction, as justification for military action against Iraq.
2. Repeatedly manipulating the sentiments of the American people by erroneously linking Iraq with the terrorist attacks of September 11, 2001 by Al-Qaeda.
3. Repeatedly claiming that satellite photos of sites in Iraq depicted factories for weapons of mass destruction in contradiction with the results of ground inspections by United Nations teams.
4. Stating that "Saddam Hussein recently sought significant quantities of uranium from Africa" in State of the Union Address after being told by the CIA that this was untrue and that the supporting documents were forged.
5. Influencing, manipulating and distorting intelligence related to Iraq with the intention of using that intelligence to support his goal of invading Iraq.
6. Repeatedly ordering the NSA to place illegal wiretaps on American citizens without a court order from FISA.
7. Retaliating against whistle-blowers who try to point out errors in statements made by President Bush.
8. Directing millions of dollars in government funds to companies associated with White House officials in no-bid contracts that pose serious conflicts of

interest. One example is Halliburton of which Vice President Richard B. Cheney was once Chairman and CEO.

Article III

In his conduct while President of the United States, George W. Bush, in violation of his constitutional oath faithfully to execute the office of President of the United States and, to the best of his ability, preserve, protect, and defend the Constitution of the United States, and in violation of his constitutional duty to take care that the laws be faithfully executed, has threatened the security of the American people, by the following acts:

1. Diverting military resources from pursuing known terrorists such as Osama Bin Laden who have repeatedly attacked the United States of America.

2. Generating ill will among the peoples of the world with an offensive and aggressive foreign policy.

3. Weakening the effects of International Law by defying the United Nations thus encouraging other nations to violate International Laws by example.

4. Diverting the National Guard to foreign wars and making them unavailable to serve the needs of American citizens at home who, for example, are suffering from Hurricane Katrina.

5. Appointing unqualified personnel to tactical government positions as political favors where their incompetence places American citizens at risk. An example being the appointment of Mike Brown as head of FEMA.

6. Proposing military strategies involving the first use of tactical or low yield nuclear weapons in violation of the Nonproliferation Treaty, which is an inherently destabilizing strategy that encourages participants in a conflict to strike before the other side can do so.

Wherefore, President George W. Bush, by such conduct, warrants impeachment and trial, and removal from office, and disqualification to hold and enjoy any office of honor, trust or profit in the United States.

THE IMPEACHMENT OF VICE PRESIDENT RICHARD B. CHENEY

House Resolution No. 333
Filed by Rep. Dennis Kucinich
Impeaching Richard B. Cheney, Vice President of the United States For High Crimes and Misdemeanors

Resolved, That Richard B. Cheney, Vice President of the United States, is impeached for high crimes and misdemeanors, and that the following Articles of Impeachment be exhibited to the United States Senate.

Articles of Impeachment exhibited by the House of Representatives of the United States of America in the name of itself and of the people of the United States of America, against Richard B. Cheney, Vice President of the United States, in maintenance and support of its impeachment against him for high crimes and misdemeanors.

Article I

In his conduct while Vice President of the United States, Richard B. Cheney, in violation of his constitutional oath to faithfully execute the office of Vice President of the United States and, to the best of his ability, preserve, protect, and defend the Constitution of the United States, and in violation of his constitutional to take care that the laws be faithfully executed, has purposely manipulated the intelligence process to deceive the citizens and Congress of the United States by fabricating a threat of Iraqi weapons of mass destruction to justify the use of the United States Armed Forces against the nation of Iraq in a manner damaging to our national security interests, to wit:

1. Despite all evidence to the contrary, the Vice President actively and systematically sought to deceive the citizens and Congress of the United States about an alleged threat of Iraqi weapons of mass destruction:

(A) "We know they have biological and chemical weapons." March 17, 2002, Press Conference by Vice President Dick Cheney and His HIghness Salman bin Hamad Al Khalifa, Crown Prince of Bahrain at Shaikh Hamad Palace.

(B) ". . . and we know they are pursuing nuclear weapons." March 19, 2002, Press Briefing by Vice President Dick Cheney and Israeli Prime Minister Ariel Sharon in Jerusalem.

(C) "And he is actively pursuing nuclear weapons at this time . . ." March 24, 2002, CNN Late Edition interview with Vice President Cheney.

(D) "We know he's got chemicals and biological and we know he's working on nuclear." May 19, 2002, NBC Meet the Press interview with Vice President Cheney.

(E) "But we now know that Saddam [Hussein] has resumed his efforts to acquire nuclear weapons . . . Simply stated, there is no doubt that Saddam Hussein now has weapons of mass destruction. There is no doubt that he is amassing them to use against our friends, against our allies, and against us." August 26, 2002, Speech of Vice President Cheney at VFW 103rd National Convention.

(F) "Based on intelligence that's becoming available, some of it has been made public, more of it hopefully will be, that he has indeed stepped up his capacity to produce and deliver biological weapons, that he has reconstituted his nuclear program to develop a nuclear weapon, that there are efforts under way inside Iraq to significantly expand his capability." September 8, 2002, NBC Meet the Press interview with Vice President Cheney.

(G) "He is, in fact, actively and aggressively seeking to acquire nuclear weapons." September 8, 2002 NBC Meet the Press interview with Vice President Cheney.

(H) "And we believe he has, in fact, reconstituted nuclear weapons." March 16, 2003, NBC Meet the Press interview with Vice President Cheney.

2. Preceding the March 2003 invasion of Iraq and Vice President was fully informed that no legitimate evidence existed of weapons of mass destruction in Iraq. The Vice President pressured the intelligence community to change their findings to enable the deception of the citizens and Congress of the United States.

(A) Vice President Cheney and his Chief of Staff, Lewis Libby, made multiple trips to the CIA in 2002 to question analysts studying Iraq's weapons programs and alleged links to Al Qaeda, creating an environment in which analysts felt they were being pressured to make their assessments fit with the Bush administration's policy objectives accounts.

(B) Vice President Cheney sought out unverified and ultimately inaccurate raw intelligence to prove his preconceived beliefs. This strategy of cherry picking was employed to influence the interpretation of the intelligence.

3. The Vice President's actions corrupted or attempted to corrupt the 2002 National Intelligence Estimate, an intelligence document issued on October 1, 2002, and carefully considered by Congress prior to the October 10, 2002 vote to authorize the use of force. The Vice President's actions prevented the necessary reconciliation of facts for the National Intelligence Estimate which resulted in a high number of dissenting opinions from technical experts in two Federal agencies.

(A) The State Department's Bureau of Intelligence and Research dissenting view in the October 2002 National Intelligence Estimate stated "Lacking persuasive evidence that Baghdad has launched a coherent effort to reconstitute its nuclear weapons program INR is unwilling to speculate that such an effort began soon after the departure of UN inspectors or to project a timeline for the completion of activities it does not now see happening. As a result INR is unable to predict that Iraq could acquire a nuclear device or weapon."

(B) The State Department's Bureau of Intelligence and Research dissenting view in the October 2002 National Intelligence Estimate also stated that "Finally, the claims of Iraqi pursuit of natural uranium in Africa are, in INR's assessment, highly dubious."

(C) The State Department's Bureau of Intelligence and Research dissenting view in the October 2002 National Intelligence Estimate references a Department of Energy opinion by stating that "INR accepts the judgment of technical experts at the US Department of Energy (DOE) who have concluded that the tubes Iraq seeks to acquire are poorly suited for use in gas centrifuges to be used for uranium enrichment and finds unpersuasive the arguments advanced by others to make the case that they are intended for that purpose."

The Vice President subverted the national security interests of the United States by setting the stage for the loss of more than 3300 United States service members; the loss of 650,000 Iraqi citizens since the United States invasion; the loss of approximately $500 billion in war costs which has increased our Federal debt; the loss of military readiness within the United States Armed Services due to overextension, lack of training and lack of equipment; and decades of likely blowback created by the invasion of Iraq.

In all of this, Vice President Richard B. Cheney has acted in a manner contrary to his trust as Vice President, and subversive of constitutional government, to the prejudice of the cause of law and justice and the manifest injury of the people of the United States.

Wherefore, Vice President Richard B. Cheney, by such conduct, is guilty of an impeachable offense warranting removal from office.

Article II

In his conduct while Vice President of the United States, Richard B. Cheney, in violation of his constitutional oath to faithfully execute the office of Vice President and, to the best of his ability, preserve, protect, and defend the Constitution of the United States, and in violation of his constitutional duty to take care that the laws be faithfully executed, purposely manipulated the intelligence process to deceive the citizens and Congress of the United States about an alleged relationship between Iraq and Al Qaeda in order to justify the use of the United States Armed Forces against the nation of Iraq in a manner damaging to our national security interests, to wit:

1.   Despite all evidence to the contrary, the Vice President actively and systematically sought to deceive the citizens and the Congress of the United States about an alleged relationship between Iraq and Al Qaeda:

(A) "His regime has had high-level contacts with Al Qaeda going back a decade and has provided training to Al Qaeda terrorist." December 2, 2002, Speech of Vice President Cheney at the Air National Guard Senior Leadership Conference.

(B) "His regime aids and protects terrorists, including members of Al Qaeda. He could decide secretly to provide weapons of mass destruction to terrorists for use against us." January 30, 2003, Speech of Vice President Cheney to 30th Political Action Conference in Arlington, Virginia.

(C) "We know he's out trying once again to produce nuclear weapons and we know that he has a long-standing relationship with various terrorist groups, including the Al Qaeda organization." March 16, 2003, NBC Meet the Press interview with Vice President Cheney.

(D) "We learned more and more that there was a relationship between Iraq and Al Qaeda that stretched back through most of the decade of the '90s, that it involved training, for example, on biological weapons and chemical weapons . . ." September 14, 2003, NBC Meet the Press interview with Vice President Cheney.

(E) "Al Qaeda had a base of operation there up in Northeastern Iraq where they ran a large poisons factory for attacks against Europeans and U.S. forces." October 3, 2003, Speech of Vice President Cheney at Bush-Cheney '04 Fundraiser in Iowa.

(F) "He also had an established relationship with Al Qaeda providing training to Al Qaeda members in areas of poisons, gases, and conventional bombs." October 10, 2003, Speech of Vice President Cheney to the Heritage Foundation.

(G) "Al Qaeda and the Iraqi intelligence services have worked together on a number of occasions." January 9, 2004, Rocky Mountain News interview with Vice President Cheney.

(H) "I think there's overwhelming evidence that there was a connection between Al Qaeda and the Iraqi government." January 22, 2004, NPR: Morning Edition interview with Vice President Cheney.

(l)   "First of all, on the questions of -- of whether or not there was any kind of relationship, there clearly was a relationship. It's been testified to; the evidence is overwhelming." June 17, 2004, CNBC: Capital Report interview with Vice President Cheney.

2. Preceding the March 2003 invasion of Iraq the Vice President was fully informed that no credible evidence existed of a working relationship between Iraq and Al Qaeda, a fact articulated in several official documents, including:

(A) A classified Presidential Daily Briefing ten days after the September 11, 2001 attacks indicating that the United States intelligence community had no evidence linking Saddam Hussein to the September 11th attacks and that there was "scant credible evidence that Iraq had any significant collaborative ties with Al Qaeda."

(B) Defense Intelligence Terrorism Summary No. 044-02, issued in February 2002 by the United States Defense Intelligence Agency, which challenged the credibility of information gleaned from captured Al Qaeda leader al-Libi. The DIA report also cast significant doubt on the possibility of a Saddam Hussein-Al Qaeda conspiracy. "Saddam's regime is intensely secular and is wary of Islamic revolutionary movements. Moreover, Baghdad is unlikely to provide assistance to a group it cannot control."

(C) A January 2003 British intelligence classified report on Iraq that concluded that "there are no current links between the Iraqi regime and the Al Qaeda network."

The Vice President subverted the national security interests of the United States by setting the stage for the loss of more than 3300 United States service members; the loss of 650,000 Iraqi citizens since the United States invasion; the loss of approximately $500 billion in war costs which has increased our Federal debt; the loss of military readiness within the United States Armed Services due to overextension, lack of training and lack of equipment; the loss of United States credibility in world affairs; and the decades of likely blowback created by the invasion of Iraq.

In all of this, Vice President Richard B. Cheney has acted in a manner contrary to his trust as Vice President, and subversive of constitutional government, to the prejudice of the cause of law and justice and the manifest injury of the people of the United States.

Wherefore, Vice President Richard B. Cheney, by such conduct, is guilty of an impeachable offense warranting removal from office.

Article III

In his conduct while Vice President of the United States, Richard B. Cheney, in violation of his constitutional oath to faithfully execute the office of Vice President of the United States and, to the best of his ability, preserve, protect, and defend the Constitution of the United States, and in violation of his constitutional duty to take care that the laws be faithfully executed, has openly threatened aggression against the Republic of Iran absent any real threat to the United States, and done so with United States proven capability to carry out such threats, thus undermining the national security of the United States, to wit:

1.   Despite no evidence that Iran has the intention or the capability of attacking the United States and despite the turmoil created by United States invasion of Iraq, the Vice President has openly threatened aggression against Iran as evidenced by the following:

(A) "For our part, the United States is keeping all options on the table in addressing the irresponsible conduct of the regime. And we join other nations in sending that regime a clear message: We will not allow Iran to have a nuclear weapon." March 7, 2006, Speech of Vice President Cheney to American Israel Public Affairs Committee 2006 Policy Conference.

(B) "But we've also made it clear that all options are on the table." January 24, 2007, CNN Situation Room interview with Vice President Cheney.

(C) "When we -- as the President did, for example, recently -- deploy another aircraft carrier task force in the Gulf, that sends a very strong signal to everybody in the regime that the United States is here to stay, that we clearly have significant capabilities, and that we are working with friends and allies as well as the international organizations to deal with the Iranian threat." January 29, 2007, Newsweek interview with Vice President Cheney.

(D) "But I've also made the point and the President has made the point that all options are still on the table." February 24, 2007, Vice President Cheney at Press Briefing with Australian Prime Minister in Sydney, Australia.

2. The Vice President, who repeatedly and falsely claimed to have had specific, detailed knowledge of Iraq's alleged weapons of mass destruction capabilities, is no doubt fully aware of evidence that demonstrates Iran poses no real threat to the United States as evidenced by the following:

(A) "I know that what we see in Iran right now is not the industrial capacity your can [use to develop a] bomb," Mohamed El Baradei, Director General of International Atomic Energy Agency, February 19, 2007.

(B) Iran indicated its "full readiness and willingness to negotiate on the modality for the resolution of the outstanding issues with the IAEA, subject to the assurances for dealing with the issues in the framework of the Agency, without interference of the United Nations Security Council." IAEA Board Report, February 22, 2007.

(C) ". . . so whatever they have, what we have seen today, is not the kind of capacity that would enable them to make bombs." Mohamed El Baradei, Director General of International Atomic Energy Agency, February 19, 2007.

3. The Vice President is fully aware of the actions taken by the United States towards Iran that are further destabilizing the world as evidenced by the following:

(A) The United States has refused to engage in meaningful diplomatic relations with Iran since 2002, rebuffing both bilateral and multilateral offers to dialogue.

(B) The United States is currently engaged in a military buildup in the Middle East that includes the increased presence of the United States Navy in the waters near Iran, significant United States Armed Forces in two nations neighboring Iran, and the installation of anti-missile technology in the region.

(C) News accounts have indicated that military planners have considered the B61-11, a tactical nuclear weapon, as one of the options to strike underground bunkers in Iran.

(D) The United States has been linked to anti-Iranian organizations that are attempting to destabilize the Iranian government, in particular the Mujahideen-e, Khalq (MEK), even though the state department has branded it a terrorist organization.

(E) News accounts indicate that the United States troops have been ordered into Iran to collect data and establish contact with anti-government groups.

4. In the last three years the Vice President has repeatedly threatened Iran. However, the Vice President is legally bound by the U.S. Constitution's adherence to international law that prohibits threats of use of force.

(A) Article VI of the United States Constitution states, "This Constitution, and the Laws of the United States which shall be made in Pursuance thereof; and all Treaties made, or which shall be made, under the Authority of the United States, shall be the supreme Law of the Land." Any provision of an international treaty ratified by the United States becomes the law of the United States.

(B) The United States is a signatory to the United Nations Charter, a treaty among the nations of the world. Article II, Section 4 of the United Nations Charter states, "All Members shall refrain in their international relations from the threat or use of force against the territorial integrity or political independence of any state, or in any other manner inconsistent with the Purposes of the United Nations." The threat of force is illegal.

(C) Article 51 lays out the only exception, "Noting in the present Charter shall impair the inherent right of individual or collective self-defense if an armed attack occurs against a Member of the United Nations, until the Security Council has taken measures necessary to maintain international peace and security." Iran has not attacked the United States; therefore any threat against Iran by the United States is illegal.

The Vice President's deception upon the citizens and the Congress of the United States that enabled the failed United States invasion of Iraq forcibly altered the rules of diplomacy such that the Vice President's recent belligerent actions towards Iran are destabilizing and counter-productive to the national security of the United States.

In all of this, Vice President Richard B. Cheney has acted in a manner contrary to his trust as Vice President, and subversive of constitutional government, to the prejudice of the cause of law and justice and the manifest injury of the people of the United States.

Wherefore, Richard B. Cheney, by such conduct, warrants impeachment and trial, and removal from office.

• U.S. MAINSTREAM MEDIA ABDICATE DUTY TO CRUSADE FOR TRUTH AS PUBLIC WATCHDOG

If Joseph Pulitzer were still alive, war criminals George W. Bush and Richard B. Cheney would not get away with murder and crimes against humanity which they committed while serving as president and vice president in 2000-2008.

Thanks to the inept U.S. mainstream media, now that they are out of office and have not yet been criminally prosecuted, if at all, they remain in effect merely fugitives from justice enjoying their freedom and retirement from their illegal and immoral imperialistic military aggressions.

Certainly, Pulitzer would put today's mainstream media to shame for abdicating their role as public watchdog whose mission, as in legal parlance, is to seek the truth, the whole truth, and nothing but the truth in the best tradition of the press and canons of journalism.

Tragically, the state of journalism in the United States leaves much to be desired. The mainstream media no longer crusade for truth and freedom and justice. They may at times report government abuses and then forget about them and let the wrongdoers in power get away with their shenanigans.

The golden era of American journalism is gone. Terribly missed, along with Pulitzer, are such other icons of the press like Drew Pearson, Walter Winchell, Walter Lippmann, Edward Murrow, Jack Anderson, and Walter Cronkite.

Today's mainstream journalists pale in comparison to them, Nobody has filled the void. Nobody is effectively fiscalizing the government of the United States, whether under the Republican Party or the Democratic Party, whose leaders are both captive of lobbyists referred to as the "Invisible Government."

What is going on? Graft and corruption are taking place in the corridors of power in Washington. But they remain unchecked because today's traditional journalists generally don't care, or are cozy with ruling politicians, or are sleeping in their job. That is the tragedy.

If Pulitzer Were Still Alive, Bush and Cheney Won't Get Away With Murder

With Joseph Pulitzer still around, the situation would have been different. To better understand the situation then and now, a glance at his life and career is in order. He was the greatest journalist not only of the United States but also of the world. He had no equal in his time or now.

His story is also inspirational and beyond compare. He came to America without knowing a single word of English. A Hungarian son of a Jewish father and German mother, he smuggled himself to the New World as America was referred to then, as a volunteer for the Union Army during the Civil War.

At first he was rejected for health reason, but somebody who had already passed the physical examination and changed his mind from immigrating, allowed Pulitzer to assume his name. That was his passport to America in 1864.

Pulitzer's first job was a grave digger. He lived in a German community where his roommate was a person of high academic education. A curious person, he learned English and U.S. history from him by asking a lot of questions and spending hundreds of hours in public libraries.

In 1868 he worked for Westliche, a German-language newspaper in St. Louis, Missouri. After saving some money, in 1879 he bought St. Louis Dispatch and the St. Louis Post, and then merged the two as the St. Louis Post-Dispatch.

His Newspaper Crusades for Truth, Exposes Scandals, and Champions Cause of Common Man

As editor and publisher, Pulitzer developed a populist approach to journalism. He crusaded for truth and championed the cause of the common man with exclusive exposés and hard-hitting opinions. It paid off with increased circulation and advertising. He became rich.

Then Pulitzer set his eyes on New York, the epicenter of American journalism. In 1882 he purchased the New York World for $346,000. With the power of the press, he exposed scandals in government and also focused on human-interest stories.

Under his stewardship, he introduced the first newspaper comic in color. World circulation grew from 15,000 to 600,000 copies and became the largest newspaper in the United States at the time. At the peak of his success, his circulation skyrocketed to one million copies.

In 1895, a battle of newspapers broke out in New York. Rival publication New York Sun criticized Pulitzer in print and branded him as "The Tucker who abandoned his religion" to alienate his Jewish readership, apparently motivated by professional jealousy.

Then William Randolph Hearst came along. As publisher of the San Francisco Examiner, he imitated Pulitzer's New York World by championing the cause of the common man and exposing scandals in government and big business. Hearst became the newspaper kingpin from the West.

And like Pulitzer, he extended his influence to the East. Hearst bought the New York Journal and improved on Pulitzer's journalistic and business strategy. This led to their circulation war and the birth of "yellow" journalism as espoused mainly by Hearst.

President Roosevelt Has Pulitzer Sued for Libel Over Panama Canal Scandal, Wants Him Jailed

Highlight of Pulitzer's journalistic career reached its peak when his World exposed an illegal payment of $40 million that the United States had made to the French Panama Canal in 1909.

Pulitzer debunked President Theodore Roosevelt's claim that the U.S. did not pay a cent to any American citizen, that the money was paid direct to the French government, and that there was no business syndicate involved.

But the World in a hard-hitting editorial demanded to know, "WHO GOT THE MONEY?"

Pulitzer asserted that the United States had paid $40 million for the canal properties, and $10 million for a "manufactured" Panama republic (as breakaway from Columbia), not to the French government, but to J.P. Morgan & Company, a group of American lobbyists.

The World report and editorial angered President Roosevelt who branded them as "a libel upon the United States Government . . . and the good name of the American people." He had Pulitzer and his newspaper criminally indicted for libel with the intention of using the full force of the government to put him in prison.

Pulitzer to President Roosevelt: You Cannot Muzzle "The World"

But Pulitzer in another defiant World editorial retorted:

"Mr. Roosevelt is mistaken. He cannot muzzle The World.

"While no amount of billingsgate on his part can alter our determination to treat him with judicial impartiality and scrupulous fairness, we repeat what we have already said -- that the Congress of the United States should make a thorough investigation of the whole Panama transaction, that the full truth may be known to the American people.

"It is a most extraordinary circumstance that Mr. Roosevelt himself did not demand such an inquiry.

"The World fully appreciates the compliment paid to it by Mr. Roosevelt in making it the subject of a special message to the Congress of the United States. In the whole history of American Government no other President has ever paid such a tribute to the power and influence of a fearless, independent newspaper . . .

"If The World has libeled anybody we hope it will be punished, but we do not intend to be intimidated by Mr. Roosevelt's threats, or by Mr. Roosevelt's denunciation, or by Mr. Roosevelt's power . . .

Even in Jail, "The World" Will Not Cease to be a Fearless Champion of Free Press – Pulitzer

"As far as The World is concerned, its proprietor may go to jail . . . but even in jail The World will not cease to be a fearless champion of free speech, a free press, and a free people.

"It cannot be muzzled."

Author W.A. Swanberg who wrote the book "Pulitzer" reported on the Roosevelt-Pulitzer controversy in great detail:

"On February 17, 1909, a District of Columbia grand jury indicted Joseph Pulitzer, Caleb Van Hamm and Robert Hunt Lyman of the World, as well as the Press Publishing Company (the corporate name of the World) on five counts charging criminal libel of Theodore Roosevelt, J.P. Morgan, Douglas Robinson, Charles P. Taft, Elihu Root and William Nelson Cromwell . . .

"The World replied in a Frank Cobb editorial characterizing the indictments as a 'political proceeding' and defining the status of The World in a manner dear to the owner's heart:

"Mr. Roosevelt is an episode. The World is an institution. Long after Mr. Roosevelt is dead, long after Mr. Pulitzer is dead, long after all the present editors of this paper are dead, The World will still go on as a great independent newspaper, unmuzzled, undaunted and unterrorized."

Pulitzer Wins U.S. Supreme Court Victory Against Roosevelt

The libel case against Pulitzer dragged on for two years and was elevated to the U.S. Supreme Court which, on January 3, 1911, decided in his favor, The World had the last say:

"The unanimous decision handed down by the United States Supreme Court yesterday in the Roosevelt Panama libel case against The World is the most sweeping victory won for freedom of speech and of the press . . .

"The decision . . . is so sweeping that no other President will be tempted to follow in the footsteps of Theodore Roosevelt, not matter how greedy he may be for power, no matter how resentful of opposition . . ."

To celebrate his court triumph, Pulitzer offered Columbia University president Seth Low funds to set up the world's first school of journalism. However, Columbia later amended the plan with his approval to include prizes for outstanding journalists, now called Pulitzer Prize.

The first Pulitzer Prizes were awarded in 1917 in accordance with his wishes. They are awarded yearly and remain as the most prestigious and coveted honors today's journalists aspire for.

At the height of his success as editor and publisher of the New York World, Pulitzer became blind and suffered from poor health. Yet he still actively managed his newspapers either from his vacation retreats or from aboard his yacht Liberty while sailing around the world.

In a fitting tribute, it was said of him:

"Joseph Pulitzer stood out as the very embodiment of American journalism. Hungarian-born, an intense indomitable figure, he was the most skillful of newspaper publisher, a passionate crusader against dishonest government, a fierce, hawk-like competitor who did not shrink from sensationalism circulation struggles, and a visionary who richly endowed his profession. His innovative New York World and St. Louis Post-Dispatch reshaped newspaper journalism."

Which Member of Mainstream Media Would Dare Do What Pulitzer Did?

In the backdrop of the Roosevelt-Pulitzer controversy, who in the mainstream media today have the courage to take on war criminals George W. Bush and Richard B. Cheney for their illegal, immoral and phony war on terror that led to their invasions and occupations of Iraq and Afghanistan that killed thousands and damaged billions of dollars of their entire infrastructures, not to mention the 9/11 casualties and huge costs that they neglected and failed to prevent?

As in the case of mythical Greek philosopher Diogenes who walked through the streets of Athens carrying a lamp in search of an honest man, it is asked, who in today's U.S. mainstream media has the same crusading spirit and fierce devotion to journalistic duty and the courage to do what Pulitzer did in his time?

Where is that honest practitioner of American journalism?

The answers have already been given, and it is not good.

Mainstream Media Censor Book "The Prosecution of George W. Bush For Murder"

Tim Arango of International Herald Tribune on July 7, 2008 reported on the newest book of famed California prosecutor Vincent Bugliosi, "The Prosecution of George W. Bush For Murder" under the headline "Mainstream Media Silent on Bush Book" as follows:

"As a prosecutor, Vincent Bugliosi was perfect in murder cases: 21 trials, 21 convictions, including the Charles Manson case in 1971.

"As an author, Bugliosi has written three No. 1 bestsellers and won three Edgar Allen Poe Allen Poe awards, the top honor for crime writers.

"But what happens when a big-name author, who more than 30 years ago co-wrote the best seller 'Helter Skelter,' publishes a book that the mainstream has shied away from?

"Bugliosi's latest, a polemic with the provocative title, 'The Prosecution of George W. Bush For Murder,' has risen to best-seller status with a nary a peep from the usual outlets that help sell books: cable television and book reviews in major daily newspapers.

ABC, MSNBC, Comedy Central Refuse Ad, Interview; Newsweek Explains

"Internet advertising has been abundant, but ABC Radio refused to accept an advertisement for the book during the Don Imus show, said Roger Cooper, the publisher of Vanguard Press, which put out the book.

"Bugliosi, in a recent interview by telephone from his home in Los Angeles, said he had expected some pushback from the mainstream media because of the subject matter -- the book lays a legal case for holding Bush 'criminally responsible' for the deaths of American soldiers in Iraq -- but did not expect a virtual blackout . . .

"Bugliosi said that bookers for cable television, where he has made regular appearances to promote books, have ignored his latest offering. MSNBC and Comedy Central were two outlets Bugliosi thought would show interest, but neither did.

"They are not responding at all," he said. "I think it all goes back to fear. If the liberal media would put me on national television, I think they'd fear that they would be savaged by the right wing. The left wing fear the right, but the right does not fear the left."

"A spokesman for Comedy Central declined to comment. A representative for MSNB said, 'We get many pitches to interview authors, and very few end up on our programs.'

Source: Philpress Columns   146

"The editor of Newsweek, Jon Meacham, said he had not read the manuscript, but he offered a reason why the media might be silent: 'I think there's a kind of Bush-bashing fatigue out there.'"

Bugliosi's Book Blacked Out by Mainstream Media, CNN's Larry King Passes on Interview

The Raw Story, an Internet press, on July 15, 2008 also published a book report bylined by David Edwards and Muriel Kane under the headline, "Bush murder trial book, blacked out by mainstream media, thrives on Internet." The report revealed:

"Former Los Angeles district attorney Vincent Bugliosi became widely known as the prosecutor of Charles Manson and later wrote bestselling books about that case, the O.J. Simpson trial, and other topics. However, Bugliosi's latest effort, The Prosecution of George W. Bush for Murder, has faced what CNN calls 'a virtual media blackout.'

"Bugliosi says that no one in the mainstream media would review his book, which argues that Bush should be charged with murder for the deaths of over 4000 American soldiers in Iraq if he lied to get the nation into war. 'My book was completely rejected across the board by network and cable,' Bugliosi told CNN.

"Larry King passed up the chance to interview Bugliosi, and neither MSNBC nor Comedy Central's The Daily Show expressed any interest when the book came out in May. (Bugliosi did finally appear on MSNBC's Morning Joe last Friday.) ABC Radio even refused an ad for The Prosecution of George W. Bush for Murder.

"'So how did the book become a bestseller?' asks CNN.

"The answer is that Bugliosi's publisher, the Vanguard Press, started advertising on liberal blogs. The blogs themselves then began discussing the book, and it sold 130,000 copies in six weeks.

"'I'm very, very encouraged, and very grateful to them,' Bugliosi stated. 'Without them, the book would not be a New York Times bestseller.'

"'There was a decision that was made by the media that was actually really out of sync with the demand,' Isabel MacDonald of Fairness & Accuracy in Reporting told CNN. 'With the rise of the Internet and the blogosphere, we've really seen books take off without any reviews.'

"Bugliosi insists that his book was not merely overlooked by the media because of 'Bush-bashing fatigue,' but that he was the victim of a deliberate blackout. 'I've had national coverage for every one of my other books,' he notes. 'People are extremely interested in this book, but they're terrified of it.'"

Alex Jones' InfoWars.com on July 8, 2008 also reported: "Bugliosi and his publicity team can't get him booked on Today or Good Morning America, let alone Countdown or The Colbert Report. Book review publications, so far including the New York Times (it's "under consideration"), won't write up his manuscript.

Mainstream Media Are "Sleeping With The Enemy"

Arianna Huffington, co-founder and editor-in-chief of The Huffington Post, the Internet newspaper,   bluntly accused the mainstream media of "sleeping with the enemy" in her Op-Ed on April 24, 2008 headlined "The Self-Loathing 'Liberal' Media".

The nationally syndicated columnist, author of 12 books, and in 2006 named to Time magazine's list of the world's 100 most influential people, bewailed that the mainstream, aka liberal media, instead of doing their duty as the people's watchdog, were giving aid to the enemy. She stated:

"Newsweek hires Karl Rove, the New York Times hires Bill Kristol, CNN hires Tony Snow. What is it with these media outlets? Have they been so cowed by the Right's relentless branding of them as 'liberal' that they feel compelled to show that they are not sleeping with the enemy?

"And make no mistake, Rove, Kristol, and Snow are the enemies -- of honesty, truth, facts, reality, and the public's right to know. Anything. By embracing the unabashed propagandists, the mainstream media have revealed a self-loathing streak a mile wide.

"The prerequisite for any TV pundit is credibility. Viewers won't agree with any opinion expressed, but they need to trust that the opinion expressed is not some pre-packaged PR pitch cooked up in the White House to keep us in the dark."

Huffington Blasts Mainstream Media for Complicity With Bush on Iraq War

Huffington, who established herself in the forefront of a crusade to reform journalism in the United States and declared war on the self-anointed elites of the mainstream media, followed up with another blistering Op-Ed attack on April 30, 2008 headlined: "Shameful Days: Why Won't the Media Pursue the Pentagon Propaganda Scandal?" She lamented:

"The last ten days have been the most shameful in the history of American journalism.

"On April 20th, the New York Times published its exposé of the Bush administration's use of Pentagon-approved, prepped, and financially-enriched 'military analysts' to appear on TV to help sell the invasion of Iraq, and then put a positive spin on the occupation -- even as conditions on the ground deteriorated.

"It was a powerful illustration of the Bush administration's commitment to propaganda and disinformation. But it was also a damning indictment of the mainstream media's complicity in the wholesale deception of the American public on the single most important decision a country can make -- the decision to go to war.

Scandalous Pentagon Paper of the Iraq War Meets Near-Complete News Blackout

"How big was it? John Stauber of the Center for Media and Democracy called it the Pentagon Paper of the Iraq war.

"So it stands to reason that a story this explosive would quickly become the subject of extensive follow-ups by TV and print journalists, and endless debate on the political talk shows, right? [Arianna herself is occasionally featured as a news analyst on cable TV].

"Wrong."

"Instead of opening their reportorial and analytical floodgates, the mainstream news media have all but ignored the story.

"The Times did a brief follow-up to its original story and, six days later, published a single editorial. Howard Kurtz wrote about the story the next day in his WaPo column and discussed it on CNN, Keith Obermann [MSNBC] and Wolf Blitzer [CNN] gave it brief mention. And that's about it.

"A Lexis-Nexis search turned up no other coverage of this should-be major story. Nothing from Brian Williams [NBC] or Kati Couric [CBS] or Charlie Gibson [ABC]. Nothing from Anderson Cooper or Lou Dobbs or Larry King or Campbell Brown [all of CNN]. Nothing from Chris Matthews or Dan Abrams [MSNBC]. Nothing from Tim Russert [NBC] or George Stephanopoulos [ABC] or Bob Schieffer [CBS]. Nothing from anyone on Fox News.

"This near-complete blackout imposed by the culpable news organizations is a despicable abdication of their central role in our society -- and has raised the ire of many in the blogosphere."

ABC Rejects Paid Opposition Ad During White House Health Care Presentation

A more recent example of mainstream media's pro-Obama leaning is when on June 17, 2009 ABC television network owned by Disney refused to air paid opposition advertisement during a health care presentation at the White House, which violated the fairness doctrine in news coverage.

Billed as President Obama's special promoting his administration's health care program, the paid ad would have featured alternative viewpoint on the health care issue. But the network rejected a request by the Republican National Committee to present contrary opinion.

Drudge Report disclosed that the Conservatives for Patients Rights earlier requested ABC for rates to buy a 60-second spot immediately preceding "Prescription for America". However, the network denied the request.

Rick Scott, chairman of the group, in a statement said: "It is unfortunate -- and unusual -- that ABC is refusing to accept paid advertising that would present an alternative viewpoint during the White House health care event.

"Health care is an issue that touches every American and all potential pieces of legislation have carried a price tag in excess of $1 trillion of taxpayers' money. The American people deserve a healthy, robust debate on this issue." He added:

"ABC's decision -- as of now -- to exclude even paid advertisements that present alternative view does a disservice to the public. Our organization is more than willing to purchase ad time on ABC to present an alternative viewpoint

"Our hope is that ABC will reconsider having such viewpoint be part of this crucial debate for the American people. We were surprised to hear that paid advertisements would not be accepted."

ABC network issued no explanation for its violation of the fairness doctrine in broadcasting and news coverage which is supposed to be objective and impartial. This is another black eye to the mainstream media.

Mainstream Media Enjoy a "Love Affair" and "Honeymoon" with President Obama

Still fresh in the mind of keen political observers is how the mainstream media during the 2008 presidential campaign gave the Republican Party ticket of Senator John McCain and Governor Sarah Palin a hard time and treated Democratic Party candidate Senator Barack Obama like a rock star.

Anchor Charles Gibson of ABC World News and anchor Katie Couric of CBS Evening News both used "Gotcha" strategy in their interviews of Governor Palin to trip her off, but gave Senator Obama a pass.

In their news coverage, the mainstream media were lavish in their treatment of Obama and the Democratic Party ticket, but not so with the Republican Party slate. They were virtually campaigning for him to get elected president.

Now that Barack H. Obama is president of the United States, their "love affair" has blossomed into a "honeymoon" unprecedented in the history of White House relationship with print, broadcast and Internet journalists.

And because of their cozy ties, President Obama and his Press Secretary Robert Gibbs are able to control and manipulate the mainstream media. For example, while before White House correspondents could shoot questions to the president in a free-wheeling fashion without being pre-screened, now they are pre-listed and scripted.

Veteran and legendary reporter Helen Thomas who usually ask tough questions was yanked out of the front-row seat and can no longer shoot question without prior permission. She has covered the White House since President John F. Kennedy's time.

Journalists with chummy relation with Obama or Gibbs have no problem, They enjoy their preferential treatment and don't mind being seduced by the powers that be.

The Bottom Line: Corporate Mainstream Media Owners Are In Business with the Government

In fact, media critics like Ralph Nader, Robert McChesney, Jim Hightower, Jeff Chester, Noam Chomsky, Ben Bagdikian and Amy Goodman point out that the main national networks NBC, CBS and ABC are owned and controlled by large corporate conglomerates in cahoot with the government.

They operate not to serve the cause of journalism or the public interest, but are governed by the capitalist imperatives of maximizing profits for the investors, stockholders, and advertisers. They don't care about truth in news reporting. Their corporate agenda dictates they must side with the government on burning issues to do good business.

The impact of Corporate Media government propaganda on world events is alarming. A research that the Centre for Public Integrity conducted after

9/11 shows that the Bush administration made over 935 false statements about Saddam Hussein's weapons of mass destruction and threat to U.S. national security.

During the next two-year period the mainstream media reported as facts without checking their veracity false statements the White House, CIA, FBI and other U.S. officials had made in support of the Afghanistan and Iraq wars.

Thus in effect the corporate media conspired with the Bush-Cheney government by serving as its propaganda outlets to justify their illegal invasions and occupations that violated international laws.

Corporate media owners do good business with the government, especially in times of war. The best example is General Electric which owns NBC, CNBC, MSNBC, Telemundo, Bravo, and Universal Studios as part of its $43 billion media empire.

Wars Are Big Business for General Electric Media Empire

General Electric or GE, for short, makes household appliances, plastics, water treatment systems, lighting, medical equipment, etc. But more than these, GE is one of the world's top three producers of jet engines, supplying Boeing, Lockheed Martin and other military aircraft makers for the powering of airplanes and helicopters.

Wars are good business for GE. The Bush-Cheney illegal, immoral and phony wars on terror in Iraq and Afghanistan have increased GE's military contracts and revenues to $134.2 billion in 2003.

GE has designed 91 nuclear power plants in 11 countries which have been questioned for their "fatal flaw." Yet the U.S. Nuclear Regulatory Commission continues to license GE nuclear reactors. With GE, it pays to be a good business partner of the government.

Not to be outdone, the Fox News of Rupert Murdoch brazenly served as the Republican propaganda machine of war criminals George W. Bush and Richard "Dick" Cheney while they were in power in 2000-2008.

The conservative news cable network led by talk show hosts Bill O'Reilly and Sean Hannity mouthed Bush-Cheney propaganda and attacked the then opposition Democratic Party. At one point in 2006 Hannity, along with other radio guys, even went to the White House and received talking points from no less than President Bush himself on how to propagandize his phony war on terror.

Now Fox News appears to be the only news outlet that is fiscalizing the Obama administration as the mainstream, aka liberal media, have replaced Fox News as the propaganda mouthpiece of the government in reverse role.

Today's Journalists Have Become Subdued and
Compromised Lapdogs -- Helen Thomas

The last say on this subject comes from legendary journalist Helen Thomas, who more than any other media practitioners in Washington has been around for 60 years. She is currently a columnist and reporter for the

Hearst Newspapers, a long-time member of the White House Press Corps, former bureau chief for United Press International, and bestselling author of four books.

She used to start and end presidential press conferences at the White House in recognition of her iconic stature for her continuous coverage of the nation's premier news assignment since the time of President John F. Kennedy in 1960, and has covered all other presidents since then.

Thomas is coming up with her latest book titled Watchdogs of Democracy?: The Waning Washington Press Corps and How It Has Failed the Public, which says a lot.

She asks tough questions of presidents and never defers to them, unlike most other reporters during the Bush regime and now the Obama administration. So not surprisingly, Thomas has bad opinion of her colleagues in the mainstream media.

In a succinct statement, Thomas said, "Without an informed people, there can be no democracy."

As one Washington observer puts it, "Thomas delivers a hard-hitting manifesto on the precipitous decline in the quality and ethics of political reportage -- and issues a clarion call for change.

"In the course of more than sixty years spent covering Washington politics, Helen Thomas has witnessed firsthand a raft of fundamental changes in the way news is gathered and reported. Gone are the days of flying in Air Force One with JFK, as she once did.

"Now, Thomas sees a growing -- and alarming -- reluctance among reporters to question the government and probe for the truth. The result has been a wholesale failure by journalists to fulfill what is arguably their most vital role in contemporary American life -- to be the watchdogs of democracy.

"Today's journalists, to hear Thomas tell it, have become subdued, compromised lapdogs."

Well, there you have it. The naked truth -- the news behind the news -- of the shameful state of American journalism today. Too bad there is no more Joseph Pulitzer around.

• OBAMA VOWED TO CHANGE WASHINGTON. INSTEAD, WASHINGTON HAS CHANGED HIM

President Obama is an astute disciple of history. He knows the subject at heart. During his inauguration as president, he even swore on the same Bible that President Lincoln had used, and the symbolism couldn't be sweeter.

Obama is also a constitutional lawyer, having taught on the subject at Harvard. So he knows what is legal and what is illegal, what is constitutional and what is unconstitutional, or what are violations of international laws. Make no mistake about that.

As legendary journalist Helen Thomas -- who has covered all presidents since John F. Kennedy -- puts it, "President Obama is very smooth."

So why the hell would he embrace war criminals George W. Bush's and Dick Cheney's illegal, immoral and phony wars in Iraq and Afghanistan as his own, in light of the historical lesson of the Vietnam war?

Obama knows that four of his predecessors -- John Kennedy, Lyndon Johnson, Richard Nixon, and Gerald Ford -- failed to win that Indochina conflict. So what makes him think that he could win where they all failed? Does he really think that he is more super-duper than them?

Not really, Obama is that smart. So again it is asked, why is he doing this?

His sudden transformation from antiwar to pro-war is puzzling to many, including his own supporters. But in a closer look at Obama the president and politician, not the Obama the presidential candidate, one might find the answer to this paradoxical question.

Obama is Like Dr. Jekyll and Mr. Hyde With Split Personalities

Like we said in our recent online regular column "Mr. President", Obama is like Dr. Jekyll and Mr. Hyde with split personalities.

It is a horror film about the strange tale of Dr. Jekyll who experiments with drug that turns him from a mild-mannered man of science into a crude homicidal maniac Mr. Hyde, and back. Which shows that within each man lurks impulses for both good and evil.

Or President Obama can also be likened to a two-faced Janos, a Greek deity. or to a Chameleon lizard with a projectile tongue and the ability to change color or blend into any color, thus fooling the onlooker.

Simply stated, Obama is a Democrat who now walks and quacks like a Republican duck. As iconic White House journalist Helen Thomas also lamented during a radio interview on June 18, 2009 by Ron Reagan of Air America, "I really regret that he [Obama] is following in the footsteps of [President] Bush on Iraq and Afghanistan."

The transformation of President Obama from antiwar to pro-war advocate in violation of his pre-election pledge to end the "stupid" Iraq war as soon as possible, apparently took place after he received highly classified briefings on defense and national security after his election, which is a traditional government practice during a change of administration.

During such closed-door classified briefings, U.S, defense, security, intelligence, military officials and think tank advisers no doubt laid their cards on the table and told new President Obama the bottom line: Immediate pullout from Iraq and Afghanistan is not an option.

The reason is that the United States is already deeply embedded in the infrastructures, economies, and oil industries of Iraq and Afghanistan, so much so that U.S. withdrawal would result in huge financial losses in gains and investments, as well as projects for hordes of 250,000 war contractors who benefit from no-bid contracts by billions of dollars.

After all, in Iraq the Bush-Cheney Mafia clique has already privatized its economy and oil industry, while in Afghanistan the two still unindicted war criminals have already built pipeline project across Afghanistan for their buddy and oil corporation Unocal that needs continued U.S. protection.

With this bottom line situation pounded on President Obama's head during such classified intelligence and national security briefings, with so much at stake, could he now in conscience let the United States down in Iraq and Afghanistan?

The "Invisible Government" of Top Lobbyists in Washington

This is where the "Invisible Government" that controls Washington comes in. It is composed of elite and exclusive club of top lobbyists who contribute political campaign funds to both Democratic and Republican candidates for the White House and Congress and thus, in effect, decide United States elections.

It doesn't matter which of the two major political parties is in power. The "Invisible Government" has a proven magic formula to actually call the shots and expand its imperialistic and business tentacles in foreign countries like Iraq and Afghanistan.

It was behind World War One, World War Two, the Korean war, the Vietnam war, and now Iraq and Afghanistan wars. In fact, the United States has been involved in countless wars and up to now has military bases all over the world. Why is that.

President Dwight Eisenhower, himself a five-star general in World War Two, in his last farewell address to the nation, warned against the danger of letting this mighty Military-Industrial Corporate Complex composed of war weapons producers and manufacturers control Washington.

Why? Because they rob the national treasury of billions of dollars in no-bid war contracts and overpricing with no oversight due to their closeness, political and business partnership with the powers that be. In fact, they also own and control the mainstream media.

While campaigning for president last year, Obama attacked the Olé Old Club in Washington and politics as usual. Now that he is part of the Establishment, he has changed his tune. Is it like, all for one and one for all, or birds of the same feather flock together.

Obama vowed to change Washington. Instead, Washington has changed him.

• SUMMING UP: WILL BUSH AND CHENEY GET AWAY WITH WAR CRIMES?

By historical precedent, branded war criminals George W. Bush and Richard "Dick" Cheney should be indicted for war crimes by the United Nations for illegally invading and occupying Iraq and Afghanistan and violating international laws while president and vice president of the United States in 2000-2008, just as war criminals of World War Two were dealt with at the Nuremberg and Tokyo war crimes trials.

UN Secretary-General Ban Ki-moon of South Korea, and before him his predecessor Kofi Annan of Ghana, have been swamped by petitions to do just that. However, to understand why up to now Bush and Cheney have not yet been prosecuted for war crimes, if at all, despite overwhelming evidence of their guilt, it is therefore necessary to know more about the UN, how it is structured, how it operates relating to war crimes and human rights violations, what is its performance record so far, and know the status of past and current war crimes trials.

UN History at a Glance

Formerly the United Nations Organization (UNO), the United Nations (UN) was founded in 1945 to replace the League of Nations which had failed to prevent World War Two. U.S. President Franklin Delano Roosevelt and British Prime Minister Winston Churchill actually used the name in reference to the Allies during the war with a January 1942 Declaration by the United Nations even before its formal ratification.

The UN officially came into existence on October 24, 1945 after its Charter was ratified by five permanent members of the Security Council -- the Republic of China, France, Soviet Union, United Kingdom, United States -- and by majority of then 46 member-state signatories.

The permanent members (or their successor states) of the UN Security Council with veto power were the main victors of World War Two. Thereafter the People's Republic of China replaced the Republic of China in 1971, and Russia replaced the Soviet Union in 1991.

In the 1950s the United Nations replaced the United Nations Organization as member states got used to calling it by the shorter name.

As an international organization whose members have now grown to 192, the United Nations aims to facilitate cooperation among countries in international law, international security, economic development, social progress, and human rights issues by providing a platform for dialogue.

The UN headquarters is based in New York City which is considered an international territory. The UN is mainly divided into the General Assembly, the Security Council, the Economic and Social Council, the Secretariat, and the International Court of Justice, which is the UN primary judicial organ.

The UN is financed from assessed and voluntary contributions from member states. Major contributions to the regular budget are: United States, 22%; Japan, 19.47%; Germany, 8.66%; United Kingdom, 6.13%; France, 6.03%; Italy, 4..89%; Canada, 2.81%; Spain, 2.52%; China, 2.05%; Mexico, 1.88%; Australia, 1.59%; and Brazil, 1.52%.

The operating budget is $4.19 billion. Other expenditures include $5 billion for Missions for Peace and Security, with 70,000 troops for 17 missions around the world.

General Assembly

The UN General Assembly is the main deliberative body composed of member states. It meets in regular yearly sessions under a president elected from among member states. Over a two-week period at the start of each session, all members have the opportunity to address the assembly.

Traditionally, the Secretary-General makes the first statement, followed by the assembly president. On important issues relating to peace and security, election of members to UN organs, member admission, suspension, expulsion, and budgetary matters, a two-thirds vote majority of those present is required. On other matters, just a majority vote would suffice.

Security Council

The UN Security Council is made up of 15 member states, five with permanent seats and veto power, and 10 with temporary seats on two-year terms voted by the General Assembly on a regional basis. The Security Council president is rotated alphabetically each month.

The five permanent members of the Security Council -- China, France, Russia, United Kingdom, and United States -- have veto power over substantive but not procedural resolutions (decisions) allowing them to block adoption, but not block a debate of a resolution unacceptable to them.

Secretariat

The Secretariat is headed by the Secretary-General who is assisted by a staff of international civil servants worldwide. It provides studies, information and facilities needed by UN organs for meetings. It also carries out tasks as directed by the General Assembly, Security Council, and other UN organs.

The duties of the Secretary-General include helping resolve international disputes, administering peacekeeping operations, organizing international conferences, getting information on the implementation of Security Council resolutions (decisions), and consulting with member governments on various initiatives.

The Secretary-General may also bring to the attention of the Security Council any matter that may threaten international peace and security.

International Court of Justice

The International Court of Justice (ICJ), which is the UN primary judicial organ, is located in The Hague, Netherlands. It was established in 1945 by the UN Charter as successor to the Permanent Court of International Justice.

However, the ICJ has adopted its predecessor's statute called the Statute of the International Court of Justice as the main constitutional document constituting and regulating the court.

The purpose of the International Court of Justice is to adjudicate international disputes among nations. The ICJ has heard cases related to war crimes, illegal state interference, and ethnic cleansing.

International Criminal Court

A related court under the ICJ is called the International Criminal Court (ICC). It began operating in 2002 through discussions that the UN General Assembly had initiated.

It is the first permanent international court that is tasked with trying violators who commit the most serious crimes under international law, including war crimes, crimes against humanity, and genocide.

The International Criminal Court is functionally independent of the United Nations in terms of personnel and financing. But some meetings of the ICC governing body, the Assembly of States Parties to the Rome Statute, are held at the UN under agreement between them on how they regard each other legally.

Human Rights Council

The Human Rights Council is a relatively new UN organ that the General Assembly established in March 2006 to succeed the United Nations Commission on Human Rights. The duty of the HRC is to address human rights violations.

It has 47 members distributed by region, each serves on a three-year term and may not serve three consecutive terms, and must be approved by the majority members of the General Assembly.

UN Controversies

Chief Judge Niloufer Bhagwat of India who presided over the Tokyo "War Crimes Trial" of George W. Bush by the International Criminal Tribunal for Afghanistan that found him "guilty" of genocide in the Afghanistan war, has challenged the United Nations to revise the concept of permanent membership of the UN Security Council.

The internationally acclaimed jurist criticized the current system as "not in the interest of peaceful solution of disputes" among nations. Instead she advocated all rotational membership of the Security Council, and also proposed to enhance the powers of the General Assembly. The judge emphasized:

"The Security Council continues to reflect the historically outdated principle of 'balance of power' among Permanent members; the legacy of the Second World War, giving disproportionate status to certain governments.

"This no longer reflects the real world and its democratic aspiration. As a consequence, the Security Council at crucial moments has either been paralyzed or has been utilized to camouflage military occupations of countries in private interests.

"The General Assembly of the United Nations, where the democratic principle prevails, must assume its rightful role in the resolution of conflicts. The Security Council should function on a rotational principle, and the concept of permanent membership be abolished, to restore democracy in the world body, reflecting the 21st Century realities."

Judge Bhagwat said that adherence to the letter and spirit of Article 33 of the UN Charter must be followed. She concluded:

"Article 33 of the United Nations Charter provides for mediation, conciliation, arbitration and adjudication prior to resort to war. Any legal defense or justification by any government of waging a "just" war must be subject to the test of Article 33 as to whether these alternative dispute mechanisms were resorted to. The Security Council and the General Assembly must secure compliance."

The United Nations has not acted on the proposal.

• U.S. Boycotted, Then Joins UN Human Rights Council

The Bush administration in 2006 shunned the newly formed UN Human Rights Council and accused it of admitting member states with bad human rights records like Cuba and Libya, The U.S. also charged the council with anti-Israel bias.

Based in Geneva, the 47-member council replaced the UN Commission on Human Rights which had widely been observed as ineffective in dealing with violations.

The Obama administration has reversed the Bush policy. In May 2009 Secretary of State Hillary Clinton and U.S. Ambassador to the UN Susan Rice both announced the U.S. decision to join the Human Rights Council.

Subsequently the United States has been elected to a seat on the UN Human Rights Council for the first time since its creation in 2006, along with 17 other countries.

After the vote, BBC reported Rice said the U.S. was not blind to the council's flaws, stating:

"Obviously there will always be some countries whose respect and record on human rights is sub-part." She added:

"We have not been perfect ourselves but we intend to lead based on the strong principled vision that the American people have about respecting human rights [and] supporting democracy."

• Other Controversies

The United States and the United Nations have had other controversies in the past. In the 1950s the John Birch Society launched a "Get US Out the UN" campaign charging that its aim was to establish a "One World Government."

In 1967 Richard Nixon while campaigning for president criticized the UN as "obsolete and inadequate" in dealing with international crises like the Cold War.

President Ronald Reagan's ambassador to the UN, Jeane Kirkpatrick, in a New York Times opinion piece, charged that the Security Council's discussion process "more resembles a mugging" of the U.S. "than either a political debate or an effort at problem-solving."

President Bush, in a February 2003 speech just before the U.S. invasion of Iraq, after failing to get UN approval, declared: "Free nations will not allow the the United Nations to fade into history as an ineffective, irrelevant debating society."

In 2005 Bush appointed John R. Bolton as acting ambassador to the UN although he had criticized the UN in 1994, saying: "There is no such thing as the United Nations. There is only the international community which can only be led by the only remaining superpower, which is the United States."

UN Failures in Security Issues

In many cases some UN members refuse to enforce Security Council resolutions (decisions). Such failures are due to UN's intergovernmental nature. In many respects, it is an association of 192 member states which must reach consensus not as an independent organization.

This has led to serious security failures such as:

• Failure to prevent the 1994 Rwanda Genocide that killed a million people because the UN Security Council had not approved military action.

• Failure to implement UN Security Council Resolution 1291 to effectively intervene during the Second Congo War which killed nearly five million people in the Democratic Republic of the Congo in 1998-2002, and to distribute humanitarian aid.

• Failure to intervene in the 1995 Srebrencia Massacre despite being designated by the UN as a "safe haven" for refugees and assigned 600 Dutch peacekeepers to protect it as they were not authorized to use force.

• Failure to successfully deliver food to starving people in Somalia which were seized by warlords. A US-UN attempt to arrest them sparked the 1993 Battle of Mogadishu.

• Failure to implement provisions of the UN Security Council related to the Israeli-Palestinian conflict.

• Failure to prevent or help sufficiently in the area of Darfur genocide, crisis which, as this is written, still exists.

Criticisms Against UN Security Council

The Security Council is criticized for failure to act in clear and decisive way when confront by crises. The veto power of the five permanent members -- China, france, Russia, United Kingdom, and United States -- are cited as the cause of the problem.

However, under the interpretations of the UN Charter made into law by the General Assembly's "Uniting For Peace" Resolution adopted on November 3, 1950, the General Assembly may recommend steps necessary to restore peace and security where the Security Council, because of lack of unanimity among permanent members, failed to act on situations that threaten international peace.

The makeup of the UN Security Council dates back to the Second World War, and the division of power is often said to no longer represent the current power realities in the world.

Critics question the effectiveness and relevance of the Security Council because responsibility for enforcement of its resolutions (decisions) lies primarily with its members themselves, and there are no consequences for violating them.

How the UN Court Work

The International Criminal Court (ICC) at The Hague, Netherlands, and the Rome Statute provides for the tribunal to have jurisdiction over genocide, war crimes, and crimes against humanity.

Article 7 of the Treaty states that for the purpose of this Statute, "crime against humanity" means any of the following acts when committed as part of a widespread or systematic attack directed against any civilian population, with knowledge of the attack:

(a) Murder;
(b) Extermination;
(c) Enslavement;
(d) Deportation;
(e) Imprisonment or other severe deprivation of physical liberty in violation of fundamental rules of international law;
(f) Torture;
(g) Rape, sexual slavery, enforced prostitution, forced pregnancy, enforced sterilization, or any other form of sexual violence of comparable gravity;
(h) Persecution against any identifiable group or collectively on political, racial, national, ethnic, cultural, religious, and gender as defined in Paragraph 3, or other grounds that are universally recognized as impermissible under international law, in connection with any act referred to in this paragraph or any crime within the jurisdiction of the Court;
(i) Enforced disappearance of persons;
(k) Other inhumane acts of a similar character intentionally causing great suffering, or serious injury to body, mental or physical health.

The Rome Statute Explanatory Memorandum further states that crimes against humanity "are particularly odious offences in that they constitute a serious attack on human dignity or grave humiliation or degradation of one or more human beings.

"They are not isolated or sporadic events, but are part either of a government policy (although the perpetrators need not identify themselves with this policy) or of a wide practice of atrocities tolerated or condoned by a government or a de facto authority.

"However, murder, extermination, torture, rape, political, racial, or religious persecution and other inhuman acts, the threshold of crimes against humanity is if they are part of a widespread or systematic practice.

"Isolated inhumane acts of this nature may constitute grave infringements of human rights, or depending on the circumstances, war crimes, but may fall short of meriting the stigma attaching to the category of crimes."

The UN Charter

Under Article VI of the U.S. Constitution, Senate-ratified treaties such as the UN Charter are considered "a Supreme Law of the Land."

Then Secretary-General of the United Nations General Assembly, Kofi Annan, called the U.S. invasion of Iraq in 2003 "a violation of the U.N. Charter" and therefore "illegal."

Acknowledged experts on international law, Robert Parry and Marjorie Cohn, concurred with Annan. They asserted that this was not a war in self-defense but a war of aggression.

As such, it was contrary to the UN Charter and considered a crime against peace, and therefore a war crime.

A war of aggression refers to any war not initiated out of self-defense or sanction by the United Nations.

Such a violation of international law could constitute an impeachable offense [or war crime], according to Francis Boyle, John W. Dean of FindLaw, Marcus Raskin, and Joseph A. Vuckovich of the Institute for Policy Studies.

On the Iraq war, the Bush administration claimed that Iraq's firing at U.S. and British airplanes in the no-fly zones alone constituted an "Act of War" by Saddam Hussein.

Thus the United States was justified to invade and occupy Iraq as part of the U.S. Global War on Terror, Bush said.

How the UN Court is Structured

The International Criminal Court (or Tribunal) is established for a country where war crimes are alleged to have been committed. For example, if it were for Iraq, it would be called International Criminal Court (or Tribunal) for Iraq. If it were for the United States, it would be called International Criminal Court (or Tribunal) for the United States.

The UN court is made up of the Office of the Prosecutor, the Chambers, and the Registry. The Office of the Prosecutor (OTP) is independent of the UN Security Council.

Other organs of the UN court conduct investigations by collecting evidence and identifying witnesses. OTP officials are police, crimes experts, and lawyers.

Once the OTP issues indictments, it relies on the country where war crimes were committed to make the arrest.

If the Prosecutor referred a case for action before a Pre-Trial 1 Chamber, the bench would announce the Presidency of the Court. The Presiding Judge of the Pre-Trial Chamber 1 will give an oral summary of the decision to indict at a public hearing in The Hague, Netherlands.

If the chamber decided that there is sufficient evidence to establish substantial grounds to believe that a defendant was criminally responsible for the war crimes brought up, it would issue an arrest warrant.

Once arrested, the defendant is transferred to the UN court's detention centre at The Hague. Later the defendant will be required to make a first appearance before the Pre-Trial 1 Chamber.

Defendants cannot be tried in absentia. Trial proceedings can only begin once the defendant is brought to The Hague. The case can be tried in one of the UN court's three trial chambers.

Decisions can be appealed to the Appeals Chamber. Each of the trial chamber has a panel of three judges. They are selected by the UN General Assembly for a period of four years after which they can be reelected.

The Registry houses all the documents and evidence collected by the UN court or tribunal. It also manages the detention centre where defendants are held following their arrests and during trials.

Judges must determine that the defendant is guilty beyond a reasonable doubt. It takes majority of the three-judge panel to convict a defendant.

The maximum sentence is life imprisonment. Sentences will be served in one of the countries that have been approved by the UN court to house prisoners, which are Austria, France, Finland, Germany, Italy, Norway, Spain, and Sweden.

The Geneva Convention

Following what was widely believed to be Osama bin Laden's Al Qaeda terrorist attacks on the United States on September 11, 2001, better known as 9/11, President Bush designated Al Qaeda and the Taliban in Afghanistan as "unlawful" enemy combatants.

As such, he contended they were not protected as Prisoners of War under the Geneva Convention with regard to the treatment of detainees.

To address the mandatory review by a "competent tribunal" as defined by Article V of the Third Geneva Convention, Combatant Status Review Tribunals were established.

The American Bar Association, Human Rights Watch, the Council on Foreign Relations, and Joanne Mariner from FindLaw dismissed the use of the "unlawful" enemy combatant status as not compatible with U.S. and international laws.

The U.S. Congress passed the Military Commission Act of 2006 to provide a legal framework for the designation of "unlawful" enemy combatants, their detention, and trial through military commission.

The Nuremberg War Crimes Trial

After the Second World War ended in 1945 with the Allied Powers (United States, Great Britain, France, and Russia) defeating the Axis Powers (Germany, Italy and Japan), enemy war criminals were brought to trials for war crimes.

A Moscow Declaration in October 1943 signed by U.S. President Franklin Delano Roosevelt, British Prime Minister Winston Churchill, and Soviet leader Josef Stalin, called for bringing up top German officials to trials for war crimes in Nuremberg, Germany.

In their first joint declaration, the Allied powers officially noted the mass murder of European Jews in gas chambers and mass shootings which amounted to genocide.

Judges for the International Military Tribunals (IMT) were drawn from each of the Allied powers.

Between October 18, 1943 and October 1, 1946, the IMT tried 22 "major" German war criminals on charges of conspiracy to commit crimes against peace, genocide, war crimes, and crimes against humanity.

The IMT defined crimes against humanity as "murder, extermination, enslavement, deportation . . . or persecution on political, racial, or religious grounds."

Twelve of those convicted were sentenced to death by hanging. Among them were Hans Frank, Governor General of the General Government; Hermann Goering, Luftwaffe commander; Martin Bormann, Nazi Party secretary general; Wilhelm Frick, Adolf Hitler's Minister of the Interior; Alfred Rosenberg, and Julius Streicher.

Hitler escaped trial because he had committed suicide as Allied forces led by U.S. five-star General Dwight Eisenhower closed in on Berlin. (He was later elected U.S. president.)

Other war criminals were tried by the courts of those countries where thy had committed their war crimes.

The efforts of Nazi hunters such as Simon Wiesenthal and Beate Klarsfeld led to the capture, extradition and trial of Adolf Eichmann, held in Jerusalem in 1961, captured worldwide attention.

Strangely, the manhunt for other Nazi war criminals not yet captured still continues.

The Tokyo War Crimes Trials

The court proceedings last over two years from May 1946 to November 1948. All Japanese Class A war criminals were tried by the International Military Tribunals for the Far East (IMTFE) in Tokyo.

The Prosecution team was composed of justice from all Allied nations, namely: Australia, Canada, China, Great Britain, India, the Netherlands, New Zealand, the Philippines, the Soviet Union, and the United States.

Other war criminals were of lower level were tried in their respective victim countries.

Of the 80 Class A war criminals detained in the Sugano prison in Tokyo after 1948, 28 defendants were brought to trial before the IMTFE.

They included four former prime ministers, three former foreign ministers, four former war ministers, two former navy ministers, six former generals, two former ambassadors, one former admiral, and one former colonel.

The charges against them were: unprovoked war against China, waging aggressive wars against the United States, British Commonwealth, the Nothorlands, Franco (Indochina), the Philippines, the USSR, inhuman treatment of prisoners of war, and widespread atrocities.

Seven death sentences by hanging were carried out against General and Prime Minister Hideki Tojo, War Minister Itagaki Seishiro, Foreign Minister Hirota Koki, Air Commander Doihara Kenji, Muto Akira, commander of Philippine Expeditionary Force; General Kimura Heitaro, commander of

Burma Expeditionary Force; and General Watsui Iwane, commander of the Shanghai Expeditionary Force.

Their war crimes occurred during a period of Japanese imperialism and were notorious and labeled as "Asian Holocaust" along with the "Rape of Nanking" and the "Rape of Manila."

Slobodan Milosevic War Crimes Trial

The trial of deposed President Slobodan Milosevic of Serbia (formerly Yugoslavia) at the UN International Criminal Tribunal for the former Yugoslavia (ICTY) at The Hague, Netherlands, was the first international war crimes trial since the Nuremberg and Tokyo war crimes trials after the Second World War.

The ICTY was established by a resolution of the UN Security Council in 1993 and funded by the UN General Assembly. Although thousands of soldiers were involved in atrocities, the tribunal was charged with prosecuting only those ultimately responsible for having ordered those crimes.

The Tribunal's powers included jurisdiction over war crimes since 1991 in the former Yugoslavia and had authority to prosecute grave breaches of the Geneva Convention of 1949, violations of law and customs of war like murder and other crimes committed against those who were not involved in military hostilities, genocide like murder and other crimes committed with the intent to destroy a national ethnic or religious group, and crimes against humanity like murder and other crimes committed against civilians, populations, before or during the war, on political, racial or religious grounds.

Milosevic was the first sitting head of state to be indicted by a United Nations international tribunal of justice. He was charged with 60 counts for crimes against humanity, genocide, and war crimes committed during the Balkan war of the 1990s in which tens of thousands of Bosnian Muslims were killed or forced to flee.

Because of the gravity of his war crimes, the nationalistic dictator was nicknamed the "Butcher of the Balkans."

But on March 11, 2006, on the 5th year of Milosevic's trial for war crimes in Serbia, while jailed at the UN detention centre at The Hague, he was found dead in his prison cell.

Congo War Crimes Trial

On January 29, 2007 the Pre-Trial Chamber 1 of the International Criminal Court (ICC) operating under the auspices of the United Nations, confirmed the three charges brought by the Prosecutor against Thomas Lubanga Dyilo, former militia leader of the Forces Patriotiques pour la Liberation du Congo.

Judge Claude Jorda of France gave an oral summary of the decision at a public hearing held in The Hague. The chamber decided that there was sufficient evidence to establish substantial grounds to believe that the defendant was criminally responsible for the war crimes of enlisting and conscripting of children under the age of 15 years into his FPLE, the military wing of the Union des Patriotes Congolais (UPC) and using them to participate actively in hostilities in Ituri (Democratic Republic of the Congo) from September 2002 to August 13, 2003.

On February 10, 2006, the Pre-Trial Chamber 1 issued a court warrant for Dyilo's arrest. After he was nabbed, he was transferred to the UN Court's Detention Centre at The Hague. On March 20, Dyilo made his first appearance before Pre-Trial Chamber 1.

The other judges were Akura Kuenyehia of Ghana, and Sylvia Steiner of Brazil. The Pre-Trial Chamber 1 heard the submissions of participants and observations of legal representatives of victims during the confirmation hearing held on November 9 to 28, 2006.

Rwanda War Crimes Trials

The UN International Criminal Tribunal for Rwanda (ICTR) was created on November 8, 1994 by the UN Security Council to try people responsible for acts of genocide and other violations of international law in Rwanda by Rwandan citizens in nearby states.

The UN Security Council decided to conduct the Tribunal in Arusha, Tanzania, where the African Court on Human and Peoples' Rights was also located.

The Tribunal's jurisdiction included genocide, crimes against humanity, and war crimes, which were defined as violations of Common Article Three and Additional Protocol II of the Geneva Conventions dealing with war crimes committed during internal conflicts.

So far, the Tribunal has finished 21 trials and convicted 28 accused persons. Another 11 trials were in progress. Fourteen in detention are waiting for trials. Eighteen others are still at large.

The first trial of Jean-Paul Akayesu began in 1997. Jean Kambanda, interim prime minister, pleaded guilty.

The trial established precedents that rape is a crime of genocide. The Trial Chamber held that "sexual assault formed an integral part in the process of destroying the Tutsi ethnic group and that the rape was systematic and had been perpetrated against Tutsi women only, thus manifesting the specific intent required for those act to constitute genocide."

Presiding Judge Navanethem Pillay said in a statement after the verdict: "From time immemorial, rape has been regarded as spoils of war. Now it will be considered a war crime. We want to send out a strong message that rape is no longer a trophy of war."

News Media Accused of Genocide

A trial against "Hate Media" was also held and it began on October 23, 2000. It was charged with the prosecution of the media which encouraged the genocide of 1994.

On August 19, 2003, the ICTR urged life sentence for Ferdinand Nahimana and Jean Bosco Barayagwiza, persons in charge of Radio Television Libre des Mille Collines, as well as Hassan Ngeze, director and editor of the Kangur newspaper.

They were charged with genocide, incitement to genocide, and crimes against humanity, before and during period of the genocide in 1994.

On December 3, 2003, the UN court found all 13 defendants guilty and sentenced Nahimana and Ngeze to life imprisonment, and Barayagwiza to 35 years in prison. The verdict has been appealed.

The United Nations on Iraq and Afghanistan

In the backdrop of the war crimes trials in Nuremberg and Tokyo after Second World War, and also in the wake of contemporary and current war crimes trials in progress, it is now asked, how has the United Nations acted on the U.S. invasions and occupations of Iraqi and Afghanistan during the Bush administration in 2000-2008?

Will the UN consider petitions it has received urging that George W. Bush and Richard "Dick" Cheney be indicted for war crimes on charges that U.S. military forces under their command had committed genocidal killings and mass destructions in those two countries?

The United Nations, as stated earlier, has had both successes and failures in resolving international disputes among member countries and preserving peace and order in the world. As also previously noted, the UN is politics-ridden just like the U.S. Congress, if not more.

By its very nature, the United Nations has to combine diplomacy with politics to achieve harmony and survive. That is the bottom line. It is no longer what is right or wrong, or what is true of false.

So not surprisingly to keen observers, the UN has supported the U.S. invasions and occupations of Iraq and Afghanistan on the strength of its public policy pronouncements. But it is hard to believe that the UN is blind to the truth that later showed they were aggressively waged on great deceptions and motivated by oil and war profit.

Truth Behind the United Nations Façade

Sadly, the United Nations seems to have lost its backbone and moral leadership. But like it or not and despite its failures and shortcomings, the UN is still the best and perhaps the only hope for world peace and security in the absence of a better alternative.

Yet the UN has kept quiet and has not acted on the various petitions it has received from concerned international groups that have repeatedly urged it to form an International Criminal Tribunal for the United States (ICTUS to indict Bush and Cheney on charges of war crimes.

The reason, of course, is obvious. The UN Security Council has jurisdiction over such ticklish issue. The decision is actually in the hands of its five permanent members with veto power -- China, France. Russia, United Kingdom, and the United States.

Just one No vote of the United States is enough to kill any proposed Resolution to indict Bush and Cheney for war crimes. So those petitions sent to UN Secretary-General Ki-moon and before him to his predecessor Kofi Annan, were dead on arrival.

The United Nations is caught in the crossfire between those who demand that Bush and Cheney be indicted by a UN court for war crimes, and the United States, its premier member and landlord of the UN headquarters in New York City, and reputedly the world's remaining superpower,

This explains why the United Nations is pretending to see nothing, hear nothing, and know nothing about what the United States has really done and is still doing in Iraq and Afghanistan. The UN has had enough problems with the U.S. before, and apparently it does not want more of the same.

This is evident when at first then UN Secretary-General Kofi Annan in March 2003 condemned the U.S. invasion of Iraq as a violation of the UN Charter, which the Security Council did not approve. Yet later his public statement condemning the attack has disappeared from UN official record. Was his statement intentionally deleted?

Obama is Playing it Smart by Looking Forward and Not Backward

President Obama's website change.gov spells out his program of government, which is impressive. But it is in his live media interviews and public speeches that provide more food for thought and cause for debate.

On Iraq and Afghanistan, the Obama administration "will responsibly end the war in Iraq so that we can renew our military strength, dedicate more resources to the fight against the Taliban and al Qaeda in Afghanistan, and invest in our economy at home."

On Iraq withdrawal, the Obama administration "believe we must be as careful getting out of Iraq as we were careless getting in . . . Military experts believe we can safely redeploy combat brigades from Iraq at a pace of 1 to 2 brigades a month -- which would remove all of them in 16 months. That would be the summer of 2010 -- more than 7 years after the war began."

On Afghanistan, the Obama administration will "Find, disrupt and destroy al Qaeda . . . Responsibly end the war in Iraq and focus on the right battlefield in Afghanistan. Work with other nations to strengthen their capacity to eliminate shared enemies."

On al Qaeda, the Obama administration will "defeat al Qaeda in the battle of ideas by returning to an American foreign policy consistent with America's traditional values, and work with moderates within the Islamic world to counter al Qaeda propaganda."

On war crimes that the Bush-Cheney administration had committed in the Iraq and Afghanistan wars and occupations, President Obama said: "I don't believe that anybody is above the law. On the other hand, I also have a belief that we need to look forward as opposed to looking backwards."

Obama is Like Dr. Jekyll and Mr. Hyde With Split Personalities

It is worth repeating what legendary White House journalist Helen Thomas succinctly said of President Obama that he is "very smooth," but "I regret that he is following in the footsteps of [President George W.] Bush on Iraq and Afghanistan," during an interview on June 18, 2009 by Ron Reagan on Air America radio program."

Another comment, this time from the blogosphere, stated, "Face the Facts: Obama is a Neocon. Like most of my fellow progressives, my attitude towards Obama has gone from cautious optimism to ambivalence to disdain and now to disgust. He's slicker than Bush, but not very much better in most respects.

"He won the primaries as a progressive, the general election as a centrist, and is now ruling as a neocon," which is short for a moderate conservative who generally opposes big government but supports social welfare and certain other liberal goals.

Our own take on President Obama is stated in our online regular column "Mr. President" which follows:

MR. PRESIDENT:

Right now you are still popular and smell like a rose. But if you refuse to learn from history, you would be digging your own political grave and end up a one-term president just like Jimmy Carter.

You are committing the same mistakes of your predecessors. From anti-war, you have become pro-war. How times have changed. How you have changed, Mr. President.

Suddenly, you are no longer the candidate Barack H. Obama that the American people knew. As president, you have become like a Dr. Jekyll and Mr. Hyde with split personalities.

If you recall, that is a horror film about the strange tale of Dr. Jekyll who experiments with drug that turns him from a mild-mannered man of science into a crude homicidal maniac Mr. Hyde, and back. Which shows that within each man lurks impulses for both good and evil.

Pardon the analogy, Mr. President. It is hoped this jolts you a little, if at all.

Voters elected you president last year because you called the Iraq war "stupid" and promised to end it as soon as possible. But as this is written, the House just passed a $106 billion bill to further fund the wars in Iraq and Afghanistan. The Senate, of course, is expected to also approve such war funding.

Before the close 226-202 vote, you and Treasury Secretary Timothy F. Geithner forced some of 51 Democrats opposed to the bill to support it. Earlier Speaker Nancy Pelosi (D-Calif.) strongly pressured her colleagues to back the measure in a closed-door meeting. And voila, it is approved!

U.S. Is Fighting the Wrong Wars for the Wrong Reasons

Unfortunately, as the new war president you are creating your own Vietnam in Iraq and Afghanistan. That can only lead to disaster. For like Vietnam, they are unwinnable wars. Four American presidents -- John

Kennedy, Lyndon Johnson, Richard Nixon, and Gerald Ford -- all failed in that war.

Unless the U.S. pulled out without further delay, Iraq and Afghanistan might surpass Vietnam (1960-1975) as the longest and costliest wars in U.S. history.

Mr. President, what makes you think you can succeed where your four predecessors failed? The United States is fighting the wrong wars for the wrong reasons in Iraq and Afghanistan where there is no end in sight. The Bush regime created fear of and defense against terrorism as the excuse, which is a great deception.

In Vietnam, the U.S. magnified the fear of communism to attack North Vietnam, which was also a great deception. In both wars, behind the great deceptions is the U.S. Military-Industrial Corporate Complex designed to expand imperialistic and business tentacles in foreign lands and profit from wars.

Mr. President, many wonder why you have changed and broken your pre-election promise to end the wars in Iraq and Afghanistan. That makes you no different from war criminals George W. Bush and Richard Cheney. Under your own war policy, more American soldiers have died and more will die.

In your hands are the blood of those victims of war crimes who had been misled that they were fighting to protect America from terrorist attack or to help Muslim nations gain their freedom from dictators, which of course is also a myth.

Mr. President, you have disregarded the warning of President Eisenhower who in his farewell address to the nation warned against the danger of allowing the U.S. Military-Industrial Corporate Complex to control Washington as some sort of "Invisible Government."

As you should very well know, this moneyed and powerful "Invisible Government" is composed of top lobbyists that contribute campaign funds to both Democratic and Republican leaders in and out of Congress, and influence the outcome of elections.

Mr. President, you should know that they are behind the wars in Iraq and Afghanistan where their hordes of war contractors -- 250,000 -- have even increased under your administration. What does that mean? It means, like during Bush's time, no-bid war contracts continue to make wars their milking cow, so to speak.

According to new statistics that the Pentagon has released, under your watch the number of mercenaries and armed contractors in Iraq and Afghanistan has increased. Under you as the new commander-in-chief, there is a 23% increase in the number of Private Security Contractors in Iraq.

In Afghanistan, in the oooond quarter of 2009 there is a 29% increase in the number of such Private Security Contractors working for the Department of Defense. Companies like Blackwater and its successor Triple Canopy work on State Department contracts.

According to the same statistics, there is no limit to the number of contractors that can be deployed in the war zone, Mr. President. This looks like war expansion, not reduction. So it is asked, is your stated 2010 timetable for pullout of Iraq for real, or just a big joke?

Or will the United States be stuck in the quagmire of Iraq and Afghanistan wars indefinitely? Hope not. But have a nice day, Mr. President.

Obama May Let Bush and Cheney Get Away with War Crimes

Just as Speaker Nancy Pelosi let Bush and Cheney get away with impeachment in the 110th Congress and violated her campaign pledge to voters and her duty under the Constitution to uphold the law, President Obama -- by his enigmatic stance of looking forward and not backward -- is likely to shun prosecuting them for war crimes, which is also violative of his sworn duty under Article I of the Constitution which mandates that he "faithfully execute the office of President of the United States and, to the best of his ability, preserve, protect, and defend the Constitution . . ."

Of course President Obama has good reason to avoid a protracted legal and political battle that would surely embroil him if his administration were involved in a government move to prosecute Bush and Cheney for war crimes, either in the United Nations which is not possible because the United States is a permanent member with veto power in the UN Security Council which has jurisdiction over war crimes, or in the United States as famed California prosecutor Vincent Bugliosi has advocated in his bestselling book, The Prosecution of George W. Bush For Murder.

Obama's top priority is solving the nation's current economic and financial crisis, universal healthcare, immigration and the wars in Iraq and Afghanistan along with Pakistan. His foreign policy concerns also focus on North Korea, Iran, the Israeli-Palestinian conflict, and other troubled spots.

Naturally, Obama's long-range goal is his reelection as president in 2012. That will keep him busy for the next four years and has therefore no apparent interest in prosecuting Bush and Cheney for war crimes.

Prosecuting Bush and Cheney in the United States for War Crimes Looms as a Possibility

So after all has been said and done on the issue of whether or not George W. Bush and Richard "Dick" Cheney should be prosecuted for murder and war crimes they committed in Iraq and Afghanistan while president and vice president of the United States in 2000-2008, may well be resolved right in the United States.

Vincent Bugliosi in Chapter 1 of his book said: "The book you are about to read deals with what I believe to be the most serious crime ever committed in American history -- the president of this nation, George W. Bush, knowingly and deliberately taking this country to war in Iraq under false pretenses, a war that condemned over 100,000 human beings, including 4,000 young American soldiers, to horrible, violent deaths. That, of course, is the most serious consequence of Bush's monumentally criminal behavior behavior. But let's not forget that, additionally, thousands upon thousands of people have suffered injuries that have disabled them for life, hundreds of thousands of humans have sustained psychic damage from the war, and literally hundreds upon hundreds of thousands of people will involuntarily re-create in their mind's eye, over and over again, what happened to their loved ones. Assuming Bush's guilt for the sake of argument at this point, if what he did is not the greatest crimes ever committed by any public official or private citizen in this nation's history, then I ask you, what is?"

Bugliosi produced a map of the United States that shows U.S. deaths in Iraq from all corners of the nation, with the following statement: "The preferable venue for the prosecution of George W. Bush for murder and conspiracy to commit murder would be in the nation's capital, with the prosecutor being the Attorney General of the United States acting through his Department of Justice. This book, however, establishes jurisdiction for any state attorney general (or any district attorney in any county of a state) to bring murder and conspiracy charges against Bush for any soldiers from that state or county who lost their lives fighting Bush's war, which as you can see applies to every state in this nation. Since the date of this map, March 15, 2007, hundreds of other United States soldiers have died in the war."

Under the law, there is no Statute of Limitations for murder charges. So federal or state prosecutors can pursue them at any time. That means Bush and Cheney can still be indicted for murder charges in United States criminal courts arising from their war crimes although they are no longer president and vice president.

31

Osama bin Laden Executed Upon Capture Without Court Trial and Fed to Sharks After Muslim Ceremonial Burial

MR. PRESIDENT:

As the commander-in-chief you get the credit for the death of Osama bin Laden, the mastermind of the September 11, 2001 terrorist attacks on the United States. You succeeded where your predecessor George W. Bush in seven years had failed.

You ordered a Navy Seal force to go ahead and raid the suspected secret hideout of the U.S. public enemy No. 1 in Abbottabad, Pakistan, based on intelligence information and after much dress rehearsal.

It was a bold gamble on your part and it paid off. Congratulations!

However, it is disturbing to note that Bin Laden was executed in his bedroom although he was unarmed and did not reach for a weapon. He also did not resist capture and had no bodyguard.

Yet the Seal shot him to death in the head and leg in the presence of his wife and children. They dragged his body down to a helicopter and brought it to the Arabian Sea. After a ceremonial burial in accordance with Muslim tradition they dumped and fed it to the sharks.

Mr. President, apparently the elite Navy Seal was given an order to shoot to kill. In contrast, Iraq's dictator Saddam Hussein was captured hiding in a ground hole. He was tried in court, found guilty of war crimes and sentenced to death, while Bin Laden was executed upon his capture without a court trial.

While the people of the United States have reason to rejoice over his death, including us, yet the way he died leaves a stigma on the American system of justice.

A White House statement Tuesday was a change in the official account that raised questions about whether the U.S. had ever planned to capture Bin Laden alive.

The Obama administration was still debating whether to release gruesome images of his corpse, balancing efforts to demonstrate to the world that he was dead against the risk that the images could provoke further anti-U.S. sentiment. But CIA Director Leon Panetta said a photograph would be released.

"I don't think there was any question that ultimately a photograph would be presented to the public," Panetta said in an interview with "NBC Nightly News." Asked again later by The Associated Press, he said, "I think it will."

Asked about the final confrontation with Bin Laden, Panetta said: "I don't think he had a lot of time to say anything." The CIA chief told PBS News Hour, "It was a firefight going up that compound. I think it was all split-second action on the part of the SEALs."

Panetta said that Bin Laden had made "some threatening moves that were made that clearly represented a clear threat to our guys. And that's the reason they fired."

The SEALs were back in the U.S. at Andrews Air Force Base outside Washington for debriefing on the raid, lawmakers said after meeting with Panetta.

The question of how to present Bin Laden's death to the world is a difficult balancing act for the White House.

President Obama told Americans that justice had been done, but the White House also declared that Bin Laden's body was treated respectfully and laid to rest in a somber ceremony at sea.

Panetta underscored that Obama had given permission to kill the terrorist leader: "The authority here was to kill Bin Laden," he said, "under the rules of engagement they have authority to kill him."

May 5, 2011, Philpress

32

Sentenced to Death by Hanging, At Least Saddam Hussein's Head Is Not Chopped Off

MR. PRESIDENT:

In another era, Saddam Hussein would have been beheaded. But Iraq is no France of old where once upon a time heads rolled like domino.

History in fact is replete with grim tales of dictators and monarchs who ruled by the sword and perished by the sword.

In 1793, for instance, the victorious leaders of the French revolution beheaded King Louis XVI and Marie Antoinette on the guillotine at a public square in Paris.

The Revolutionary Tribunal sat without recess daily as the terror of reprisal continued for 14 months. One of those whose head was chopped off was the famous Madam Roland who, at the threshold of death, uttered her now classic curse:

"O liberte! Que de crimes on commet dans ton nom!" ("O Liberty! How many crimes are committed in thy name!")

Soon even the advocates of the guillotine were themselves executed by the same dreaded head chopper after the very people for whose cause they had fought, revolted against them.

Thus the vicious cycle continued. In 1794 another famous victim named Danton, as he faced the guillotine, ruefully recalled:

"It was about this season of the year when I caused the Revolutionary Tribunal to be set up. I ask forgiveness of God and men."

Then turning to Robespierre, his executioner and new architect of the guillotine, in the face of death Danton, exclaimed: "Infamous Robespierre, the scaffold claims you! You will follow me!"

A few months later Robespierre did — the 16,800th victim of the French guillotine.

In Saddam Hussein's death, does it really matter if he died by hanging or by guillotine? Should he been executed as a prisoner of war and not like a common criminal? As captured president of an invaded and conquered nation?

So what? When one is dead he is dead, right?

There is no question that Saddam Hussein deserved to die for killing his own people. Yet the United States and Iraq cannot escape from the more serious question, was he given a fair trial?

Let us stop kidding ourselves. Throughout his trial by an Iraqi court that handed out the death sentence he was actually in the custody of the American military. He was turned over to the Iraq government only after the judicial process was severely criticized as a violation of international law.

So did the United States railroad his trial and conviction as befit a victor in what *Washington Post* author Bob Woodward in his books labelled "Plan of Attack" and "Bush War"? It looked like it.

What Saddam Hussein got was revenge, not justice.

December 7, 2006, Philpress

To Dream the Impossible Dream

We end this thesis with a quotation from British statesman and philosopher Edmund Burke who said: "The only thing necessary for the triumph of evil is for good men to do nothing!"

And also with the lyrics and theme of the song The Impossible Dream by Joe Darion with Don Quixote as Man La Mancha, upon which spirit this is written:

To dream the impossible dream
To fight the unbeatable foe
To bear the unbearable sorrow
To run where the brave dare not go
To right the unrightable wrong
To love pure and chaste from afar
To try when your arms are too weary

Source: Philpress Columns   173

Mr. President   *by Hermie Rotea*

To reach the unreachable star!

This is my quest, to follow the star
No matter how hopeless, no matter how far
To fight for the right, without question or pause
To be willing to march into Hell, for a Heavenly cause
And I know if I'll only be true, to this glorious quest,
That my heart will be peaceful and calm,
When I'm laid to rest . . .
And the world will be better for this
That one man, scorned and covered with scars,
Still strove, with his last ounce of courage,
To reach the unreachable star!

Hermie Rotea, Rizal Day, June 19, 2009, Los Angeles, California, United States 90051-2933

--oOo--

Published by a Self-Publisher

Tatay Jobo Elizes was born in Manila, Philippines, in 1934, retiree, now based in NY, busy writing and self-publishing as a hobby. The Publisher disclaims any responsibility or liability on the writings of the Author.

Mr. President book's ISBN CODES:
ISBN-13: 978 - 1496125439   ISBN-10: 1496125436

My website - http://tinyurl.com/mj76ccq

My Book List - Contact:
job_elizes@yahoo.com - tatay@usa.com

Writings 1 Book, 2012 + + 1. Obit, *Bambi Harper* **+ + 2. Speech, UP, 2003,** *Butch Jimenez* **+ + 3. Speech, Silliman U, 2006,** *Butch Jimenez* **+ + 4. The Mission Moment,** *Dr. Phil Stack* **+ + 5. Subanon Spirits of Rice & Land** - *Noel Cornel Alegre* **+ + 6. I Look Out The Window** - *Atty. Toto Causing* **+ + 7. Ride On A Bus, Poem,** *Melanie Ferrer, et al* **+ + 8. Why Am I Doing This,** *Susie*

Barbieri + **9. How To Court A Philippine Lady**, *Rodel Ramos, et al* + + **10. Story of Bacna Surgical Mission**, *Sylvia Salvador* + + **11. Catch That Story**, *Tatay Jobo Elizes*

Writings 2 Book, 2012 + + **1. There Is Hope For The Philippines**, *Grace Padaca* + + **2. Pointers On Employment Abroad**, *Melanie Aquino* + + **3. Without KNCHS: (Love story)**, *Atty. Toto Causing* + + **4. 422 Years Ago**, *Rodel Rodis* + +**5. Filipino American History Month**, *Rodel Rodis* + + **6. A Need For Reflection, Gloom**, *Cesar Torres* + + **7. Did Ninoy Die For Nothing**, *Joey Concepcion* + + **8. Criteria - American Institute of Philanthropy**, *Charity Guidelines (Feature)* + +**9. Coming Revolution In The Ballot**, *Cesar Lumba* + + **10. 2009, A Retrospective**, *Cesar Lumba* + + **11. Strangers In Our Own Country**, *Casiano Mayor Jr.* + + **12. The Gypsy Soul**, *Casiano Mayor Jr.*+ **13. An End To Cheating**, *Sonny Coloma* + + **14. Toward Culture of Giving, Not Having**, *Sonny Coloma* + + **15. 100 Reasons to be Proud as Pinoys,***Anonymous*

Writings 3A Book, 2012 + +
1. EPIC25, Emerging Philippines Investors Coalition, *Norman Madrid* + + **2. Management Ability As An Issue**, *Dr. Rene B. Azurin* + + **3. Do We Really Want To Give Our Politicos More Power**, *Dr. Rene B. Azurin* + + **4. Will 2010 Fulfill Filipinos High Hopes For Better Life – Metamorphosis**, *Ernie D. Delfin* + + **5. Comelec Is The Root Of All Evils**, *Toto Causing* + + **6. Some Advantages of Federalism and Parliamentary Government For The Philippines**, *Dr. Jose Abueva* + + **7. Sometimes A Great Nation**, *Mar-Vic Cagurangan* + + **8. Great Conspiracy**, *Mar-Vic Cagurangan* + + **9. Of Speech & Life's Riddles**, *Casiano Mayor* + + **10. Bad Start To The Year**, *Rod Garcia* + + **11. A Dinner out**, *Rod Garcia* + + **12. One More Time**, *Roy Gaane* + + **13. Strange Noises** – *Tatay Jobo Elizes* + +

Writings 3B Book, 2012 + +
1. The Reeds and Beams of Sunset in Paite and Balangaging in Zambales, *Ceres Busa* + + **2. Memories of your Past**, *Ceres Busa* + + **3. Blowout in the Barrio**, *Ceres Busa* + + **4. Dream on Sari-sari Store Keeper**, *Ceres Busa* + + **5. O Naraniag O Bulan**, *Ceres Busa,* + + **6. Candelaria, O Candelaria**, *Ceres Busa* + + **7. Four P's … Pastillas, Pilipig, Patupat at Panan**, *Ceres Busa* + + **8. On Being Filipino American**, *John Reyes* + + **9. The Monterey Peninsula**, *John Reyes* + + **10. The Salaza Fiesta**, *John Reyes* + + **11. Salawikain: Filipino Proverbs**, *John Reyes* + + **12. Musikero (The Musician)**, *John Reyes* + + **13. Did You Know (1)**, *Bert Guiang* + + **14. Did You Know (2)**, *Bert Guiang* + + **15. Did You Know (3)**, *Bert Guiang* + + **16. Did You Know (4)**, *Bert Guiang* + + **17. Did You Know (5)**, *Bert Guiang* + + **18. Sharing Trivia**, *Bert Guiang* + +

Writings 4A Book, 2012 + +
1. The State of Our Nation and Democracy In 2010: Building 'The Good Society" We Want, *Dr. Jose V. Abueva* + + **2. Assessing the Expanded Role of AFP in Nation Building**, *Col. Dencio (Dennis) Acop, Ret,* + + **3. Assessing RP's Security Strategies, Alternative Views**, *Col. Dencio (Dennis) Acop, Ret.*+ **4. The Way We Were**, *Fred Natividad* + + **5. Veterans of Ipo Dam, A Fiction**, *Fred Natividad* + + **6. A Plea**, *Miguel Reyes Reynaldo* + + **7. International Youth Bowling, My Impressions**, *Marjorie Ann Elizes Reyes* + +

Writings 4B Book, 2012 + +
1. Mi Ultimo Adios (My Last Farewell), *Dr. Jose P. Rizal* + + **2. Aling Pagibig Sa**

Tinubuang Bayan, *Gat. Andres Bonifacio* + + **3. Rekonsilasyun Dula (Reunion in Heaven),** *A Play, Irineo P. Goce (KaPule2 or Leonidas P. Agbayani)* + + **4. Forgery of Rizal Retraction,** *Irineo P. Goce (KaPule2 or Leonidas P. Agbayani)* + + **5. Maikling Kasaysayan Ng Malas Na Bayang Pilipinas,** *Ireneo P. Goce (KaPule2 or Leonidas P. Agbayani)*

Writings 5 Book - "Best Hopes" 2010, About President P-Noy + + **I. The Challenge of a Hundred Days: Believing that Filipinos can,** *Tony Meloto* + + **II. The 2006 Ramon Magsaysay Award for Community Service,** *for Tony Meloto* + + **III. Open Letter to Noynoy,** *F. Sionil Jose* + + **IV. A History of Pain,** *Juan L. Mercado* + + **V.An Open Letter to Noynoy,** *From OFWS* + + **VI. Pursuit of Good Governance Advocacies,** *Marcelo Tecson* + + **VII. A Fervent Prayer for Peace,** *Cesar Torres* + + **VIII. A History of Betrayal,** *Perry Diaz* + + **IX. Corona's Thorny Crown,***Perry Diaz* + + **X. Dawn of a New Era,** *Perry Diaz* + + **XI. Of Mice, Boys and Men,** *Philip S. Chua, MD* + + **XII. A Hopeful Tomorrow - A Balikbayan Insight,** *Philip S. Chua, MD* + + **XIII. Global Filipinos: A Sleeping Giant,** *Philip S. Chua, MD* + + **XIV. Heart to Heart - Winds of Change,** *Philip S. Chua, MD* + + **XV. Growing Old is a Privilege,** *Philip S. Chua, MD* + + **XVI. Our Cruelty to Mother Earth,** *Philip S. Chua, MD* + + **XVII. Advice to Grads: "Never Choose Your Heroes Lightly",** *Ernie Delfin* + + **XVIII. Gawad Kalinga, A Progressive Movement,** *Ernie Delfin* + + **XIX. Why a Man Must Save and Invest,** *Ernie Delfin* + + **XX. Beautiful San Francisco, Pinoy Heaven,** *Ted Laguatan* + + **XXI. The next President and PAMUSA,** *Frank Wenceslao* + + **XXII. Philippne Budget Deficit,** *Frank Wenceslao* + + **XXIII. Money Laundering: US Tools vs. Corruption,** *Frank Wenceslao* + + **XXIV. Amid the Fighting, Clan Rules Maguindanao,** *Jaileen F. Jimeno* + +**XXV. Why I Publish Writings,** *Tatay Jobo Elizes*

Writings 6 Book, 2010 + + **I. SONA, State Of Nation Address, English,** *Pres. Benigno Aquino III* + + **II. SONA, State of Nation Address, Pilipino,** *Pres. Benigno Aquino III* + + **III. First 100 Days Speech, Pilipino,** *Pres. Benigno Aquino III* + + **IV. Finally, Another Ramon Magsaysay In The Making,** *Bert Guiang.* + + **V. A Covenant With Our President,***Tony Meloto* + + **VI. From A Grateful Heart, A Thank You Letter,** *Tony Meloto* + + **VII. The Scent of Hope For The Global Filipino,** *Tony Meloto* + + **VIII. Fleshing Out The Broad Strokes,** *Felicito (Tong) C. Payumo* + + **IX. In Search Of Leaders (Part1),** *Felicito (Tong) C. Payumo* + + **X. In Search of Leaders (Part 2),** *Felicito (Tong) C. Payumo* + + **XI. A Conspiracy of Dunces,** *Cesar Lumba* + + **XII. Only Science Can Solve Poverty,** *Flor Lacanilao* + + **XIII. Education Reform Amid Scarcity,** *Flor Lacanilao* + + **XIV. Highblood: Obituaries/Reasons,** *Flor Lacanilao* + + **XV. How Money Works,** *Edmund Lao* + **XVI. State of Economy & Society, 2002,** *Juan Dela Cruz (Txtmania)* + + **XVII. Global Filipinos,***Juan Dela Cruz (Txtmania)* + + **XVIII. Understanding Poverty,** *Juan Dla Cruz (Txtmania)* + + **XIX. Kuyakuy,** *Dr. Ramon Marquez* + + **XX. Cambodian Octopus,** *Joey Jamito* + + **XXI. Inspite Of Herself, I Still Love The Philippines,** *Joey Jamito* + + **XXII. Love Has Wings,** *Percy Campoamor Cruz* + + **XXIII. Walk For Kris,** *Rod Garcia* + +**XXIV. Coldblooded, But Alive,** *Rod Garcia* + + **XXV. It Takes A Village,** *Rod Garcia* + + **XXVI. Beauty Contest,** *Rod Garcia*+ + **XXVII. Eight Points In Enlightening The Elites,** *Orion Perez Dumdum* + + **XXVIII. Case Against "Cellphone Revolution",** *Sarah Raymundo*

Writings 7 Book, 2010 - My Vintage Pics (Biographical) Tatay Jobo Elizes

Writings 8 Book, 2010 + + I. The Church and the State: In Search of Common Ground, *Gel Santos Relos* + +II. President Aquino: "Walang Kaibigan, Walang Kamag-anak", *Gel Santos Relos* + + III. What Makes Us "Pinoy", *Gel Santos Relos* + + IV. Minsan May Isang Puta (2007), *Mike Portes* + + V. Build Our Dream, *Jose Ma. Montelibano* + +VI. Hope In Europe, *Tony Meloto* + + VII. Wealth in Canada, *Tony Meloto* + + VIII. Parenthood: A Sacred Covenant, *Philip S. Chua* + + IX. Are We, Humans, Really Civilize? (Or, are we for the birds.), *Philip S. Chua,* + + X. Save Our Nation, *Philip S. Chua* + + XI. A Time To Pause, *Philip S. Chua* + + XII. The Gawad Kalinga Virus, *Philip S. Chua* + + XIII. A Marching Order For P-Noy, *Philip S. Chua* + + XIV. "Bayan Ko" Bonds, *Philip S. Chua* + + XV. P-Noy's First 99 Days, *Philip S. Chua* + + XVI. The Practice of Quackery in the Phils, *Cesar D. Candari* + + XVII. Remember When? A Brief History of Old and Recent Past, *Cesar Candari* + + XVIII. The Philippines Before and What Now?,*Cesar D. Candari* + + XIX. The Traffic Problems are Beyond "Wang-Wang", *Cesar D. Candari* + + XX. Behind The Gold, *Eliseo Serina* + + XXI. May Angal? (Any Complaint?), *Greg B. Macabenta* + + XXII. Pagbalik-Tanaw Sa Kapatirang Masoneriya Sa Pilipina, *Irineo P. Goce* + + XXIII. Mysteries & Riddles Behind RP's Corridors Of Power, *Irineo P. Goce* + + XXIV. Wika - Diwa Ng Lahi, O, Ang Tore ni Babel Sa Pilipinas, *Irineo P. Goce* + + XXV. Can There Be Peace; Is There Hope For Progress?, *Irineo P. Coce* + + XXVI. Drama Queen, *Percival Campoamor Cruz* + +XXVII. Ang Tulay na Kahoy, *Percival Campoamor Cruz* + + XXVIII. Sa Alaala ni Maria Lorena Barros, *Percival Campoamor Cruz* + + XXIX. Text Game or Text Gambling?, *Juan dela Cruz* + + XXX. Of Husbands and Wives, *Juan dela Cruz* + + XXXI. It Must Be Love, *Juan dela Cruz* + + XXXII. Elite Triad Blocking Reform, *Demosthenes B. Donato*

Writings 9 Book, April 2011 + + I. Solidarity in Literature W/out Borders, *Simeon Dumdum Jr* + + II.Macario Sakay Vindicated, *Gemma Cruz Araneta* + + III. The Dilemma of the Last Filipino, *Larry Henares* + + IV.Ping Joaquin, Fil. Jazz Pianist, my Father, *Tony Joaquin* + + V. Bert Del Rosario, Inventor, Sing-Along, *Tony Joaquin*+ + VI. Xmas Article 2009, *Allen Gaborro* + + VII. Beaches (short story), *Allen Gaborro* + + VIII. Democracy Versus Discipline, *Allen Gaborro* + + IX. Amend the Const. Make Jury Trial, *Atty. Toto C. Causing* + + X. Dakdak Beach Resort in Dapitan City, *Toto C. Causing* + + XI. So I'm Dark-skinned, Leave Me Alone, *Mar-Vic Cagurangan* + + XII. Dig My Sexy Flip Accent, Arizona, *Mar-Vic Cagurangan* + + XIII. A Fan Mail From Prison, *Mar-Vic Cagurangan* + + XIV. Three Poems: a. Please Don't Let Her Know, b. I Have Memories of My Own, c. God Has Made Someone Only For me,*Emily Espanol Derry* + + XV. Three Love Poems: a. Some Good Things Never Last b. The Dance c. As I Trod Upon Your Ground, *Elyn Jean Felarca* + + XVI. My Advocacy, *Naysan A. Albaytar* + + XVII. Feminism: The Great Paradox,*Laura Wade* + + XVIII. A Blast From the Past, *Peter Allan Mariano,* + + XIX. Bus. Perspective: Bldg. Your Future,*Peter Allan Mariano* + + XX. An Overview of Health Connections, *Peter Allan Mariano* + + XXI. My Workspace At Home, *Marge Trajeco-Aberásturi* + + XXII. Investing on a Home Business, *Marge Trajeco Aberasturi* + + XXIII. A Brighter Day for Little Jane, *Julia Carreon-Lagoc* + + XXIV. A Consummation Devoutly to Be Wished, *Julia C. Lagoc*+ + XXV. No Birds and Beetles and Trees, *Julia Carreon-Lagoc* + + XXVI. Ang Wika, Ang Tore Ni Babel Sa Pilipinas,*Irineo Goce* + + XXVII. Scattered Thoughts - *Anonymous*

Writings 10 Book, July, 2011 + + 1. The Spratlys Are Worth Dying For, *Ted Laguatan* + + 2. Ang Siyam Na Buhay ni Felizardo Cabangban, *Percival*

Campoamor Cruz + + 3. **Old Man of the Mound,** *Percival Campoamor Cruz*+ + 4. **Walang Kamag-anak Sa Pag-ibig,** *Percival Campoamor Cruz* + + 5. **Congo and the Philippines,** *Allen Gaborro*+ + 6. **Divorce In the Philippines,** *Allen Gaborro* + + 7. **RH Production Bill,** *Allen Gaborro* + + 8. **Take the Amazing "Wow! Kay Ganda ng Pilipinas" Challenge,** *Peter Alan Mariano* + + 9. **Your Thoughts,** *MLMunoz* + + 10. **Common Money-Mistakes OFWs Make,** *Alvin T. Tabanag* + + 11. **Don't Just Save, Invest!,** *Alvin T. Tabañag* + + 12. **MRT-3: The Daily Commute Is The Destination,** *Resty Odon* + + 13. **Manila: A Glorious Mismatch, A Happy Confusion,***Resty Odon* + + 14. **Triptych,** *Resty Odon* + + 15. **The Precariousness of Being Pinoy,** *Resty Odon* + + 16. **Ode to My Alloy Nation,** *Resty Odon* + + 17. **Precious Precariousness,** *Resty Odon* + + 18. **Heart to Heart, Violence on Television,** *Philip S. Chua* + + 19. **Heart to Heart, Attitude Impacts Health, Life,** *Philip S. Chua* + + 20. **Heart to Heart, Are We Getting Enough Sleep,** *Philip S. Chua* + + 21. **Heart to Heart, Obesity: A Killer,** *Philip S. Chua* + + 22. **Are we the disappearing breed of professionals in this country?,** *Cesar D. Candari* + + 23. **If You Dream It, Do It Retirement,** *Cesar D. Candari* + + 24. **Only In America, Human Interest Story,** *Anonymous*

Writings 11 Book, August, 2011 + + 1. **SONA In English and Filipino,** *Pres. Benigno Aquino III (P-Noy)* + + 2. **Telltale Signs: SONA and the Dogfight Over Spratlys,** *Rodel Rodis* + + 3. **Why China will not bring the Spratlys issue to the United Nations,** *Ted Laguatan* + + 4. **Random Thoughts, On Website Demise and On Disunity,** *Tatay Jobo Elizes* + + 5. **Can Local Private Sector Help Reverse Philippine's Migration Addiction?,***Jeremiah M. Opiniano* + + 6. **What Fuels the Passion of Filipinos to Pursue Studies and Work in UK?,** *Ofw Journalism Consortium* + + 7. **Our Life in the Philippines,** *Bob & Carol Hammerslag* + + 8. **Reality Check: the Philippines – A Tropical Paradise for the Retiree?,** *by Bob & Carol Hammerslag* + + 9. **Filipinos Dominate Cruise Ships,** *Roger P. Olivares* + + 10. **Vargas: Hero, Villain, Tragic Figure?,** *Roger P. Olivares* + + 11. **Is it Hell to go Back Home?,** *Roger P. Olivares* + + 12. **The Filipino, now a commodity!,** *Roger P. Olivares* + + 13. **How US Can Create Jobs,** *Rob Ceralvo* + + 14. **Modus Operandi - Common Crimes (In Metro Manila, Philippines),** *Anonymous* + + 15. **Poem, Kabuhayang Bansa At Wika,** *Irineo P. Goce (aka KaPule 2 and Leonidas Agbayani)* + + 16. **Random Sayings & Advices,** *Anonymous*

Writings 12 Book, April 2012 + + 1. **Twenty Excuses Filipinos Use,** *Orion Perez Dumdum* + + 2. **One By One, The Petals Drop,** *Julia C. Lagoc* + + 3. **Religion & the Scientist,** *Honorio M. Cruz, MD* + + 4. **The Tales of the Aswang & Bangungot,** *Honorio M. Cruz, MD* + + 5. **Sex & Politics,** *Honrio M. Cruz, MD* + + 6. **Autopsy,** *Ben Gonzales, MD* + + 7. **Geekmocracy,** *Mar-Vic Cagurangan* + + 8. **Flights: Voice from the Future that Lives in the Past,** *Mar-Vic Cagurangan* + + 9. **Kaya Natin! Sanctuary,** *Marisa Lerias* + + 10. **The Days of Courage,** *Gerry Partido* + + 11. **Earth Day and the Tragedy of a Famous River,** *Cesar D. Candari, MD, FCAP Emeritus* + + 12. **Few Filipino-American NonprofitsGetting Political,** *Erwin De Leon* + + 13. **Filipino-American Political Invisibility And Community Organizations,** *Erwin De Leon* I+ + 14. **I'm 32 and I am still a Virgin,** *Jovelyn Bayubay Revilla* + + 15. **Hiding Ill-Gotten Wealth,** *Jobo Elizes*

Writings 13 Book, July 2012 + +
1. **From "Criminal" to "Doctor" in Criminal Justice,** *Raymundo E. Narag* + + 2. **The Essence of Giving, MLMunoz** + + 3. **My Prescription for Spiritual Life,** *Sonja*

Barbara dL Munoz + + **4. Anak Ng Prosti,** *Pamela Joy Agtoto* + + **5. Ang Kapangyarihan ng Kanyang Pag-ibig,** *Percival Campoamor Cruz* + + **6. Ang Tato ni Apo Pule,** *Percival Campoamor Cruz* + + **7. Rapture,** *Percival Campoamor Cruz* + + **8. Ang Taong Walang Anino,** *Percival Campoamor Cruz* + + **9. Gender Formula – Boy or Girl,** *Tatay Jobo Elizes* + + **10. The Single,** *Jhackie Eslit Bayobay* + + **11. Why I Am Angry,** *Jhackie Eslit Bayobay,* **12. Rules of Living,** *Jhackie Eslit Bayobay* + + **13. Being Alone,** *Jhackie Eslit Bayobay* + + **14. Love and Hurt,** *Jhackie Eslit Bayobay* + + **15. My First Heart Aches,** *Jhackie Eslit Bayobay* + + **16. Why the Philippines Need Sex Education,** *Reygel Saplad Perales* + +

        Timely Writings 14, 2013 + +
1. The Giant Sucking Sound and the Rise of Employnomics, *Cesar Fernando Lumba* + + **2. UP, College of Bus. Admin. and Cesar E.A. Virata,** *Eugenio Pulmano* + + **3. The Missing Element in Education Reform,** *Late Sec. Jesse Robredo* + + **4. China: Some Observations from My Recent Trip,** *Antonio Nievera* + + **5. Don't invest in stocks if you don't have these,** *Alvin T. Tabanag* + + **6. Creating Your Own Financial Plan,** *Alvin T. Tabanag* + + **7. Anti-Gay Hate Crimes on the Rise in New York City: A Call to the Community,** *Kevin L. Nadal, Ph.D.* + + **8. Native Colonialism & Subjugation,** *Anonymous (TJ Friend)* + + **9. The Way We Were - Fond Look at a Hometown,** *Fred Natividad & Bing Castillo* + + **10. Obituary: Common Sense,** *Anonymous* + + **11. Be The Best Ever,** *Anonymous* + + **12. Remembering Capt. Rene N. Jarque,** *Ellen Tordesillas* + + **13. Why I Left the Military,** *Late Capt. Rene N. Jarque* + + **14. Soldiers In Elections: From Pawns to Knights,** *Late Capt. Rene N. Jarque* + + **15. Reforming The Armed Forces -** *Late Capt. Rene N. Jarque* + +

Solo Authored Books: + + +

Book A, **Turning Points,** *Job Elizes Sr,1968 (Reissue 2009)* + + +
Book B, **Be Considerate For Once,** *Tatay Jobo Elizes (Jr), 2013*
Book C, **Piglets Unlimited - Wealth,** *Tatay Jobo Elizes, 2009* + + +
Book D, **Out of the Misty Sea We Must,** *Cesar Lumba, 2010* + + +
Book E, **Fulfilled** - *Gonzales Reynaldo, Editor, 2010* + + +

Dook F - **Reflections** - *Bert Guiang, 2010* + + +
Book G,   **Writings 7 - My Vintage Pics,** *Tatay Jobo Elizes, 2010* +
Book H, **May Bagwis Ang Pag-ibig,** *Percival C. Cruz* + + +
Book I, **Letters To Matrimony,** *Irineo Perez Coce, Ka Pule2, 2011* +
Book J, **Songs I Wish You Knew,** *Soledad R. Juan, 2011* + + +

Book K, **Make My Day,** *Larry Henares Jr., 1993, Re-issue 2011* + +
Book L, **Our Guerrero Family,** *Tatay Jobo Elizes, 2010* + + +
Book M, **Handy Jokes,** *Tatay J. Elizes, 2011* +
Book N, **FaveArt 1,** *Tatay Jobo Elizes, 2011* + +
Book O, **Beyond idle thoughts,** *MLMunoz, Sept,2011* + + +

Book P, **Cracke In The Armor,** *Mariano Ngan, Oct 2011* ı ı ı
Book Q, **FaveArt 2,** *Tatay Jobo Elizes, 2011* + +
Book R, **Balitang Kutsero,** *Perry Diaz, Jan 2012* + + +
Book S, **FaveArt3,** *Tatay Jobo, 2011* + + +
Book T, **FaveArt4** *,2012, Tatay Jobo* + + +

Book U, **Stack Family Journals,** *Phil & Fe Stack, 2012* + + +

Source: Philpress Columns   **179**

Book V, **Emily, An Adoption Journey**, *Romerl Elizes, 2012* + + +
Book W, **Hermes Alegre Art Gallery**, *TJ & Hermes, 2012* + + +
Book X, **Masaya Din, Malungkot Din**, *Jovelyn Bayubay Revilla, 2012*
Book Y, **Tiis, Sipag At Tiyaga**, *Raquel Delfin Padilla, 2012* + + +

Book Z, **Until I Meet You**, *Jhackie Eslit Bayobay, 2012* + + +
Book AA, **Buhay At Pag-ibig**, *Argel Lucero Tamayo, 2012* + + +
Book AB, **Hail to the Second Best**, *Dr. Philip Stack, 2012* + + +
Book AC, **Life Bus**, *Mommy Joyce Pineda-Faulmino, 2012* + + +
Book AD, **My Candid Musings**, *Monette Dioquino Calugay, 2012* +

Book AE, **Tickets to Life**, *Maria Lourdes Jesalva, 2012* + + +
Book AF, **The Dove Files**, *Mike Portes, 2012* + + +
Book AG, **Nursing Vignettes**, *Jocelyn Cerrudo Sese, 2012* +
Book AH, **Poor Ba Us**, *R.A. Gubalane, 2012* + + +
Book AI, **Summer Idyll**, *Avelina Gil, 2012* + +

Book AJ, **Legacy (Pamana)**, *Rachel Astrero, 2012* + +
Book AK, **Narratives Old & New**, *Avelina J. Gil, 2013* + +
Book AL, **Buhay Saudi**, *Adele J. Esic, 2013* + +
Book AM, **Buhay Ofw Atbp**, *Jessica Napat, 2013* + +
Book AN, **Mga Tula Ng Buhay**, *Angelita C. Esguerra, 2013* +

Book AO, **Not by Bread Alone**, *Judge Lily V. Magtolis, 2013* +
Book AP, **Jokes Collection-2**, *Tatay Jobo Elizes, 2013* + + +
Book AR, *My Writings Sometimes, Tatay Jobo Elizes, 2013*
Book AS, **Sa 'Yo Na Ako**, *Shayne A. Martinez, 2013*
Book AT, **My Kin's Family Trees**, *Tatay Jobo Elizes, 2013*

Book AU, **Rizal Family Tree & Others**, *Tatay Jobo Elizes, 2013*
Book AV, **Make My Day-2, Nice & Nasty**, *Larry Henares, 2013 (1993)*
Book AW, **Make My Day-3, Cecilia, Love**, *L.Henares, 2013 (1993)*
Book AX, **Handy Lyrics-1**, *Tatay Jobo Elizes, 2013*
Book AY, **Ang Biblos**, *Rev. Dr. Eugenio Guerrero, 2014 (1929)*

Book AZ, **Make My Day-4**, *Sweet & Sour, L. Henares, 2014 (1993)*
Book BA, **Life's Journey, True Stories**, *Dr. Phil Stack, 2014*
Book BB, **Diary ni Gracia**, *Gracia Amor, 2014 (pending)*
Book BC, **Mr. President**, *Hermie Rotea, 2014*

Please buy online or give as gift in paperback or kindle edition. All authors and titles are easy to search, trace or find online. Thanks. Self-Publisher, Tatay Jobo Elizes